GROWING UP
BETWEEN
1900 AND 1920

Grace Horseman

Cottage Publishing

© Grace Horseman 1996

First published in 1996 by Grace Horseman of 3 Ashburton Road, Brimley, Bovey Tracey, Devon TQ13 9BZ . Tel: 01626 832300, in association with:

Cottage Publishing
Bovey Tracey
Devon TQ13 9AE
Tel: 01626 835757

British Library Catalogue in Publication Data

A CIP Catalogue Record for this book is available from the British Library

ISBN 1-897785-06-2

Horseman, Grace
Growing up between 1900 and 1920

Horseman, Grace
Growing up in the Thirties

Madders, Jane and Horseman, Grace
Growing up in the Twenties

Typeset by
Cottage Publishing, Bovey Tracey

Printed in Great Britain by
Sprint Print Ltd, Exeter

Cover illustration and photographs
The cover illustration is from an original water colour by Miss Enid Dynes (1909-1991), a former headmistress of Chichester High School for Girls. It shows Jane and Grace in the garden at Bude where the Bobs were together for a week in 1978: overlaid are photographs of Graces mother nursing Jessie, sitting with her godparents, Grace and Percy Allott, with beach huts in the background: Karwood Dairy milk carts; Ypres mud. On the reverse side are; Maddie Stokes in her classroom; Joyce Booth sitting on chair.

CONTENTS

FOREWORD

From the Revd. The Lord Soper

"It is a pleasure for me to have the opportunity of writing a foreword to a book which opened the door into my own life as a schoolboy. It has refreshed my recollections of days so long ago, and half forgotten.

I have an unusual interest in Growing Up Between 1903 (when I was born) and 1920. I was a scholar at Swaffield Road School and at the same time my mother was the headmistress of the girls' department. School for me was an extension of home life rather that a separation from it. Of course, at the time I took it all as a matter of course.

What is written here is a fascinating view of a world in which I was growing up. Moreover, one of the values attached to the reading of it is the realisation of the interpenetration of home and school which was, for me, such a fundamental experience. For this and many other reasons I heartily commend Growing Up Between 1900 and 1920."

Donald Soper.

Authors note.

My brother John, sisters Jessie, Kathleen and Biddy all attended Swaffield Road School.

DEDICATION

With grateful thanks to everyone who has contributed to this book, to the long-suffering librarians for their patient assistance, and above all to my parents who began it all.

I much regret that some have died since writing about *Growing Up Between 1900 and 1920*.

Mr Cyril Davies, Mrs Elsie Gomm, Mrs Isobel Wookey, Mrs Marion Yates and Mrs Elsie Rive.

INTRODUCTION

The Twentieth century really began with the death of Queen Victoria on 22 January 1901, the end of a long and mostly gloomy reign. She was succeeded by Edward VII, a very different personality, self indulgent and pleasure loving.

In those days there was a great gulf between the rich and the poor, the upper and lower classes. The former spent thousands of pounds on entertainment, property and clothing, and were grossly overfed, whilst most of the population lived on the edge of poverty and starvation, if not below it.

The Edwardian period, which ended with the outbreak of war in 1914 rather than with the death of Edward VII in 1910, was also one of growth and invention. The production of cars increased rapidly, and the first flimsy aeroplanes as well as balloons and zeppelins took to the skies. The new Underground railway was built in London and Marconi experimented with wireless telegraphy. Opulent liners like the Cunard TITANIC were built, and although the steam engine reigned supreme, there were increasing numbers of cars on city streets, to join the trams and buses.

Opportunities for the poorer classes to receive education were greatly improved, especially with the introduction of the state grammar schools. The founding of new universities opened up the possibility of further education to the middle classes. However, this was still mostly beyond the means of the working classes.

The Liberals had political power and for the first time introduced social services, taxing the rich to provide at least some basic necessities for the poor. It was also a time of strikes and of demonstrations by women seeking enfranchisement. Mrs. Emmeline Pankhurst and her daughters Christabel and Sylvia led the militant suffragettes. Christabel and Annie Kenney were the first to be sentenced to a week in prison. After the failure of a new Franchise Bill in 1912, the militant campaign was intensified and more were imprisoned, where conditions were grim. When they went on hunger strike they were forcibly fed by having a long rubber tube thrust down throat or nostril. This was extremely painful. War changed everything and Suffragettes joined other women in giving great service to the country. In February 1918 they were rewarded with the vote they had failed to win by militant means.

Much of the Edwardian life-style was to change with the outbreak of war. Students at Oxford and Cambridge universities who had joined the Officers Training Corps were among the first to volunteer for the forces, and few of them survived. The flower of youth was destroyed in the bitter trench warfare. Already before 1914 women far exceeded men in numbers; now many of them were to be prematurely widowed and their children left orphans. For some it had its compensations. There was work for the unemployed and for women in the munitions factories and elsewhere.

Some poets and writers had foreseen the perils of war, others eulogised it. War time poets like Rupert Brooke became very popular.

In 1907 Sir Robert Baden-Powell established the Boy Scout movement, originally to be part of the Boys' Brigade, but it thrived as a separate entity.

Lord Baden-Powell

1. FAMILY LIFE.

By the beginning of the twentieth century the elite group of aristocrats, with their opulent life-style, had been joined by others who had made their millions during the industrial revolution. They included people like Sir Thomas Lipton, the grocer, and Sir Blundell Maple, the store owner, whom King Edward VII was willing to accept into his circle. Most of them lived lives of luxury, spending much time at balls and dances, eating enormous meals, or attending functions such as racing at Royal Ascot, Henley Regatta, the Eton-Harrow cricket match, or yachting at Cowes. They were waited on hand and foot by a bevy of servants, who catered for their every need and whim.

Life for the lower class was very different: they worked long hours for a pittance, often in very unsavoury surroundings. The housemaid had to be up early in the morning to clear and light fires, clean boots and shoes and do many other chores. To clean the floors and carpets meant kneeling on the ground and using a brush and dustpan: no vacuum cleaners and no washing machines in the early years. The valet looked after his masters' clothes, while the between maid (tweeny) did many jobs like filling the coal-scuttles and preparing vegetables for meals. Head of the staff was the butler, but even his wages were poor, and the cook earned even less. Hours were long, often 6.00 am to 10.30 pm, with only a half-day off each week. At least they had free accommodation and food, but that was often meagre unless it could be augmented by the remains from banquets. Their bedrooms in garrets were freezing cold in winter. In large houses coal had to be carried up endless flights of stairs for the fires, which made a lot of dirt and dust to be cleaned daily. Much of the work 'above stairs' was done before the master and his family were up. Hot water and early morning tea were taken to the bedrooms. Food had to be cooked on a fire-heated range and then carried to the dining room. Because conditions were so grim, many preferred to work in the new factories; at least their hours were not quite as long and the remuneration better, although conditions might be far from good.

Life for those in the middle classes was easier. At the top end were the professional men, with interesting careers, adequate earnings and leisure. Those at the other end, the clerks and shop assistants, only just managed to make ends meet and sickness or accident might well push them into penury.

For the unemployed and the old and destitute there was only the Workhouse, the ultimate degradation, where men were segregated from their wives.

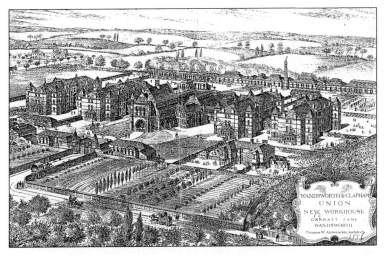

Wandsworth & Clapham Union Workhouse, built 1886.
(Men & women were seperated)

On the credit side it was a time when new suburbs were being built, with more modern accommodation and some labour-saving devices, but still there were the slums.

Much of this was to change during the First World War. Men were called up into the forces, practically ending unemployment, and older men and women had to take on their jobs, and also work in the munitions and other factories. For many women this was the first opportunity they had had to work and know financial independence. In Glasgow wages varied from 30 shillings for an electric meter reader for a forty-eight hour week, to 35s. 6d. for tram conductors for a fifty-three and a half hour week. There was a great demand for girls to work in offices to replace men who had volunteered or been conscripted. Others took voluntary work as VAD's, nursing, doing secretarial work for the St.John's Ambulance Brigade and elsewhere, whilst some joined the Women's Police Service or worked on the land.

I was born in October 1911 at a flat in Amerland Grove, near Wimbledon Common, London, a place which was to become a favourite haunt for exploring and picnicking in later years. Jessie was two-and-a-half years older than me.

Within a year we had moved to a larger ground-floor flat, one of eight in Pentland Gardens, Wandsworth, with a very pleasant communal front garden and our own back garden with side entrance. There was a large bed of irises in front of our house, with lots of wallflowers in the Spring that warmed the air with their perfume. The front door opened on to a passage on the right of which was the drawing room: mostly only used when we had guests. Ahead were the kitchen, scullery and bathroom, then the passage turned right with our bedroom on the left. Jessie and I shared a large double bed that had brass knobs at each corner. With a sheet tied to each knob this made an exciting tent when we were a little older. There was a playroom beyond it, all looking on to the back garden. Opposite was our parents' bedroom, with a cot later for the baby.

To my young eyes it was quite spacious, and I loved our garden. In the summer a sweet-scented white jasmine covered almost the whole of one side, elsewhere there were beds of roses, both still among my favourite flowers. I remember one sunny morning when I was only about two rushing indoors and crying "Mummy, Mummy, come and see what I've found in the garden." It was a wide open yellow crocus - the golden pool against the brown earth was a miracle to me then: it had arrived so suddenly.

In the adjacent garden was an enormous mulberry tree, and sometimes birds dropped the ripe fruit in our garden. They were good to eat once we had washed them!

In the front garden were lots of trees, shrubs and bushes, a delightful place for hide-and-seek when we were older, and for the first time I saw the fragile perfection of a skeleton leaf.

The kitchen was quite large and we used it as a breakfast room. Good in winter as, long before the days of central heating, the kitchen fire made it the warmest place in the house. The scullery housed the gas cooker as well as the copper and large wooden mangle. The sink overlooked the garden, which made washing up much more pleasant than it might otherwise have been. There were no detergents, just Sunlight soap and soda. Lighting was by gas.

Two months before my second birthday it was arranged that I should go and stay on my own with my godparents at Harrow. Quite an ordeal! They were very kind but so different from my own family and I felt very shy and lonely. They had only one child, Frank, who was about six years older than me. To cheer myself up I used to walk down the garden humming, until Frank sang to me:

> *'Yer penny buys yer 'ummin' top,*
> *Yer winds it up, it never stops,*
> *And don't forget the little ones at 'ome.'*

One day Auntie Grace, as I called her, had served smoked haddock for breakfast. It was the first time I had met haddock and decided I didn't like it, so left it on my plate. To coax me Auntie put a piece in my mouth. That was the last straw, so I sat through the rest of the meal with it hanging half out of my mouth, and as soon as I could went and flushed it down the lavatory. I was frequently teased about that in later years! When I returned home I discovered I had a new baby sister, Kathleen, but it was much later I realised that that was why I had been sent away on my own at such an early age.

Grace   Mummy + Kathleen   Jessie   - 1914

Soon after the war began my father enlisted in the Royal Army Service Corps and was stationed at the barracks at Winchester, so he arranged for us to move to a house there. It was three- storeyed, with a long back garden, but only an outside toilet adjacent to the house. We were glad there were commodes under the beds! You approached the toilet by a steep staircase that led to the semi-basement kitchen, where Mrs. Beard, a former cook, prepared all the meals on a kitchener. She and her husband and family used it as their sitting room when they had lodgers in the rest of the house. Their daughter, May, was a real skivvy at her mother's beck and call, and she also did cleaning at the nearby Workhouse. I still remember her red hands and sack apron! We felt very sorry for her. There were two sons, Ted who was married and had a daughter, so lived away, and Percy a sailor. We thought it wonderful when he came home on leave and would throw a ball miles into the sky and catch it, and play other games with us.

Then came a brief, harrowing interlude when we returned to London, to be met by air raids. So we returned to Winchester and then to Bath, when my father was stationed there. He had hoped to meet the train at the station when we arrived, but his leave was cancelled at the last minute and Mother was met with a message telling her to take a cab to a certain address. Again Father had managed to find accommodation for us, but it was very different from Winchester; a much smaller house but with quite a long garden, with chickens in a shed at the end. Mrs. Horton's husband had been announced missing, presumed killed, but she was sure he would return home again one day. He never did! She had three children, Maddie, who was older than Jessie, Reg, about my age, and Clifford the youngest. We three Solkhon children had to share a large double bed and none of us liked being the middle one, so we took it in turns! Mother had a very difficult time trying to keep our hair clean, as all the Horton children had head lice. From time to time she lost the battle!

There was one rather sad but humorous time, when Mrs. Horton had to go away and asked Mother to look after the chickens. She did not leave very clear instructions about their diet, so when there was porridge left over from breakfast Mother thought they would enjoy it. But it was too sloppy and one of the birds that had eaten it got croup and staggered around gurgling, and eventually died. We could not consider eating it, although food was scarce during the war.

We had a lovely Airedale dog, Barlow, who was very gentle. He would carry one of the new laid eggs from the end of the garden to the kitchen without breaking it, but unfortunately one day he accidentally knocked Kathleen down in front of the milk cart, and my father decided it was too dangerous to keep him. He found a good home with a farmer, but we were all very, very sad and missed him greatly.

Another day Kathleen, who was about three at the time, thought she would copy Mother and hold a piece of newspaper in front of the fire to make it draw better. But she used a whole newspaper and it caught alight. By the time we were able to call Mother there was a fierce blaze. She was able to put the rest of the paper into the grate, but it set the chimney on fire. Glowing lumps of soot fell into the room, and there was an acrid smell. When we went into the street we could see flames coming out of the chimney. We had to call the fire brigade, which was an exciting experience.

Early in 1917 Mother had a telegram to say that her brother Jack had been killed at the front. It was the first time I had seen her cry: until then I had not realised that adults could cry! When I asked her what had happened and she told me I, too, was very sad, because I still remembered him as my favourite uncle!

It was on 6 December 1917 that our brother Jack was born, out of the blue as far as we were concerned! Mother's sister, Kit, our favourite aunt and the youngest in the family of seven, came to help her, and we all enjoyed the addition to our family. She loved dancing and singing, as did all the aunts, and sometimes she wore a very full, crinoline type dress, pirouetted around and then collapsed on the floor, with it billowing all around her. We used to jump on to the ballooning skirt! However, Mrs. Horton's house was too small for us all so we moved to another house nearby. The thing I remember most about it was that it had a swing!

We were there when the Armistice was signed, and there was great excitement. So at last we were able to return to our own home. No telephone in those days, so Mother sent a telegram to our tenants, but when we arrived back we found that they had not vacated the flat as requested. There was Mother stranded with four children, one just a baby. We all descended on Father's brother, Harry, and his wife Hannah and their three children, all older than us: Lottie, Alice and William. Aunt Hannah kept a cane behind the dining room door, in case of need, and that terrified us!

Maddie   *Hannah Solkhon*
      William   *Alice*

Obviously we were much too much of a crowd for their average sized house, so it was arranged that Jessie and I should go and stay with one of Mother's sisters, Lily, her husband Percy, and Harold, Lily and Kit (about Jessie's age) and Frank, exactly my age. This was Christmas time, and we both felt homesick, but they had a wonderful Christmas tree and lots of presents, and did their best to make us feel at home. I remember Harold singing a song by way of entertainment, it began:

> *Rise at six, every morn,*
> *Milk the cow with the crumpled horn,*
> ....
> *Teach the nanny goat how to beg.*

We were very grateful when at last the tenants moved out and we were able to join the rest of the family in our own home.

I remember Mother had left several pounds of sugar, a very precious commodity in those days of rationing, in a locked cupboard in the kitchen. We were all devastated when she unlocked it and found the cupboard bare. The tenants had managed to pick the lock!

Early the following year Father returned home, but he was almost a stranger to us, and Jack had never seen him. He was frightened of this big man, and so were we. We had been so long with just Mother that it took a while to get adjusted. Father had some problems too! Swearing was almost universal in the army and words would slip out unintentionally. So he had a swear box and put a penny in every time he swore. He was soon cured. By 1920 we had settled down to a peaceful family life once more.

Arthur and Jessie Solkhon - 1919

Lady Helen Asquith's home is at Mells, near Frome in Somerset, a charming village where her mother's parents owned the beautiful Elizabethan Manor House. From St.Paul's Girls School she won a scholarship in classics to Somerville College, Oxford, in 1926, where she read Literae Humanioraes (Latin and Greek literature, history and philosophy) and got a Second in Honour Moderations and in 'Greats'. When she came down she was appointed to Clapham County Secondary School, where the wonderful headmistress, Miss E. A. Jones, was also a Somervillian, to teach classics. She spent seven happy years there from 1932 and was then appointed to H. M. Inspectorate of Schools. On retirement in 1971 she taught Latin and Greek part-time, mainly to sixth formers, for twelve years at St.Mary's Convent, Shaftesbury.

I was born in 1908; my father was a rather struggling barrister. We lived in a large house in Bloomsbury, 49 Bedford Square - a most beautiful Georgian square with lovely plane trees. We used to play in the gardens when we were quite young. I had a sister fifteen months younger than me. Then my mother stopped childbearing for a while as she found children rather hard work! We had a very happy childhood. Unlike most people we had a nurse, and sometimes a nursery maid as well, who looked after us. Our nurse was a very intelligent woman, keenly interested in natural history, (birds, flowers, butterflies) with a liking for literature and poetry (of a rather low brow kind). She was a devout Christian, though Low Church and very anti-Catholic. We did our early lessons with her and learned to read and write and do 'sums' without any difficulty at all. She inspired us with a liking for bible stories and singing, both sacred and secular, and she had an easy natural authority which commanded almost invariable obedience combined with strong affection and respect. The routine of daily life, both out of doors (she was a great devotee of 'fresh air') and indoors was almost always enjoyable and fun. After she came to us, early in 1914, I never remember any kind of 'corporal punishment'.

When the war began in 1914 it gradually altered our life. My father did not have to join the army for a while but when, in 1915, he insisted on going to the Front it became difficult for my mother to go on living in London. Though the London house was our home we had always spent quite a lot of time at the lovely Manor House at Mells which belonged to my mother's parents, the Horners. The house was very unsuitable for children, lofty and narrow with lots of stairs, and when we stayed there we children lived in two cottages in the garden. The front one contained a day nursery and night nursery upstairs and a spacious bathroom and another bedroom on the ground floor. It looked out on a small enclosed garden with apple trees and flower beds and a paved path up the centre. All our meals were cooked in the large distant kitchen of the big house and carried across the garden, in all weathers, by patient 'nursery maids' on large wooden trays. There was a second cottage at the back, separated by a small open yard and facing on to the village street, with fairly similar accommodation but including a scullery and a kitchen. This housed our cousins from Newmarket when they came to stay in the summer, a boy and girl of similar age to us and their nurse and nursery maid. We had a bath with hot water but for some time the lighting was all by oil lamps and candles.

One of my vivid memories is of being in the cottage at Christmas time in 1915. I woke up very early that Christmas morning. The cottage was right under the church and the eight bells began pealing about 6.30 am and moonlight came flooding in, and there was my Christmas stocking on the bed with lovely things sticking out of it. We couldn't light the lamp, but we could see them in the moonlight and feel them and wonder what they were. We were not allowed to open them until later. When the lights were on they were quite a different colour! Among other delightful presents, I had books: 'Children of the New Forest' and 'The Swiss Family Robinson', which I read from cover to cover with great enjoyment.

Then in 1916 my brother arrived. We were very well prepared by our nurse. For a long time we had thought how lovely it would be to have a baby brother. Suddenly we awoke one morning and we were told he had arrived the night before. It was a great thrill! We adored him and as he grew up we waited on him hand and foot. He had a lovely name, Julian, but he was always called Trim, because my father who came home on leave just once, when he was about a month old, called him that. Of course, in those days a 'confinement' lasted quite a long time, about a month. A monthly nurse looked after mother and baby but my mother was just recovering when my father came home on leave. I remember him looking at the baby, as men do, and saying he was very 'dusky' which rather offended us. That was the only time he saw his son. My father referred to him as Trimalchio after a somewhat disreputable character in a rather coarse Roman satire of the 1st Century AD, who was no better than he should be, greedy and lecherous! It is a famous work though not one that is much read in schools! But my father who was an accomplished classical scholar liked it very much, so after his death my mother liked to have the baby called Trim.

My father was killed in the battle of the Somme that same year. It was a very traumatic time for us all, especially my mother, because she adored him. She had all his letters, including the ones from the front, typed and put into several books with locks, which we never saw, but he wrote to us too - sweet little pencilled letters from the trenches, saying how awful it was. His father was Prime Minister, so my mother was very angry that his father didn't do more to secure him from danger. She persuaded her father-in-law to get him into the Intelligence Corps but my father disliked this and soon insisted on going back to the Grenadier Guards in the trenches. Then there was the terrible, disastrous battle of the Somme in September and he was wounded and died almost immediately.

I very vividly remember when the news came. We were living at Mells in the cottage. Trim was only four months old and my mother was sleeping in the big house and still nursing him. Early one morning we were told she wasn't well but would see us later. That evening she sent for me: I had no idea why, but I met my grandmother on the way and asked her why Mother wanted to see me. "Bad news about Daddy darling", she said. Mother had obviously been crying. She held me close but couldn't say much and I was completely bewildered and distressed. I remember meeting my grandmother in the garden on the way back and bursting into tears, but not really understanding what had happened. My father had been away so much, so although he was always very sweet to us he wasn't so much part of our lives as our mother. He was in France from 1915 to 1916. My mother in all her grief remained very loving and caring of us and she loved our brother. It made a lot of difference to her having this one son.

The nursery rhyme:

> *"Little Jack Horner*
> *Sat in a corner*
> *Eating his Christmas Pie*
> *He put in his thumb*
> *And pulled out a plum*
> *And said 'What a good boy am I"*,

has been connected with my ancestors on my mother's side. When Henry VIII dissolved the monastery at Glastonbury in 1535 and martyred the Abbot, the land was sold very cheaply to local landowners, and one of them, called John Horner, bought a fairly large estate, including Mells. To begin with he went on living at Cloford, a tiny village about six miles away, but later, about 1592, the family added on to a house adjoining the church at Mells and made it into a large manor house, probably in the shape of an H, and eventually went to live there. It was invariably suggested that the rhyme referred to the estates he bought, but my grandfather always strenuously denied this allegation and I think the rhyme is older than the sixteenth century and can't really have anything to do with our property.

The last Horner, my second cousin, entered the monastery at Ampleforth in Yorkshire and is now a member of a huge monastery in St.Louis, USA. My mother's elder brother was killed in the war, and the other died when he was 16, so when my grandparents died, the property was divided between my mother and her sister. My mother became a Catholic in 1924; my sister and I did not automatically follow her, but had to find our own way into the Church as we grew up, amid a certain amount of family opposition.

My maternal grandmother was a Scot, the daughter of a tea merchant in Glasgow called William Graham, who was a great patron and admirer of all the pre-Raphaelite artists and also bought Italian pictures. She herself was very artistic and literary minded. She had grown up in a cultured Presbyterian society and was very well educated as also was her husband, Sir John Horner, to whom the Mells property belonged. He was a darling. He was a Liberal - rather unusual for a High Church country gentleman - and gave me my first lessons in Latin when I was about seven.

After 1916 we were rather homeless. We went twice to stay with my aunt in Newmarket, and my mother became a VAD nurse. She nursed at one time at a big hospital on Wandsworth Common which later became an orphanage. She used to cycle there from Bloomsbury; then when we went to Newmarket, she worked at a hospital for the war-wounded near there. In 1918 a great friend of my grandmother, the Duchess of Sutherland, very rich and glamorous, took out a hospital to St.Omer in Flanders. She had her own hospital and staff: her daughter worked there and my mother spent the summer of 1918 nursing there. While she was doing that we were lent a bungalow in Suffolk, at a place called Thorpeness, near Aldeburgh, quite close to the sea. Our nurse, myself, my sister Perdita and Trim stayed there for about six weeks. It was almost on the sands and we used to bathe two or three times a day; we were even allowed to bathe before breakfast while our nurse kept an eye on us from the window. The sandy garden round the house was full of toads, and my brother used to pick them up and bring them in, so we all got very devoted to toads. I remember him (aged two) going up and down the stairs to the balcony reciting bits of Beatrix Potter's Jeremy Fisher, which he knew by heart.

There was a shallow lake in the village with small islands, which had been developed for children and we learnt to row about it and land on the islands, which we found fascinating.

Till that summer we had always regarded fish as very disagreeable food, to be endured rather than enjoyed. But at Thorpeness for the first time we tasted fish fresh from the sea; it was completely different from anything we had eaten before, and ever since then I have expected fish to be delicious, even though my expectations have not always been fulfilled.

Mrs. Marjorie Davies is still living in the village of Brailford, between Derby and Ashbourne, not far from the place where she was born. She is another among the many whose fathers were killed during the First World War.

I was born on 18 February 1915 in the village of Brailsford near Derby, and was christened Marjorie Constance in the old village church. My parents were Albert and Lilian Whitehurst; I was destined to be an only child.

My father was gamekeeper to Col G.A. Strutt of Brailsford Hall - a member of the famous Strutt's cotton family - and even now I can remember my father's guns in a large case hanging on the wall, and numerous stuffed animals and birds, some of which I still have.

Brailsford Hall

My mother's home at that time was in Warwickshire, where her father was head-gardener to the Phillips family. They were mine owners and became well known in more recent years through the marriage of their great-grandson, Mark, to Princess Anne. My parents met when my mother was employed as, I believe, a housemaid at Brailsford Hall. They were married in 1913 and given a house on the estate.

When war broke out in 1914 my father waited until I was born in 1915 before enlisting in the Royal Fusiliers. He exchanged the green fields of Derbyshire for the mud and hell of Flanders and, tragically, was never to return, except for brief leaves. I can very vaguely remember his last leave and crying when he left me, and still have some silver and copper coins he gave me. He was reported missing on 28 March 1918, with no known grave, so peace brought only sadness to our home, although I was too young to understand. I remember once being taken to visit my father lying wounded in a military hospital at Birkenhead, and crossing the Mersey by ferry-boat. He was wounded twice but unfortunately never received what was known as a 'Blighty one' - or bad enough to bring him home for good. I still possess heart-rending letters which he wrote to Mother from the front. I lived in three different houses in my very early years, and they could not have been more different in character and style.

Mr. & Mrs. Whitehurst with Marjorie

The first one, called Lake View, where I was born, was a comparatively modern semi-detached house in a leafy lane near to Brailsford Hall. My parents were the first occupants soon after their marriage in 1913. My father's employer, Col. G.A. Strutt of Brailsford Hall, when he heard that both his chauffeur and gamekeeper were shortly to marry, arranged for the two brand new 'semis' to be built especially for them, by estate workmen. The two couples eventually became firm friends and the chauffeur's wife, who had no children, became my beloved 'Auntie Effie'. The house even had an upstairs bathroom, rare in those days, with water heated by a solid fuel fire. We had no indoor toilet however. It was situated in the back-yard, but at least it was a WC, and all under cover with the coal-house. There was a back kitchen with a copper, in addition to a dining room, sitting room, front hall and two large bedrooms. Outside was a very large garden, with runs and cages for my father's gun-dogs.

Brailsford, Derbyshire

When my father did not return from the war, Col. Strutt decided to move my mother and me to my second home in the same lane - so close that I recall the removal men were able to carry me there on our old sofa! I must have been about four at the time. This house, called 'Woodyard Cottage' was detached and very pleasant, but was older and had no mod.cons., except for cold running water. The lavatory was outside and of the bucket variety. I have many happy memories of this house and look at it wistfully even today. It had a smaller garden, with a front lawn and very sunny aspect. Mother used to make nettle beer in those days from the large quantities of nettles growing in the fields around. We practically lived out-of-doors in the summer months.

Unfortunately, when I was about seven years old Col. Strutt decided he wanted this house also for an employee, so Mother and I were on the move again. This time he most unkindly gave my mother notice to quit and advised her to move in with her parents. In retrospect perhaps we had spent too long away. Young as I was at the time, I recall how upset she was, as she wished to keep a home together for my sake.

However, Col. Strutt relented and offered to interior decorate this old cottage where I still live for us, and Mother had no choice but to accept. The terraced cottage in the village street was vastly inferior to the other two houses in every way in those days. Ironically, after being recently modernised, and with its old oak beams and quaint doors, it now has a very much higher value than in those far-off days when beams were not admired at all! The amenities, or rather lack of them, were similar to Woodyard Cottage. We had one cold tap, and that was all, and bucket lavatory. The garden was down the road, away from the cottage - most inconvenient. We now have a new one taken from the field at the back. We had two bedrooms and a large landing, two living rooms and a wash-house. Although the estate owners have changed over the years we are still tenants and pay rent for the cottage. I found out it had once been the village Post Office, so called it Old Post Office Cottage, or 2 Main Road. The old wash-house is now a modern bath-room, and the whole place far more comfortable. I often wish it could have been like this in Mother's day!

My most enduring memories of early childhood, however, are not of Brailsford but the old gardener's home at Ansley Hall, near Nuneaton in Warwickshire where, as previously mentioned, Grandpa was head gardener. As Mother was now widowed we spent more time than ever there. Mother took me home to her parents whenever she could, which was most of the time until I started school. Ansley Hall was an historical and fascinating old building - even in those days being semi-derelict. To an imaginative child, as I was, it was a happy hunting ground for childhood games and rambles.

The building and its park land had no doubt been purchased and developed because of the rich seam of coal which lay beneath it, giving its name to the Ansley Hall Coal and Iron Company, owned by the Phillips family. Old Mr. William Garside Phillips was a kindly looking old gentleman, who always wore a button-hole. The Hall itself was never occupied by the Phillips, and in those early days they lived in a fairly modestly-sized mansion close by, known as The House. I well recall Grandpa coming over each morning from the Hall gardens, laden with produce which was handed to the housekeeper there, named Miss Little, an elderly lady in black. The House also had fairly large grounds, which Grandpa was in charge of, so he was a very busy man, with many responsibilities. Overwork may have contributed to his early death, when I was about fifteen. Tragically he was found in a collapsed state from a brain haemorrhage by a garden-boy in the old potting-shed. A sad but possibly fitting end to a wonderful life.

The main part of the old Hall was turned into a Working Mens' Club, complete with bowling green, and there were tennis courts nearby. The rest of the huge complex, including courtyards, outbuildings and stables, was used as staff accommodation. Many of the Phillips' employees were housed there. Apart from my grandparents and their family, the chauffeur and even some of the coal-miners lived in what had become almost a village-like community, where I made many childhood friends. Things were very primitive, water having to be fetched from a communal wash-house, and the only toilet facilities were earth-closets, requiring a visit by the night-soil men when we were all in bed! As many homes in Brailsford were not much better off at that time, we thought nothing of it. At least the gardener's house, which was located in an outer courtyard, was very spacious. It needed to be, for numerous relatives from all over the country visited Granny and Grandpa at various times; we were a very happy and close-knit family. My grandpa, William Richard Davies (I married my cousin, which explains my married name) was like a father to me, taking the place of the father hardly remembered.

The parkland around the Hall was full of interest. There was a sinister looking pool, known as the Temple Pool, with a small ruin nearby, where it was rumoured a hermit had once lived. It was also rumoured that a secret passage led from somewhere in the kitchen gardens beneath the road and into the Hall, but to my knowledge no-one ever found it. The annual Flower Show was held in the Park, with a fairground and colourful gipsies. This was an extra busy time for everyone connected with the gardens.

I think I must have been the most travelled child in Brailsford, for most village children had never seen a train, let alone been on one, although cars were slowly taking the place of horses on the main village high street. Granny, Grandpa, and numerous aunts, uncles and cousins made up my little world in those far-off days, and I really believe I thought they would never end, if indeed I thought about it at all. I was naturally made a great fuss of - spoilt I suppose.

Miss Betty Bindloss is another whose father was killed during the First World War, but her mother managed to provide a wonderful home for her three children.

I was born in 1910 at Edgebaston, Birmingham. My father was a civil engineer. My mother was a Devonian, from a small village (Coffinswell) between Torquay and Newton Abbot, where for generations her family had farmed Court Barton, in whose court-yard the church also stands. My sister was born in 1913 and a brother in 1915, only a few months after the outbreak of the First World War.

My father was a Territorial officer, in the 5th Warwicks, and was called up early in the war. My only recollections of him are of a tall man in uniform, of which I remember a peaked hat, leg-gings called puttees, and carrying a cane.

We had a Nanny for a time, who wore a cap with long white streamers, and a large white flannel apron at bath time. I remem-ber the delicious taste of my sister's bottle, made from Allenbury's milk powder, and also the nasty taste of senna pods and the pleasant flavour of Syrup of Figs.

A great aunt took me away while my brother was born, on a long train journey to Paignton. I was frightened by the noisy, rocking, jolting steam train, with blinds drawn over the windows and porters calling out the names of all the stations. In those days one could buy a delicious lunch basket, full of chicken sand-wiches, fruit and milk, at the station restaurants and that helped to pass the time.

The house where my two elderly great-aunts and a great-uncle, who had a long white beard, lived was full of strange things from the Far East, where Uncle Henry had lived and worked for many years. There was a glass case full of Chinese figures of nodding Mandarins, and a cabinet whose drawers were filled with large, beautiful shells.

In my bedroom I had a set of china wash basin, jug, a tooth brush holder, a soap dish and a large pail for the dirty water, all gay with a pattern of huge roses. A brass can of hot water came up for washing, and the gas fire had a high guard fender on which the towel was hung - lovely and warm and dry. A nightlight gave a comforting glimmer of light all through the night, and on the landing a gas mantle popped softly and companionably.

My mother was advised by our doctor in Birmingham to move us all to Devon, hoping that good air, good cow's milk and a milder climate might help my brother, who was very delicate. A house to rent on a hill in Newton Abbot, opposite one owned by my mother's aunt and husband, was found and at once my brother improved. Milk came every day by pony trap in great churns with a tap, and was measured into jugs by copper ladles.

Our daily walks with the pram or a push-chair round the hill gave us plenty of fresh air. We played in the large gardens of our two opposite houses, with lawns and a swing, with lots of pine trees and wide open views over the meadows and claypits, and the canal where horses drew the barges full of clay or granite from Dartmoor down to Teignmouth.

Looking the other way over the railway station we saw the marshalling yards of Newton Abbot, with a constant soft background sound of machinery, clanking and hooting, whistling and puffing.

My father was killed on the Asiago Plateau between Italy and Austria in July 1918 and so never saw my younger brother, born in May that year.

Pony traps brought farmers and wives into market for shopping. Shop deliveries were made locally by boys on bicycles. Coal and heavy deliveries were made by large carts with one or two horses - a difficult business on winter's slippery roads! Very few roads were surfaced - most were gravel - muddy in winter, dusty in summer.

Country walks were in lanes thick with wild flowers, where we met the stone-breaker sitting by his pile of big stones that he broke up with a hammer; or the lengthman who had the hedges to cut and the ditches to clear. There were always horses working in the fields, ploughing, harrowing. Haymaking time was specially lovely - the ricks smelled so good and it was fascinating to watch them, and the straw stacks when the corn was cut, being thatched.

I look back on the first ten years of my life in Devon with great thankfulness for its fullness and zest. We were a happy family, with a wonderful mother who had to be father as well, and we lived in rural surroundings with friends from all walks of life. It has good memories.

Miss Eileen Karwood was born in 1915 at Shepherds Bush, but is now living in Bexhill-on-Sea. She is among the many children whose fathers were tragically killed during the First World War.

My father worked in his father's dairy business, with hand-drawn carts to deliver milk to the customers. There was also a shop in which bread and groceries were sold.

When war was declared he was called up into the King's Royal Rifles and stationed at Winchester, but then just nine months after my birth, in 1916, he had embarkation leave. That was the only time he saw me, as he was killed in the battle of the Somme. So

Eileen Karwood's father with the K.R.R's

I have sadly no personal memory of him, but am grateful for the photographs, especially the one of him taken with me and my mother. This he had in a wallet in his breast pocket, and it protected him from injury from shrapnel on one occasion. Many years later I was able to go to France and visited the cemetery where he was buried among so many other soldiers at that time. So I was able to put flowers on the grave and take a photograph.

It is good to have one of his father's shop, too. His mother is standing in the doorway, and my father in front of the left-hand churn. This was taken between 1909 and 1910. The lady in the separate photograph is my father's sister. In the photograph of KRR recruits at Winchester, taken in 1916, my father is in the back row, third from the left.

Life was difficult for my mother, being left widowed and with a small baby to care for. Pensions were very inadequate but she managed somehow.

Mrs. Doris E. Russell is another whose father died during the First World War. She spent her early years in Bexhill-On-Sea and returned to live there after her husband's death.

I was born on 16 June 1907 at Western Road, Bexhill. My father died of TB during the war, which meant my mother was left on her own to bring up eight children: she had ten children but a boy and girl died in infancy. Life was a great struggle without a father. My older sister went out to work as soon as she left school

Mr. & Mrs. Karwood with Eileen   *Eileen Karwood's aunt.*

and my mother, who was a trained nurse, spent as much time as she could nursing private patients. As she was away from home so much, it meant that I, as the oldest daughter available, had to keep the home clean and see the children off to school, then look after them when they returned.

There was a small entrance hall to the house, a scullery, breakfast room and kitchen downstairs, and five bedrooms, a sitting room and bathroom upstairs. The sitting room was large and had

Eileen Karwood's family dairy business.

21

a veranda facing the main street. The iron cooking range and copper were joined to the same chimney and flue system. I cleaned out the flues but the chimneys were swept by a local sweep. The outside of the copper was smooth cement and was kept white by using hearthstone. The range was kept black and shining with Zebo, and the fireguard, fire-dogs and kerb were also cleaned with Zebo, the brass parts with Brasso.

The washing was done on a Monday, mostly by me, as Mother was out at work nursing. I passed the special examination when I was twelve so was allowed to leave school before the age of fourteen to look after the house and family.

The house was Victorian and had an entrance off the main pavement, with shops at both sides. I cleaned the front doorstep with hearthstone. Trams ran along the street very close to the pavement. The shops were situated in similar Victorian houses.

Most of the food we needed was delivered to the door. The local coalman brought coal once a week by horse and cart, and we had fresh milk and eggs daily from a local dairy. When my father was alive he had an allotment which kept us well supplied with vegetables.

I well remember the gas lighter. He was an old man who rode a bicycle and carried a long pole which he hooked onto rings on the side of the gas lamps. It was amazing how he could do this job, as he had only one leg. I also remember the muffin man ringing his bell, the hot chestnut seller, and the organ grinder with his monkey.

Most of my time when I was not at school was spent looking after the family and doing housework. On Saturdays and holidays we usually stayed at home, but sometimes our uncle who had a farm would take us there for a day out. Saturday was the day for the weekly shopping, and in the evening I was sent to the local baker's just before closing time to buy cheap bags of buns. On Sundays we went to church and if the weather was fine visited the local cemetery with flowers for my father's grave.

We played with iron hoops and a hook made by the local blacksmith. My brothers had tops made of wood.

Mary Shirley was born in 1922, but shares memories that her sister, Isobel Brooks Wookey, deceased, had of life before 1920. Isobel, who was born on 4 August 1911, had silver blond hair, and blue eyes.

It was the custom in 1911 to name children after royalty, so my full names were Ena (Spain), Isobel (Portugal), Louise (France).

My parents' name should not have been Brooks! My grandfather's name was Taylor, but apparently he was a womaniser and his wife divorced him. He was so ashamed of his behaviour that he moved away, changed his name to John Brooks, and began a new life with someone else. He died suddenly in his forties, leaving my grandmother with six small children and a farm to run. She could not continue to live that way for very long, so she moved to a sub-post office at the top of Bridge Street, Barrow-on-Soar, Leics., which she ran. She was granted a licence to make and sell her own wine.

Grandma wore red flannel petticoats and had a four-poster bed in her bedroom. It was in the front of the house, over the parlour. She also had *two* grandfather clocks.

My father was born at Brook Farm, Wilson, Derbyshire in 1880. The timbered farm is now Brook House, restored to a high standard. The last I heard was that it was a conference centre, with a ballroom on the first floor. A few years later a party was being held by young people who were so heavy on their feet that the ceiling in the room below came down!

My mother's first husband, a Gilman and the licensee of *The Bell* at Horsley, Nailsworthy, Stroud was much older than her. He had died before she met my father.

My father loved clothes and so did my mother - especially hats! He always drank his first cup of tea of the day out of the saucer, saying "What's good enough for Queen Victoria is good enough for me!"

I remember soldiers being billeted on my parents. Charlotte Sophia and William Henry Brooks, when they were living at 87A Albert Road, Wellingborough, Northants, during the First World War. These soldiers taught me to read and write. They were sadly missed when they marched off on their way to Flanders, many of them never to return.

War songs included *Tipperary, Pack Up Your Troubles, Keep The Home Fires Burning,* and *The Sunshine Of Your Smile.*

Another was:

> *(Chorus) God send you back to me,*
> *Over the mighty sea.*
> *He knows I want you near;*
> *God dwells above you,*
> *Knows how I love you,*
> *He will send you back to me. (Verse)*
> *Dearest you've left me,*
> *Weary and lonely,*
> *Sailing so far away ....*

Large families were more common at the beginning of the 20th century than they are now. Florence Slade (née Fowler) was born in London, the youngest of nine children. She was so unhappy at the orphanage she was sent to when her father died, that she has few memories of her childhood there. She now lives at Wealdstone in Middlesex.

I was born in July 1901, the year that Queen Victoria died, in Finchley on the outskirts of north London. I was the youngest of nine children, having four older sisters and four brothers. When I was only five my father died of cancer at the age of forty-five. He was a builder and in those days there were no pensions. I still remember my father taking us all out in his pony and trap. In those days there were hardly any motorised vehicles on the roads.

As my mother had a large family to support and I was the youngest, I had to go into an orphanage at Haverstock Hill until I was sixteen. My curly locks were cut off to a bob. We had dormitories with wooden floors and iron bedsteads. The food was plain but adequate. After breakfast we all went into the chapel, where we were joined by the boys for morning prayers. The regime at the orphanage was very strict. During the First World War we watched the Zeppelins from the dormitory windows. These airships were much used to bomb parts of England, until later in the war the Germans changed to aeroplanes as too many of their Zeppelins were being shot down in flames.

My family visited me occasionally, but I have few happy memories of those days, though we were allowed to go out with a supervisor and walk round Regents Park.

Mr Gerry Lott enjoyed the peace and quietness of life in the country when he was young.

I was born in 1907, in Bayswater, London, the youngest of four boys. My next oldest brother died very early, so I did not really know him. Both my parents were from Plymouth, but my father was working in the Admiralty. When they agreed to separate in 1909 my mother returned to Devon with her three sons, first to Exeter, where we lived for two years. Then we moved to a small village, Upton Pyne, about three miles from Exeter, into a little brick-built terraced house. The rear garden adjoined the church. Opposite us was a large farm and I used to go there to collect the milk.

We had running water in that house, but when we moved to a detached house in its own grounds we had to use a pump in the front garden. Then the water had to be boiled on the kitchener in the kitchen. We were allowed to collect any fallen wood for the fires, but not to fell trees. I remember my older brothers sawing up logs: we used no coal. The villagers could not afford it!

This house probably proved too expensive so we moved to a small cottage, one of three with thatched roofs. There was a hornets' nest in our roof, but we were told that if we left them alone they would not trouble us - and they didn't. We had two large orchards at the rear of the cottage, and handpicked most of the apples, then packed them into sacks. Mother would hire a cart to take a ton of them to Exeter, where they sold for £4. We also picked mass (acorns), which the farmer bought from us for a few coppers a peck. Like nearly all the villagers, we kept chickens, and knew the delight of free range new-laid eggs. Blackberries were abundant in the hedgerows and we gathered them for tarts and jam. They went well with the apples. I also caught a mole occasionally, which I skinned and dried, then sold to the plumber. Plumbers used the moleskins to wipe the soldering on the joints of lead pipes whilst red hot, to make a good seal, so they were always in demand. Sometimes we found young rabbits, took them home and fed them until they were big enough to be released. Rabbits were abundant and a good source of meat. I found that if I approached one quietly, down wind, I could touch it. Then instead of bolting off it would somersault backwards, where I was ready to catch it. Another source of nourishment. During the war there was plenty of meat around. The butcher would call on Mother to order her joint for the week-end. Late on a Saturday night he would call and say, "Mrs Lott, here is the joint of lamb you ordered," notwithstanding that she had asked for beef! Sugar was the only item in short supply, but we were fortunate in having plenty of bread. Wounded soldiers in their pale blue uniforms were a common sight in those days - so many of them around.

The local policeman was also the gamekeeper, and a friend of the family. He brought pheasant and partridge eggs to my mother, who hatched and reared them under her hens, then handed the young birds back to the gamekeeper. I used to go out with him when I was free and act as a beater during the shooting season. If he found any finches' nests he watched over them, then when there were eggs he substituted sparrows eggs for them. Men came from Exeter and collected finches' eggs, to sell them to people who liked to keep finches in cages in those days. My gamekeeper friend did not approve!

All the children and many of the adults helped with the haymaking and harvesting on the farm. A firkin of cider was hidden in the hedge to quench the thirst of the adults. One day I discovered it and much enjoyed drinking the cider. When I was missing

Mother alerted the farmer and all the village searched for me. When they found me I was completely drunk and unable to stand. It took a long time to live that down!

Periodically a lorry came to the top of the hill in the village and dumped a quantity of large stones. Then the stone breaker would sit and break them very skilfully into 2" pieces. Eventually a lorry would come to collect them, ready for use on the cobbled roads.

The village school cattered for children of both sexes from the ages of three to thirteen. There were about thirty of us. The boys wore corduroy knee breeches (a revolting smell when new!), a woollen jersey and hobnailed boots. The girls wore pinafores, black woollen stockings and laced boots. On Sundays I had to wear a 3" stiff collar. Mother made sure that all we three boys were ready for church in good time.

The Headmaster and his staff were called up during the war, and two young lady teachers took their place. Mother got them accommodation in the cottage next to us. It was their first time away from home and she used to mother them. There was a local reading competition among the seven-year olds, and when I was awarded an Easter egg for reading, I was accused of favouritism!

The Earl and Countess of Iddesleigh, who owned Upton Pyne, were living in America and Lady Rosalind Northcote had presumably been delegated to look after the estate. From time to time she would summon all the children in the village to the mansion, up to two miles' walk for some. I think it was to do with the Band of Hope, but we had no other meetings. When we were all gathered she marched us to Barnfield Hall at Exeter, where we were shown lantern slides ('magic lantern') and given a lecture on how to look after animals - horses' hooves, etc. - and the countryside. She bought us buns when we were outside the city boundary, then walked us back to her home where we were directed to the kitchen; there the servants provided a welcome meal. All the men and boys doffed their caps to her and to the Headmaster's wife, and the Rector and his wife, whilst the girls curtsied.

I was the only chorister in the church during the war, and when the rheumaticky elderly lady who pumped the organ was in too much pain to do so, I took her place.

Mrs Marion Yates is a real Devonian; she was born near Plymouth in 1907 and although she moved away when she was married she has returned to the area.

My father was a farmer at Cornwood. He had a mixed farm - arable, cattle, horses and pigs, but no sheep. We had a very pleasant farm building, comparatively new as the house had been burnt down not long before we moved there, especially the kitchen area. The latter was very modern for those days, with a large range and a boiler by the side, which heated the water. It was marvellous! When the water was boiling mother drew it off by a tap at the bottom. None of our friends had one like that in those days.

As well as the large kitchen, there were two more rooms downstairs and four bedrooms on the first floor. My sister Winifred was eight years older than me and we shared a room together. She was a dear and looked after me when my mother died: she was always very good. Father was not called up during the war as farmers were needed to help produce food for the nation. Nor was he required to do fire watching or other national service.

He became ill and had to go to Plymouth hospital: it was stomach cancer. The doctor asked if he had had an injury at some time. "No," said my mother, but then Father remembered that some years earlier he had been kicked in the stomach by a horse he was breaking in. That was the beginning of the growth, and he died later on in the Twenties.

Maidie Stokes spent her very early years in Cheltenham but is now living in Ledbury, Herefordshire.

I was born in Brimscombe, Stroud, as my father was working in that area. He found a tiny cottage in Brimscombe. It is a very hilly place, so when they were first married my parents walked everywhere. Mother lost her first baby, which would have been a boy. She soon became pregnant again with me. As soon as she was fit they moved to Cheltenham and I was christened in Leckhampton. Father borrowed money from his mother to buy a small house there. He had a younger brother, Walter, who had a severe spinal deformity. There were no other children.

Mother had three sisters and four brothers. They were very poor so she was adopted when about twelve by the Teague family. They loved her and taught her to play the piano and violin. That is how she eventually met my father as he played the violin and called in their shop for a G string. Father could not get a job in Cheltenham as an engineer, so in 1912, when I was two years old, we moved to Liverpool. Father's cousin, Cotterell, was manager of the Cunard line in Liverpool and suggested Father took his engineer's examinations. He passed well and went on the INVERNIA, travelling to New York and back. We found a terraced house in Bootle but we were lonely without Father and he missed us, too. He came home once a month. The area was rough and although we got to know our neighbours life was very different from Cheltenham.

Mrs Gwendoline Harris (née Long) was born in Truro but now lives in Bovey Tracey, Devon, with her daughter Joyce Pook.

I was born in 1906 in the shadow of the unfinished cathedral in Truro city, and was christened in St.Mary's chapel in the cathedral. I was an only child so enjoyed playing with my cousin Florrie, of my age. I also visited my grandmother and aunties and uncles, as well as cousins who lived in and around Truro. A special treat was a boat trip on the river with Granny and Florrie; I also went for walks with her and her Mum and enjoyed cooking and making pastry in their kitchen. Later, due to poor health, we moved away from the river and went to live in a house on higher land near the railway viaduct in Truro.

The women used to compete with one another to see who had the shiniest black lead range and the brightest brass handles and knobs on their ovens and fireplaces. Also they competed to see who could scrub their door-steps the whitest. The stone floor of the kitchen was scrubbed with carbolic soap and a well-beaten or shaken coco matting put down on top.

Before I was old enough to go to school, my family and a lodger moved to St.Austell to look after my maternal grandmother. Once we went to Truro for a day's visit and missed the last train home. We were very proud of our independence in those days and rather than ask a relative if we could stay the night my parents walked the fourteen miles back to St.Austell, whilst the lodger carried me all the way.

I went to a day school when I was five and walked a mile each way. I stayed there until I was fourteen.

Our house in St.Austell shared an outside toilet with three other houses. When we went there we took a bucket of water to flush it. The night bucket usually had a lid and was emptied early each morning. Sometimes it was necessary to walk back to the outside tap for more water. The cold water tap was shared with three other houses: there were no taps or sinks indoors. In the winter we had a bowl on the scrubbed wooden table top to wash in in the kitchen, where the fire was always lit. In the warmer weather we used the marble wash-stand in the bedrooms with a china basin. An iron kettle on the range provided hot water, which was carried to the bedrooms in a jug. Bedroom rugs or mats were made from pieces of odd bits of cloth.

On bath night we had a zinc bath on the kitchen floor, in front of the range, either on a Friday night or Saturday - the latter especially for those attending church or Sunday school. People kept their Sunday best clothes just for Sundays - always very clean and with well polished shoes. Hats were worn by all ladies and girls. Poor families made their own clothes and cut them down for their children. They would buy a linen flour bag cheaply, boil it until the print was gone and then make it into white shirts and white dresses for the children to wear to Sunday school. Girls had a best ribbon for their hair. The prize of a lovely story book was treasured when given for good attendance. For Sunday School Treat days clay wagons would be scrubbed to take children and their mothers to the seaside. A mug of tea and a huge saffron feast bun would be given to each child. Mothers put their umbrellas up to protect them from the smuts from the railway engine - sometimes the umbrellas caught fire!

My father worked with shire horses, carting logs down to the river. Some of the logs were used for telegraph poles along the roads. Men were very proud to lead the horses in the local carnivals and spent hours cleaning the brasses and 'tracing' the tails and manes and grooming the horses. The brasses and rosettes were proudly displayed until the gypsies were in the area selling clothes pegs and paper flowers. The French onion sellers were also looked upon with suspicion.

Doctors charged for their time and medicines, so most people used home remedies when ill. Many men and also widows bought pieces of leather to sole and heel shoes.

Bread and cakes were baked at home. Women with large families could be all day at the washtub. Most people kept chickens to eat and for the eggs. We could take a milk jug to the nearest farm and have it filled for a penny or two, and a dish of clotted cream cost a few pennies. The butcher delivered to the house and six pennyworth of meat was sufficient to make a pie or several pasties.

In the 1914-1918 war my father lost an arm, but he was fortunate to have a job to go back to, whereas many wounded men never worked again.

Elsie Gomm (née Lucas) was born on 12 December 1903 and appreciated living in the country.

When I was young I lived with my parents in a rented cottage at Upper Studley, Wiltshire. Life was hard and my mother had had several miscarriages. I was the only child to survive.

The cottage had a thatched roof, which was later replaced with tiles. There was a passage inside the front door, with a parlour and kitchen on the ground floor. Upstairs were two bedrooms, one for my parents and one for me. There were no washing machines at that time: all the clothes were washed by hand and mangled outside in the yard. At first we had no running water in the cottage, but then we were the first in the village to have it laid on, with a tap in the scullery: a great improvement. We used an oil stove for cooking and oil lamps. There was plenty of wood around so Dad filled the copper with water and then burned wood underneath to heat it. We also used wood for the fire in the parlour. We had a large garden with three or four strips of land, and in the summer Dad worked for an hour in the garden before going to work. So we had all the vegetables we needed. Across the road there lived a large family, and I was particularly friendly with Dollie and Irene, so I was not lonely.

My father worked as a farm labourer; he was up between 5.0 and 6.0 am to milk the cows then make the butter,etc. Later he worked on the Great Western Railway as a mason's labourer, but he still had to begin at 6.0 am. As he was in a reserved occupation he was not called up when war was declared in 1914, but did firewatching once a week. Like everyone else, we were affected by food rationing and had to queue for fruit and biscuits, but as we kept chickens we had our own eggs and chicken to eat so were better off than those living in towns.

Mrs Frances P. Huxtable has spent most of her life in Devon, and now lives in Bovey Tracey.

My father was one of six brothers born into a farming family in Gloucestershire, but eventually he came to Devon and bought an ironmongery business in Newton Abbot. It was situated in Bank Street and formed part of Ridgeways shoe-shop. My maternal grandfather was an architect and surveyor. He had four daughters, the second of whom became my mother. My father was very fond of horse-racing and attended many local race meetings - as an onlooker, of course. When I was born in 1910, a year after my brother Phelps, he announced my arrival as 'a fine filly foal'. When we were taken to one of the meetings at Newton Abbot, we were so small that we entered under the stile!

My earliest memory is of my third birthday. I was sitting on my mother's knee as she fastened a silver bracelet on my wrist.

We had quite a large lawn, so many children came into our garden to play. One of our playmates at that time eventually became my husband. My father used to get very cross as they and we always climbed over the hedge and railings, so the hedge had a big gap in it. In the Second World War the railings were all taken away for munitions purposes to help the war effort.

When I was five or six years old I went to a small private school, called St. Catherine's. It was very near my home and also close to St. Mary's church in Abbotsbury. I was christened and confirmed, and later married there. In those days the roads were not tarmacked and watering carts had to sprinkle water to lay the dust when it was dry. When the weather was wet, the roads became very muddy.

One night my brother and I were awakened by my parents and carried up to the attic to watch flames leaping to the sky from Vicary's wool mill and tannery in Bradley Lane. It was burnt to the ground.

Paper boys came down the streets shouting out late news if any disaster had happened later in the day. Bennets bus used to travel to and from the station and we would catch it to board a train to Teignmouth and an afternoon on the beach. In those days the entrance to Newton Abbot station was further over, opposite the big main gates of Courtenay Park, no longer there (presumably also taken for the war effort).

On 1 April my father hired a carriage and we went for a lovely drive over the moor. This was to celebrate his birthday and my parents' wedding anniversary. I also have vague memories of my mother going for a trip on a wagonette, and someone standing up and blowing a long horn, evidently to announce their arrival. My father always wore a top hat and frock coat when attending a funeral. What a contrast to these days!

My uncle stayed with us when on leave from the Mounted Police during the First World War. I was fascinated to watch him putting his puttees on! This was a form of leg bandaging to act as gaiters.

When the chimneys needed sweeping Mother left one shilling on the mantle piece, prepared the room by dust-sheeting everything, and then the sweep was ordered. He came very early in the morning, let himself in and out again, so we never saw him. Our milk and also the bread were delivered by horse and cart each day.

Iron and wooden hoops were very popular when I was small, but I was only allowed to use a wooden one. An organ-grinder came along the streets with his small organ on wheels, with a little chained monkey hopping about on top. When we gave him a penny he played his organ and gave us small coloured pieces of paper. I do not remember what was written on them.

We used to rent our pew in church and one day, when Mother took communion I was left alone in the pew. I howled as I really thought she had gone: we were in the last pew in St. Mary's church, Abbotsbury, and it was a very long way to the communion rail. In those days children did not accompany their parents. I understand now that all the pews have been replaced by chairs.

Phelps and I enjoyed a very happy childhood, except when we were expected to lie quietly on the rug in front of the fire while Father had his customary snooze. We would then be taken for a walk in our finery, which consisted of a sailor suit for my brother and white frock, shoes and socks for me.

E. C. was born in Cumberland but is now in a nursing home in Herefordshire.

I was born on 1 May 1903 and looking back my childhood in Cumberland seems to have been enchanting. This wasn't entirely true, of course, but it was when compared to the moral and general behaviour of today. It was easier for us then as there were definite rules of behaviour which we never questioned.

Home life was so different. If we came home from school and my mother was out at some function it seemed dreadful, as it disturbed the accepted pattern of life. Monday was washing day. The wash house was down the garden, a dear little building with climbing roses growing over it. The boiler had a fire to heat the water. Everything possible was boiled after it had been slushed around with a dolly stick in a tub. The clothes were then mangled and rinsed in clean water complete with blue bag. Everything was starched and dried in the garden; then endless ironing even of stiff collars, until my father said they were not well enough done and they were sent to the laundry. Tuesday was baking day. A lovely smell of bread filled the house and the tea cakes were rubbed on top with a butter paper. They were delicious.

On market day we went to the square with a linen napkin for the butter - 'Mrs Barwises' best' (a family joke!). At Michaelmas the market square was very busy for the hiring of new maids who wanted to change their jobs.

Once a year Miss Graham came for a week to make our summer frocks and do alterations. We were quite fascinated because she had a peg leg. She was very patient and kind when we had to try on the clothes.

Spring cleaning was a great upheaval and we quite expected to live in disorder for a week. The mattresses and carpets all went into the garden and were left in the sunshine to air (it never seemed to rain!). The curtains were changed from winter into summer and nothing was left undone.

One day when I was going for my piano lesson Mother said Miss Moore would be on the couch with a rug over her legs, and I was not to ask any questions. I asked "Is she ill?" and was told she had been jilted. "What is jilted?" I asked. Mother said "That is all you need to know, so be off."

We cycled everywhere. My father had tin boxes made to hang on the paraffin lamp hook so that we could keep rare flowers fresh. I only remember Hare's Foot now. There was great emphasis on wild flower collections at school.

We cycled to Silloth to see the pierrots. If we sat on benches on the Hill it was free; otherwise we had to pay for a deck chair. When we returned home we played pierrots in the summer house, dressed in clothes made out of crinkly crepe paper. Another favourite ride was to Caldbeck, through John Peel country in the Fells. We always had to rest on a steep hill, Rotten Row, and once I fell asleep with my head in a gorse bush!

Every Christmas about eight of us, all friends, walked three miles to skate on a little frozen tarn, which was great fun. Another time I remember dropping my purse down the loo at the Pheasant Inn at Bassenthwait lake: we had great difficulty fishing it out!

We are all now terrified of thunder because my father made us sit on Friars Crag at the end of the lake to watch the lightning darting among the mountains. After that I always covered the kitchen fender with newspaper when we had a storm, and to this day I prowl about when there is a thunder storm.

Other interesting things I remember are my sister fainting during her first violin lesson; picking enamel plates off the swimming bath floor and being praised by Mr. Bell, who taught us; passing life-saving exams and going to parties in Mr. Brough's horse-drawn bus. A very special memory is of my brother coming home on leave from the war.

Mrs Elsie Rive was born in 1900 in the beautiful Channel Island of Jersey. A brother was born in 1904 and a sister the following year. She now lives in the Zelah area of Cornwall.

I had a very happy childhood as we lived at a seaside town in Jersey. We spent our days by the sea, shrimping, swimming, diving off the pier, and low water fishing. If the weather was bad we played tiddlywinks, card games like Happy Families, ping pong and skittles. We had hardly any toys as we did not need them - we made up our own games; but I do remember having a dolls' house, a few dolls, a teddy bear and a dolls' tea-set. I also had a wheelbarrow.

We always wore a 'pinny', black woollen stockings and black boots. My cousin made us dresses out of red and white check French cotton. We also had plenty of underclothes! Our hair was worn long, in plaits with a ribbon.

My father was a gardener, so we had plenty of home-grown fruit and vegetables - potatoes, apples, strawberries and melons, which grew well in the milder climate. My father was very strict but kind. He had a BSA motorbike and sidecar. He would sit my mother on the carrier, fill the sidecar with tomatoes and sell them. He also took the sewing machine in the sidecar to a cousin, who did all the sewing for the family. I think he also piled the Jersey Royal potatoes into the sidecar. Later we had a car, as my mother did not like riding on the carrier.

She would bottle fruit and preserve a lot of the garden produce. Pork from a pig that was killed was put into a big earthenware pot with salt, to preserve it. She had a hay box to help with slow cooking. We also kept chickens. Crabs cost twopence each. Mother had a washer-woman, who came in to help. This was the old lady's only source of income. The First World War did not have much effect on us in Jersey, so things were not too bad.

A lot of the people on the island spoke Jersey-French patois, and French visitors would come over from Brittany to buy 4 lb. loaves and fruit, etc.

We had coal fires and paraffin lamps. My mother had a monthly account for groceries, which were delivered by a boy on a bicycle. She ordered a hundredweight of Tate & Lyle sugar at a time, for all her preserving.

We did not have much pocket money, but my friend's mother used to make butter to sell, so my friend sometimes pinched a pound of butter and sold it; then we went to a restaurant to have afternoon tea. At the age of fourteen we did have boy friends, but we always paid for ourselves.

We had a wind-up gramophone with a horn and cylinder records. I kept having to change the needles, which cost fourpence a box. There was also a lot of home-made music, with concertinas, mouth organ and piano.

At Christmas we had a Christmas tree and hung up our stockings. In the early morning we were very excited to discover what they contained. We also had crackers. My grandparents came to visit us, arriving in a 'Victoria' - a horse-drawn carriage. They sat very upright - the tight stays grown-ups wore in those days meant it was not possible to slouch!

There were no tourists at that time, so we had the place to ourselves. We did not go away but walked and cycled. Sometimes for a treat we went on a Sunday school outing in a horse and coach. Once the driver got tight so we all had to get out and walk. We went to the Church of England Sunday school from the age of four, but we were taken out of church during the sermon. I wonder what the vicar would say if he saw what was going on on Sundays nowadays!

We, as girls, did not have much schooling, but we all sat in desks and did reading, writing, arithmetic, composition and dictation.

Mrs Mary A. Blott was brought up in the beautiful environment of Hampton Court, where her father was assistant Clerk of Works, maintaining the buildings and surroundings. She was born there in 1904. Now she is living at Kings Lynn.

It so happened that I was the only girl living in the Palace, although the head gardener had five boys and the fireman three. This was a great anxiety to my mother, who tried to bring me up to be ladylike. So when I was eight I was sent away to an aunt's for the summer holidays. I was put on the train to Ayr at St. Pancras station, in charge of the guard. There was a lady in the carriage who took me to the restaurant car for lunch and tea. On another occasion I was put in charge of the guard when I went to Norfolk. I loved it.

At the time of King George V's coronation in June 1911 I was taken to see a unit of the Indian Army arriving at Hampton Court. They were in tents in the Home Park. On the morning of the coronation (I think about 4 a.m.) I was taken to the Long Gallery overlooking the river to watch them march to the station. They had such colourful uniforms with a lot of gold.

My elder brother was a chorister in the Chapel choir. He had a good voice but Frank, the younger one, had no note of music in him. However, when they were short of a boy he was called upon to make the number up, just mouthing the words!!

Mrs Grace H. Knight (née Ashford) was born at her paternal grandmother's house in Stratford, East London.

My father was a painter and decorator. He was well-known in the building trade as a 'grainer and marbler' - that is, someone who can imitate the grain in different kinds of wood and the various patterns and colours in marble. We were not well-off, but certainly not poor. My elder sister, Ellen, my brother, Alfred, and I were well nourished and clothed, and our family was respected in the neighbourhood.

Grandma was a formidable figure, dwarfing my grandfather, and a veritable matriarch. She had a wonderful singing voice and had an extensive repertoire of songs which she sang almost continually in her rich, contralto voice. Her songs were usually romantic and often so heart-rending that anyone listening could be moved to tears. She was not the usual doting grandmother, and sometimes if we were sent down to see her, she would say, "Aren't you going for a walk?" and when, grudgingly, she let us in, she found jobs for us to do. The one I usually got - and hated doing - was scraping a block of rock salt into powder so that it could be stored in a jar. We never received any reward for these chores.

If she felt more kindly disposed towards her unfortunate grandchildren, she would tell us all to sit down, warn us to be quiet, and then tell us hair-raising stories of supposedly true events. It might be about the time when it rained frogs and toads, and hobgoblins hid in dark corners waiting to grab naughty children, or ghosts appeared with shriekings and moanings. She was an inveterate collector and hoarder - the place was stacked with boxes of buttons, buckles, and odd bits and pieces 'which might come in handy'. She was almost a recluse and only went out on momentous occasions, looking like a galleon in full sail, with her black, heavily-beaded cape and matching bonnet.

Her shopping was done by my cousin, Edie Ashford, who had been brought up by Grandma as her parents separated when she was tiny. She was a wild creature, with startlingly blue eyes and a mane of curly, black hair. Grandma was very strict with her, and kept her well under control most of the time. I was allowed to go downstairs on Sunday mornings and have my breakfast of a boiled egg and 'soldiers' with Edie, whom I adored and thought very funny.

Thursdays were called 'Bread pudding day', when aunts Lizzie and Florrie and my mother (Nellie) took tea with Grandma. The grandchildren, my cousins Winnie, Bibbie and Alfie Collingwood, my sister and brother and I played in the passage and up the stairs. We were given large pieces of Grandma's bread pudding, which was absolutely wonderful - hot and spicy, crammed with raisins, sultanas, currants and peel. Edie was always there and organised games, which were enormously funny and kept us in fits of laughter. This often interfered with the adults' conversation in the sitting-room, when we were ordered to be quiet.

The flat at Grandma Ashford's house became too small for a family of five, with three growing children, and the time came when we had to move to larger accommodation. This was just round the corner at 123 Gurney Road. The move was made through the garden fences at the back! By taking down a section of fence from Grandma's garden and another section into the garden of our new home (and with the permission of the owners of the house backing onto our new house) we were able to pass all our effects from one house to another. I got stuck in the gap in the fence with a large, tin tray whilst endeavouring to help in the activities.

My father, whom I loved very dearly, worked extremely hard to give us a good life and, looking back, I realise what a dull, hard life he led, working all through the hours of daylight, often not getting home until after dark. His only 'vice' was a pint at the local pub, called 'Dew Drop Inn'. My mother disapproved and this, unfortunately, led to quarrels. My mother was only a girl of eighteen when she and Dad married, and by the time she was twenty she had borne him three children. Three babies in two years and four months!

I can imagine how desperate she must have been to avoid a further pregnancy, and I conclude that she must have refused to risk another one. For eight years she bore him no more babies, and during this time their marriage got steadily worse. Sometimes we could hear raised voices in the night, and we three children suffered much misery in the unhappy atmosphere that brooded over the house. As much as I loved my father, I hated to see him the worse for drink but I being a child could not understand the reason for his drinking.

Mrs. Hilda Morgan (née Gibbs) was born in Southfields and spent much of her life there.

I was born in Southfields, London, in 1909. My parents had four daughters, Gladys, Hilda, Maisie and Brenda. They adopted an orphaned nephew, Bert, when he was seven years old.

Hilda Joyce Gibbs.
= Mrs. Morgan
in 1913

My father, a Wiltshireman by birth, came to London to join the Metropolitan Police. At first he rode a motorcycle as a Dispatch rider, going from police station to police station in the south-west district. As a young man in Hampshire he learned to play a wind instrument in the Marquis of Winchester's private band; therefore he soon found himself a member of Wandsworth Police Band as a cornet player.

This was great for the family, for it meant we attended many fêtes during the summer months. Dad used to practise his music at home, with the score propped up against the potted Aspisdistra in the centre of the mahogany dining table.

Father was very strict with his children. I was reproved for idly picking a leaf overhanging a neighbour's fence. He even bought a small cane 'to tickle our legs' when we misbehaved, but we used to hide it under the ottoman! He was a very loving father really and always was most concerned if anyone of us were ill in bed. When on leave he took us on outings to museums or the Zoo.

There was one memorable occasion when in Regent's Park he bought a bag of broken biscuits, with which we could feed the animals. An astute elephant, giving children rides on his back, came up from behind us and, lifting the flaps of Dad's jacket pocket, removed bag and biscuits and conveyed them speedily into his mouth. Outside the Zoo I recall seeing a horse-bus - no wonder we afterwards called 'buses' motorbuses!

Mother was an expert seamstress and made all our clothes when we were young. She made us pretty blue overalls, trimmed with braid. We had to put them on as soon as we came home from school. I always wished we could have the magnificent white frilled pinafores that the heroines in our Victorian picture books wore!

Christmas was a magical time, beginning well before light, when Father brought a little oil lamp into the bedroom. We were awake so early, trying to find what Father Christmas had left in our pillow cases, hung up the night before! The lamp was necessary because there were no gas lights upstairs. We probably had a roast chicken, a great treat, for dinner and a Christmas pudding with silver threepenny pieces for the lucky ones to find. We called the threepence 3d Joeys.

Having been allowed to eat oranges and nuts during the afternoon, I felt it a pity that I was not hungry when I saw the festive tea-table, with the beautiful Christmas cake that Mother had made. She always provided an extra surprise - 'Jack Horner's pie', or a huge cracker which contained little gifts for each of us. Mother did not claim to be anything but a plain cook, but she provided much appreciated seedy cake on Sundays.

Across the road from St.Michael's School there was a ditch and Hawthorn hedge, with a field beyond. In spite of being told to walk straight home by the road we often played there and squeezed through a broken fence to reach our home.

We loved to hear the muffin man's bell as he came along carrying his tray of muffins, covered with a green baize cloth, upon his head. As we ran along beside him we sang:

Have you seen the muffin man,
The muffin man, the muffin man?
Have you seen the muffin man
Who lives in Drury Lane?

The milkman shouted, 'Milk-o, Milk-o' as he pushed his hand cart or drove a horse-drawn one on which a large churn stood. Housewives took jugs into the street to be filled with milk. I remember the rows of graded blue and white jugs that hung on the dresser at home.

Gypsies used to call out;

'Lavender, sweet lavender, who'll buy?'

Family history says that once I said to the gypsy, "Won't you please come in?" Fortunately she refused.

There was a fish shop in the Merton Road. It was lit by gas fishtail flares, which branched out from the wall. They sold winkles, which we ate for Sunday tea. They also sold bloaters, which were smoked herrings.

Our house was lit by gas in two downstairs rooms. They had incandescent mantles around the jets, but they were terribly fragile and would shatter at the merest touch of a taper when we tried to light them. It was great progress when pilot lights were introduced. They were controlled by two chains hanging from the fitting.

In the corner of the scullery stood a large copper. Water, heated by a coal fire underneath, was boiled there on wash days. Sheets, etc. were pushed down using a copper-stick, so that the suds would not boil over. On children's bath nights hot water was ladled into a tin bath placed in front of the black kitchen range. There was a fixed bath alongside the copper, but it had no taps.

Mrs. Winifred M. Chandler was born on 7 July 1896 in Wood Green, North London, and is still very bright and interested in life.

At the opening of the twentieth century, my parents already had two children, my brother aged four and sister aged two. So when I came along my father thought it was time my mother had some help in the home. He worked in the Civil Service. We were not well off but never lacked any necessities. So, in due course, Leila, a child of fourteen, came to help in the house, living in. She looked after we three babies for the princely sum of two shillings and sixpence a week! However, she was quite happy in her job and glad of a good home.

On washing day the big copper in the scullery was filled with water and a fire lit underneath by Leila. The clothes were boiled with shavings of Sunlight Soap added. Afterwards they were rinsed in the sink and then put through the heavy wooden rollers of the mangle. It was a laborious process, and Leila had to be careful not to get her fingers caught in the rollers.

When I was four we moved to a semi-detached house at Bowes Park. The new home had a large garden, with a summer house, apple trees, raspberries, and other fruit and vegetables, as well as roses. My father was the gardener.

When my brother and sister went to school, I was left alone with the maid. One day I wandered into the pantry and saw a large bag of sugar. I wanted to see whether it contained lump or soft sugar, so put in my hand. Leila came in and caught me and said, "You naughty girl, you are stealing." I replied, "I wasn't stealing, because I didn't get any!"

One day I went to a party and was wearing a new dress. Mother did not want me to soil it, so said "Don't have any jam if you are asked. There is plenty of jam at home." So when I was offered jam on my bread and butter at the party I said primly, "No thank you. We have plenty of jam at home!!"

Leila stayed with us for seven years until she got married. For the next three years we saw her only once a year; she pushed the pram the three miles to her old home to see us with first one child, then two, and then three. After this we presumed the pram would not hold any more and we never saw her again.

Our childish joys then were very simple. We loved the milkman with his cheery Milko' and large churn, from which he poured a pint of milk into the jug we held out, with a little drop over 'to show he gave good measure'.

Then there was the lamplighter, who came at dusk with his long pole which he wiggled about till the light came on. The postman, too, in his smart uniform and sharp rat-tat on the door were all very exciting to a small child.

Mr. Bill Hogg, Jenny's husband, is now living in Salisbury but was born a Londoner.

I was born on 6 April 1910 in West Norwood, London, but the first home I remember was at Brixton Hill, SW2. I was the middle one of three boys. We lived in a three-storeyed house with other similar buildings round a garden. There was the usual aspidistra in the window. We had gas for lighting and cooking.

Milk was delivered in two-wheeled milk vans and the milkman baled out the milk into a metal container. It was then poured into our own jugs. Sainsbury's shop had a marble-topped butter counter, and the assistant would cut a piece off the block of butter, weigh it and add or subtract some as necessary, then pat it up and very skilfully wrap it. When you were buying cheese you could always taste a piece beforehand if you so wished. Francis' was another popular shop. The butcher wore a white apron and a butcher's hat: the grocery manager wore a bowler hat.

Jenny Hogg (née Brown) was born at Dulwich in 1907.

We had an upstairs flat, with a kitchen and one bedroom, which I shared with my parents. Twins were still-born, so I was an only child. We had a gas stove and gas lighting.

My father was a carpenter who worked for a Scottish ship-building company. He was sent to London to make seats in Hyde Park for Queen Victoria's jubilee. Joe Lyons wanted a good carpenter and my father went to work for them in Paisley and then their Picadilly shop. My mother was a waitress there and that was how they met. As suffragettes had been causing damage to property at night, my parents were given a flat above Joe Lyons on High Hill so that my father could keep an eye on them.

He did very well with Lyons. They provided a chauffeur driven car to take him as far as the Cumberland Hotel when they needed work done there. We watched the débutantes queuing up to go into Buckingham Palace to be presented to the King.

We played rounders, skipping, hoops and balls, and went for walks in Hyde Park. In High Holborn there were horse-driven open-topped buses. One-decker trams went under Kingsway through a tunnel and came out on the Embankment.

Mrs. May Goodman (née Clark), who now lives in Bovey Tracey, has some endearing memories of life in the London area between 1910 and 1920.

I was born in 1905 and lived in Dulwich with my parents and sister. Our little house had two bedrooms, bathroom, sittingroom, breakfast room and a small kitchen. The latter contained a gas cooker, copper boiler (no washing machines or central heating in those days), a sink and small table. It was a terrace house, but ours being the end one we were semi-detached. There was a small garden with a wonderful black morella cherry tree, and we kept a few chickens. We were fortunate to have a street lamp right outside!

It was a happy childhood and Dulwich was then a pleasant suburb of London in which to live. 1911 was the coronation year of King George V and I can recall the procession of the King with Queen Mary along Dulwich Common. This was not a common as we know it nowadays, with vast open playing fields etc., but just a wider than usual country lane, unpaved, leading to Dulwich village via the park. School children lined the route, with we six-year-olds in the front row.

For many years Queen Mary made an annual visit to Dulwich Park to view the wonderful display of rhododendrons. The park is not large, but boasts a small boating lake, tea-house, tennis courts, bowls, cricket, and a small 'Rotten Row' for horse riding. To this day it is still the same - well cared for and patronised.

In my early school days the summers were very hot and the winters very cold, with heavy falls of snow. The lake in the park used to freeze over and ice-skating was allowed. Also I remember the November fogs: we could not see the sky or find our way around - thick yellow swirling fog, which seemed to last for days, so while it lasted, no school. Our street lamps were gas, as was all our lighting. The lamp-lighters came around at dusk with a long pole to pull down the chain to ignite the light.

Our milkman called daily, his transport a two-wheeled vehicle, horse drawn. He came to the door with a metal container and measured out our needs, pouring the milk into our own jug - not very hygienic.

Mrs. Florrie Healey has lived in the Dulwich/Sydenham area all her life.

I was born in 1901 and went to the village school from 1906 - Dulwich really was a village in those days! There was a farm with cows nearby, and also a slaughter house, where we could get pigs' liver for black puddings. There was a blacksmith's forge - but no restaurants! There is still a pond in the village, which was originally a millpond: the nearby cottages are still called Millpond cottages. We paid 15s 6d a week rent for our house in Dulwich. It had bells in the kitchen to summon the servants. The house I am now living in was once occupied by Logie Baird, who invented TV.

I believe the toll gate in College Road is the only remaining one in London. When I was a child it cost 1d to go through: now it is 50p and no longer manned but with an automatic gate. An old sign shows that it originally cost $2 \frac{1}{2}$ d to take a flock of hogs through!

Many city merchants had country houses along Sydenham Hill and in Dulwich. The former Lord Vestey's house, which now accommodates the public library, has some of the original panelling. The large houses each had big staffs, with a housemaid, kitchen maid, scullery maid, nursery maid, butler, footmen, coachmen and gardeners. My father ran a carriage hire firm, so knew a good deal about the gentry. The maids earned £10 a year, had one Sunday off a month, and once a month were allowed to go home to visit their families. They did not receive personal Christmas gifts from their employers, but always had new uniforms or something useful for their work.

There were no buses, but cars were just being introduced, and a tramcar went from West Norwood to Victoria. There were also two trains a day and we used to rush up from school to Union Bridge (as it was then called) to see the trains - and get covered with soot at the same time! My mother was the first in our road to have a gas stove for cooking, and of course lighting in the streets was by gas. Some people had gas lights at home, but many just used paraffin lamps. Every Saturday night a man came round selling gas mantles and paraffin oil.

There was no radio or TV, and we entertained ourselves by singing around the piano. We were a musical family and during the First World War entertained many soldiers and sailors from Canada, Australia and New Zealand.

I left school at fourteen and earned 8s 4d a week, working from 8.0 am to 6.0 pm, with an hour for lunch. There were no tea breaks! In the Second World War I worked in the Department of Food based in County Hall for 25s a week, for fewer hours. In 1918 I had an account at the Army and Navy store, for which I had to pay £1.

Mrs. Doris Thorneloe is now living in Littlehampton, but describes life as it was in her young days, when she lived in Addiscombe, Croydon.

I was born in 1914, one of two children. Homes in those days were cold. We had gas cooking, gaslights downstairs and a gas boiler for washday. Washing was a big thing on Mondays. The large galvanised bath was lugged in from where it hund in the outhouse, and the gas copper lit. Mother's arms seemed just to reach over the edge of the bath to scrub with a brush, rub and rub, and then heave out the things into a bucket. Finally they went into the copper.

Eventually everything would be strung out down the garden; then the kitchen had to be cleared up and washed. The whole house smelled of the boiling of clothes! In the evening, there was the ironing; then the airing, all put on a 'horse' around the fire, outside the fireguard.

We had linoleum all over the house, with mats. Bedroom day was Thursday. As a tiny girl I was parked on a bed with dolls or some other toy, whilst the floor was swept and the room cleaned and dusted. Then it was on to another bedroom, Mother had to get down on her knees and wash the floors.

Downstairs there was the black-leading of fireplaces, hearth-stoning of parts around the sink and copper, etc. Womens' work was very hard indeed, but in spite of this my mother was always singing. She would sing hymns a lot, or very, very old music hall songs.

At bedtime we were taken upstairs with a candle, then a night-light in a saucer of shallow water was left on a fairly high piece of furniture, out of reach. Because of these conditions, family life was much closer; everyone did most things in the warmer living or dining room. Children did not have toys in their bedrooms, and in my very young days there was not even a radio. Bedrooms were too cold to linger in, or practice an instrument, or do any-thing except dive into bed as quickly as possible. All the bedrooms in our house had little fireplaces, but fires were only lit if someone were seriously ill.

For breakfast sometimes we had the cereal 'Force' (which was like small cornflakes). The packet would be on the table and the logo on it was a cheery man called 'Sunny Jim'. He had his hair done like a little ponytail, which turned up at the neck. He was very well known, as was the golliwog on Robertson's marmalade. Other days 'Shredded Wheat' was on the table and I sat trying to spell out all the words on it. In the winter more often we had porridge. Then the golden syrup tin would be there for study and I know it by heart still. It is exactly the same to this day, with the lion lying surrounded by the words 'Abram Lyle and Sons, Sugar Refiners'. In small print are the fascinating biblical words; 'Out of the strong came forth sweetness'.

Mother kept a cane hanging on a picture in the living room. I don't think it was ever used on me, but my brother Arthur had it across his bottom or legs on a few occasions. When he was going on to grammar school at ten or eleven years of age, he decided that he was too old to have the cane, so defiantly broke it in two. Mother insisted that he should go down to the local hardware shop (known to us as the oilshop) and buy a new cane. He per-suaded me to go with him, as he felt rather foolish. I think the cane only cost a halfpenny, and as Arthur had just gone into long trousers he pushed it down his 'longuns', so that no-one saw it on the way home.

Father spent a lot of time at the piano and I used to go into the room with him with some of my toys. He was an organist, too, and occasionally I sat with him on the long organ seat, with a pencil and paper to amuse myself during the long service. On Sunday evenings we all sang around the piano at home.

Dad used to take us for many bus rides to parks in different places and also for picnics in the country. Sometimes we took the bus into Croydon and went to the aerodrome. There, for a few coppers, we could go up onto the roof of the airport building and watch as the planes came and went - they were all biplanes in those days. The Crystal Palace was another favourite - a wonderful place.

About Christmas time in 1919 I was told that we were 'saving up' for a new baby, but Mother said that we should not have it until the winter was nearly over, about when the daffodils were out. Immediately I wanted a little sister, named Freda, as I had a small school friend with that name. Arthur's reaction, at nearly twelve years old, was that he would run away to sea. However, on learning that for his impending birthday he was likely to get the bicycle he had been longing for, this anchored him down. Sister Freda did arrive in March, 1920.

Mrs. Eileen Amsdon now lives at Bristol, but was born in the married quarters of Chatham Barracks.

I was born on the hottest July day for fifty years. My father, a Royal Marine, had come back from service in Wei-Hei-Wei, in China and friends who came to see the newborn exclaimed, "Oh, she looks exactly like a Chinese baby!" as they glanced doubtfully at my father. For I had black hair, slitty eyes, and a pale complexion. Fortunately I changed as I grew up. I was looked after quite often by the only child of a service friend of my father's. She lived in another flat and was several years older than me.

I was a proper tomboy, always trying to climb trees and fences, and spoiling my clothes in doing so. It was the custom in the summer for the Royal Marine band to play in the recreation area each Sunday afternoon. The wives and their children always went to listen, and tried to outdo each other in their best clothes. My poor mother never had a chance with me!

When air-raids began during the First World War my mother thought I would be safer with my auntie Lou, her sister, who lived in Camberwell, outside London. Auntie Lou's husband was one of my father's brothers, so there was a close relationship between my cousins and myself. Auntie Lou had two boys, older than me, and a daughter Madge some ten years older. I thought she was too bossy but I adored the boys and tried to do whatever they did, with dire results sometimes. I remember watching searchlights. One night Tom and I were in bed together when there was a loud crash outside. In the morning we all rushed into the garden to see where the anti-aircraft shrapnel had broken off a piece of the roof guttering.

My only sister, Betty, was born in 1917, while Mother was in barracks in Dover. She had blue eyes, fair curly hair, and a docile disposition. She was my mother's favourite - even my Auntie noticed it, for I remember her saying, in front of me, "You know, Ellen, that Eileen always has to do what Betty wants, and it isn't fair." I don't suppose my aunt knew that I always had to go to bed at the same time as my sister, as Betty refused to be in the bed alone. I wasn't sleepy, of course, so I passed the time telling stories. I slept with my sister until I was twenty-five and got married - to-day, girls (and mothers) would think this a very unhygienic arrangement.

Dad left the Service, and we moved to a house in Chatham and acquired a dog. The house was at the top of Silver Hill, and the garden went all the way down the hill. Dad now worked in the Bank of England and went to London and back by steam train. After he had left one morning Mother found his dentures. She wrapped them up, gave them to me, and told me to run to the station as fast as I could (I was seven then and a good runner), so I should be in time to give them to him before the train left.

At the station I told the official by the platform gate he *must* let me through, as I had my father's false teeth to give him. The official must have been amused, but he let me pass. I ran up and down the platform until my father spotted me, and I could hand over the precious package.

Soon after I was eight, we moved to Dulwich village, to a large house with four bedrooms. Mother made ends meet by taking in lodgers, usually young men from the Bank of England. I was forbidden to go near their bedroom and also had to keep away from the dining-room, as it was their's for meals and leisure. We had our meals in our large kitchen, where the range kept us warm in winter. There was a large table, with a couch to one side. The table served as a house or ship or castle for my play-times. It was on that very table that my sister had her tonsils removed by our own doctor. I saw her lying on the couch afterwards, only half conscious, with a bloody mouth.

The drawing-room, heated by gas-fire, was kept for special occasions. I could, however, do my piano practice there.

Mrs. Cleone Heath, now living near Kingsbridge, Devon, describes life in a doctor's house at Walton-on-the-Hill, in Surrey, before 1920.

My father was a doctor and, before the introduction of the National Health Service, a doctor's family was very much involved in his work. His patients came to his private house.

Two rooms were given up for the practice, one as a consulting room off the hall and connecting with another large one, as a waiting room. In between these was the dispensary, a little room where the doctor made up his own medicines. 'Private' patients came to the front door and were brought straight through the hall into the consulting room. The 'Panel' patients came down the patients' path, through a separate gate, into the waiting room, where they sat around on hard chairs. As children, whenever we had to go through to fetch something, we were always extremely polite and compassionate to these people who were 'Daddy's patients' - a very special and important race, different from other people. When gypsies came to him from Epsom at Derby time they were given cups of tea: I remember being very interested that they preferred to drink from the saucer rather than the cup!

In the days before the NHS, my father made his own charging system. At that time when there was a particularly large gap between the rich and poor, he charged the impoverished as little as possible, while giving them as much care and attention as he did to the better off. The latter could make up the difference by paying him higher fees, because they were more able to afford them.

The telephone was constantly ringing from patients needing a visit in their own homes. My father would leave a list of his intended visits; urgent messages had to be passed on to him at one of these houses to catch him on his round. They were usually phoned through by one of the maids, but if they were not available at the time, one of the family would have to do so. When domestic staff became less available, the doctor's wife was tied to the phone.

My brother, who is older than me, remembers that the main illnesses at that time were scarlet fever and measles, which were usually treated at home. Children with poliomyelitis, pulmonary tuberculosis and diphtheria were taken by horse-drawn ambulance to hospital. Hospitals at that time were very different from today, and it was customary for operations to be performed in a private house. Our nursery was at times turned into an operating theatre. The place was scrubbed and clean dustsheets hung over the furniture. I, myself, had my tonsils and adenoids removed on the nursery table by an ENT surgeon. My father had previously driven me round to the fishmonger to get some ice for me to suck after the operation.

The doctor made up his medicines himself, putting them usually in bottles with tablespoon doses marked off by ridges on the glass. The bottles were corked, labelled and expertly wrapped in shiny white paper, which was sealed with a dab of hot sealing wax melted over a little methylated spirit lamp. On one occasion my father had to mix up something for some poor old soul, for whom he was particularly sorry, so he decided to make the medicine taste nice. The patient came back and said, "Doctor, I know mistakes can occur, but did you forget to put the medicine in?" So he had to make it taste horrible for her to feel that it was doing her good!

Later on he was able to change to giving his prescriptions to the chemist to make up. This he did by telephoning from his upright telephone, with the earpiece which hung from a hook on the instrument. He was always anxious not to be kept waiting (no direct dialling in those days), and if the telephone exchange did not answer at once there was much rattling of this hook to attract the operator's attention.

Growing up in a doctor's house, with a caring and compassionate attitude engendered by such contact with the sick and suffering from an early age, must have made a very deep impression. Three of his five children (and even his grandchildren) entered the medical and allied professions.

Mr. Kenneth R. Jones is now living in Watford, Herts., but was born near Cardiff in 1904, one of a large family.

My father was born in Pembroke in 1870. His father was the miller at nearby Carew, the French mill below the castle. He died in 1870, aged thirty-nine, and my grandmother was left with seven children, one only a few months old, to care for. She moved to Cardiff and later to Merthyr, where she married the local brewer. My father and one brother were sent to the London Orphan School at Watford. He met my mother, who was from Dulwich, London, and they were married in 1898. They lived at Croes Faen, near Cardiff, but I cannot remember anything of this village.

Hill Cottage, Croes Faen, Glamorgan. Kenneth Jones' family home from 1898 to 1907. Maes Mawr Farm. Croes Faen means Bridge of Stone.

Around 1908 we moved to a farm at Warlingham, Surrey, 700 feet up, as my father's step-sister married a man who took over the farm at Croes Faen. My brother and I had a governess at Beech Farm and my father drove into Croydon for supplies. The farm belonged to Lord Hastings, but was a poor one, with fields covered in flints. Previous owners had sold the flints to the council for roads but, with the introduction of tarmac, this stopped. Being so high up, snow remained on the roads until April. Once when we were out with a governess a car came by and the occupant threw a bar of chocolate to us. That year there were six weeks of rain and the harvest failed, with stooks of corn sprouting, so my father left the farm.

We moved to Dulwich, where my mother had been born, and my father started a furniture shop. When I was old enough, I went to Alleyns school. We lived in a flat next to Alleyn's school, belonging to St. Barnabas church, as my father was a sidesman. In 1918 Father became manager of a stores at Watford.

We used to go shopping in Lordship Lane, Dulwich, and bought bacon No. 7, sliced, for only a few pence. Sometimes we went to David Greig, the grocers. When the 1914 war broke out they put up the price of eggs: people revolted and threw eggs at the shop. We used the Dulwich library. When you went in you were not allowed to see the books, but a number index stood outside. If the book were available, the number was blue; if on loan, the number was red. The Suffragettes usually held a stormy meeting outside the library on Sunday evenings.

We went to cinemas at Goose Green and later the Tower Cinema, Peckham. At the former I saw Madam Butterfly. She waded out to sea at the end. My parents went to the Tower Cinema, where almost the first rising organ was used; as they came home the first Zeppelin raid began.

Mr. William Paterson was born at Auchinleck, Ayrshire, but he is now living in Falkirk, Stirlingshire.

I was born in a farm cottage at High Glenmuir, Lugar, Auchinleck, in the spring of 1909, the eldest of five children. My father was a ploughman and mother a dairy woman.

My earliest recollection is of being perched on my father's shoulders at Craigendoren Pier as we waited to board a ferry-boat to cross the Clyde. This was in November 1910. The following year my parents moved to a farm about three miles from the village of Muirkirk, eastern Ayrshire. I recall the walk from the station over moorland, and being carried part of the way to what was to be our home for the next nine years. Muirkirk is situated in a mining area: it had Iron Works (which ceased operations after the 1921 miners' strike). It was a busy railway junction and station, with frequent services to neighbouring communities and larger towns farther afield. The junction and station no longer exist. Road transport in those days was practically nil: just pony-traps and a few horse-drawn vehicles, and bicycles. While we were there I remember vividly the sinking of the *Titanic,* as I looked at the huge letters on the front page of a newspaper.

My father was seasonally employed in the local gas-works, when demand was heavy. Gas was the only means of street and domestic lighting. Coal and gas were used for heating and cooking.

Then in 1914 came the outbreak of the First World War. From this point I developed an acumen for listening and absorbing the conversation of my elders. The general opinion then was that war would be over by Christmas. However, as the war progressed the rationing of sugar, butter, flour, etc., took place. New names and situations such as French, Kaiser, sinking of the Lusitania, Somme, Ypres, Arras, Dardanelles, Mesopotamia, the Russian revolution, and General Foch registered in my mind.

During those war years I would lie on my tummy on the hearth rug, under the paraffin lit lamps and candles, spread the newspaper in front of me and scan the faces and names of those 'killed in action'. Slowly the horror of warfare dawned on me.

By 1916 I had two brothers and a sister. This was the year Father 'joined up'. After this, Mother took over the wintering of the cattle, attending to the foddering, and I had the task of 'mucking the byre'. Such winter duties for the farmer enabled my parents to sit rent free.

Sunday school trips and soirées were annual events. Local farmers provided transport with bedecked horses and carts. On arrival at our destination, usually a farm where a field was provided for the afternoon's entertainment, we received our packs of goodies and soft drinks. Such outings were always enjoyed, no matter what the weather.

In general terms, apart from the gloom of war years, I had a joyful boy-hood, free to roam the fields, moors and woodland and in springtime search for birds' nests, watch the eggs hatching and the young being fed. In the long sunny summer days my favourite was the skylark, listening to its song as it soared skywards and then dived to the ground.

Quite a large stream flowed past the farm, a tributary of the river Ayr, rich in fish life. In spate I fished it with bait, in drought I waded and guddled for trout, and snared graylings. Fish was always on the menu, so was hare soup. The latter I was adept at snaring. Potatoes and carrots were in ample supply, harvested and stored in field pits. The farm threshing machine was brought into use during the winter period, the corn being milled into oatmeal, which was our staple food. The straw provided fodder. Fresh water was collected from a well about 250 yards from the farm: this was a daily trek for one of us.

Finally father secured a job as a full-time shepherd on a sheep farm in another district. By this time I had three brothers and a sister, and we all moved to take up our new abode and went to another school on 28 May 1920.

Mrs. Jessie Young spent her early years in Hopeman, Moray, a village in north-east Scotland.

I was born in 1906 and was the sixth child and the fourth daughter of my parents. I have seen many changes in my life and lived under five monarchs, the first being King Edward VII. I remember the coronation of King George V and Queen Mary, which was celebrated by a picnic in our village. I was glad to find a place on my father's lap when my older brothers and sisters grew too big!

My mother was not one of the proverbial bustling housewives; she was a lovely, gentle person, caring for her large brood as well as she could. Often she employed the help of a 'big girl', or, as we called her in our local dialect, 'a big quine'. They came from poorer families and used to work for their keep and perhaps a little pocket money.

My father was a sailor, though not in the Navy, like most of the others in our village, and was away for weeks at a time. How we looked forward to his return, knowing he would give us a penny! A half-penny was the pocket money for the younger members of the family, so we could go to two shops to spend a whole penny.

We were not impoverished in any way. My father owned our two-storey house and part-owned the boat he sailed in, employing ten men. We were always well-clothed and had Sunday clothes as well as week-day ones. These latter never saw the light of day during the week.

Cars were unknown in those days. Even our doctor used a bicycle. When the first car came down our street a woman scrubbing her doorstep jumped up and ran into the house shouting, "There's something coming down the road without nothing" (i.e. no horse to draw it).

We were a very healthy family on the whole. Colds were a nuisance, not an illness, and did not keep us away from school. Germs had not been invented and we never seemed to worry about such things. Not like the present day when everything has to be sterilised! We used to walk to a farm for milk, wait for it to be brought from the byre, and carry it home in a milk pail, still warm. We even sampled it on the way and we did not come to any harm.

Jessie Young on right, aged 7.
Jane   Bella   Jessie
Alex

As my father got his livelihood from the sea, we lived quite close to it, so spent our long summer holidays on the lovely golden beaches, collecting shells, catching small crabs in the pools, and finding shell fish which we boiled in an old syrup tin. We learned to swim from each other: no life-saving belts or arm bands, we just did as we were told. "Keep your chin up," a more clever older sister would shout. And doing just that I learned eventually. I loved the water, which was bitterly cold at first, but again had to obey the "Get under, don't just stand there" command - and we all accomplished the art. The weather always seemed lovely, or do we only remember the fine days?

Mrs. Elspeth Burns is a Scot, at present living in Edinburgh.

I was born at 4 pm in May 1906: a very civilised time to join my family! A younger sister was born in 1912. My native town was Falkirk in Sterlingshire, where the Burns family can trace its roots back to 1530. Grandfather and Uncle Jim carried on a lawyer's business in Burns Court, off the High Street. The office was on the ground floor and the old family home upstairs. From the upper windows the family are said to have watched the second battle of Falkirk being fought in 1746. Prince Charley won. The battle took place near the fever hospital, now Princes Park. There was a triangular small wood almost opposite, known as 'Dead Man's Wood'.

My father was the second of seven brothers and he also had one sister. My mother and her brother lived on the same Arnothill. Both had lovely gardens and tennis courts, so we were very lucky as there were always cousins to play with. Granny's parties were wonderful! We greatly envied cousins who lived in Hertfordshire, as they ate strawberries in June at home, then in the summer holidays they came to Granny Hillside's at Falkirk and were able to eat strawberries again from her excellent garden. After that they went to their other Granny in Aberdeen, whose fruit was just ripe! In 1911 I remember being lifted out of my bed by my father and carried up to the drawing room, where several guests were with my parents. We watched a huge bonfire being lit for the coronation of King George V and Queen Mary. Earlier our daily walks had often taken us to see the bonfire being built.

Another favourite walk was along the canal bank, near the High station railway line, to wave to the drivers as the trains rushed past. Some of them looked out for us, too, and returned our waves!

Mrs. Hannah Bruskin, who is now living in Berkhamsted, Herts., was born in 1903.

I have a vivid memory of the time when I was about five years old and my mother asked me to go to the shop to buy some cream. In those days there was no problem concerning young children going to the shops on their own! We took a cup with us to buy provisions like that. However, instead of buying cream I bought ice cream. I walked along licking it. Mother was looking out of the window to see if I was all right and saw me licking the ice cream: I got a smack. When I look back I realise it was the first time I'd ever been smacked. The second was when I would not let Mother wash my hair. These were the only times I was ever smacked by my darling mother, who was really a wonderful Mum and also a very brave woman. She could not do much for herself but always said 'I am strong as iron' if she were asked how she was.

I was about eleven when we moved, at the beginning of the First World War. One of my brothers joined up but sadly was killed on his twentieth birthday, which really made my parents ill. As for me, every time I went out it was as though he were still alive and I looked for him.

Mr. David Leach was born in Tokio in 1911; his father was Bernard Leach, the well-known potter. It was 1920 before the family returned to England.

The first home I remember in Tokio was at Harajiku - a typical Japanese residential bungalow built on legs to raise it off the ground. There were paper doors and windows, no glass, and matting 1" to 2" thick on the floor. We had two maids, one did the cooking and the other looked after me.

My brother Michael was born in 1913, then a year or two later we went to China. My father was interested in a German philosopher, Dr. Westharp, who was in China at that time, and was anxious to meet him there. Dr. Westharp offered to provide accommodation for my parents, my brother and myself, but it was very hot that first summer and the conditions primitive. Later we moved elsewhere. Dr. Yanagi, a Zen Buddhist, was a great friend of my father in Japan, and he felt he was making a mistake in going to China. My father later agreed he was probably right.

We were pestered with wild cats, which invaded the pantry. One day my father caught one and, with the help of Wong, tied a tin can on its tail. An unkind thing to do, and it clattered over the roofs dragging the can behind him. But at least the cats never returned.

After a year my father decided to return to Japan. We went to Tientsin, from whence we would catch the boat to Japan the following morning. We had to leave all the luggage on the wharf and Father told one of the servants to look after it. In the morning he discovered the boy still sitting on top of the pile of luggage, and he was freezing. We moved outside Tokio, near the river, to Sumidagawa, and were there until 1920. My father wanted me to go to the American Grammar School, and to get there I went right across Tokio on my tricycle or later a fixed-wheel bicycle. Sometimes my wheel got caught in a tramline!

One day on the way home from school I had to cross as usual the main street (the Oxford Street of Tokio), but this time the Emperor was expected and troops were lining the road and had a rope to keep the people back. I took no notice but wriggled through the crowds and across the road, disappearing before anyone could stop me.

David Leach and Michael - held by his Mother, Karvizawa. Sept. 1914.

University students used to waylay us on the way home from school and invite us to go out with them in their sampans. They liked children and also wanted us to help them speak English. We came to no harm and found the young Japanese full of kindness.

When he first went to Japan my father was interested in painting, but one day his great friend, Dr. Yanami, invited him to a tea ceremony. An itinerant potter demonstrated the art of Raku pottery and invited the visitors to draw something on the pots. The Japanese inscribed a poem or something, but as my father could not write Japanese he painted a scene. He found this entrancing and asked his friend if he could introduce him to someone who would teach him how to throw similar pots. The Sixth Kenzan, an outstanding potter in Japan at that time, agreed to give him some lessons. He also built him a little pottery by the house. One day the pile of wood caught fire, and the pottery was burnt down, but when everything had cooled down the pots emerged unscathed. A wealthy friend, Count Kuroda, built him another pottery. My father became a very talented potter and later held an exhibition in Japan.

Eearly in the summer of 1920 my father decided we should return to England as he wanted his sons to be educated at an English public school. He brought with him a talented young Japanese potter, Shoji Hamada, and together they set up a pottery at St. Ives in Cornwall. Hamada later became the foremost potter in Japan. At that time the National Museum of Wales was being built, and my grandfather became the Director. He died in 1927. My maternal grandmother had sadly died whilst we were in China in 1915, a great loss to my mother.

Davis Leach's Mother Murial Hoyle, with her parents William Evans Hoyle and Edith Hoyle. 1900.

Mrs. Anne Porter Hales is an American, now widowed and living in England. She met her English husband when he was in America reading history at Yale University. They returned to his home in England. He was a brilliant historian and became an H.M. Inspector of Schools. He also wrote many books.

I was born in 1908 in the home of my mother's parents. They lived in Rochester (near Lake Ontario) in Upper New York State. An ancestor had gone there from Connecticut, with his family, in a covered wagon drawn by oxen and had built the first log cabin there in 1812. The following year there were eleven houses; then it mushroomed and is now one of the largest and richest cities in America, with the Eastman orchestra and University known world wide. Eastman made his fortune with Eastman, Kodak and Eastman colour. I was born there because my mother had nearly died of tuberculosis a year after my sister was born, so she went to stay in Rochester where she could be nursed and coddled till after the birth. They even built a sleeping porch on to their house for her. She lived to be ninety-four!

Our own house was a modest one, with a typical front porch, in the town of Middletown on the Connecticut river. When I was six we moved across the river to a larger house as another baby was expected. I was told I could pray for a little brother or sister, and was shown the lovely little garments and bassinet that were ready for the baby. Sadly the baby, a boy, was stillborn. My father told us with tears running down his face: I had not known that men could cry.

The house was stone with lofty rooms and interesting out-buildings, a tennis court and gardens. My teenage sister and her friends would sit under the trees playing the ukelele and singing such songs as *Poor Butterfly* and *I'm For Ever Blowing Bubbles*. We had a Swedish cook, an Irish house-maid, an Italian gardener, and a German laundress. This mixture seemed normal at the time!

All middle class American houses by that time had central heating, running water, electricity and gas, and refrigerators that were called 'iceboxes', as they were cooled by large blocks of ice, delivered once a week by a brawny man with an ice wagon. I imagine in the 19th century our house had no central heating, as it had open fire places in all rooms, including the main bedrooms. We had a vacuum cleaning system and even a clothes washing machine. This was unusual before 1920.

I became aware of the Great War from newspaper pictures and posters. My mother worked hard collecting for the Red Cross and the 'Liberty Loans'. Food rationing was called 'Hoovering', for Herbert Hoover (later President) who organised it. We were told to 'think of the starving Armenians' and not waste food.

We all went to the local railway station to see off our local boys going to the war. There was a band and a small crowd. When the armistice was signed there were bonfires and celebrations in the main street of the village. A cousin of ours was killed in the war and also the son of our German laundress. It was doubly a grief for her in that he had had to fight against other Germans.

A seamstress came each spring and worked in the house for several days, making our summer dresses (the winter ones were smocked on fine wool by a place in Boston). The every day dresses had bloomers to match. Under the best dresses were elaborately tucked petticoats and drawers, with tatting lace on them: these were made by my paternal grandmother. We had laced shoes for school and buttoned shoes for Sundays. Every

Easter we had new chamois gloves and straw hats with floral wreaths.

My father's ancestors had come from Messing, Essex, England, in about 1634. I imagine they were Puritans. Altogether I had a very English background and when I married an Englishman and came to live in England, it was easy for me.

2. EDUCATION

The Education Act of 1870, providing free elementary school-ing for all children, had led to widespread improvement in the general level of education by 1900. The schools were run by local councils, but many children went to the popular church schools. Classes were large, up to fifty under a single teacher. Senior boys and girls still at school helped with the teaching. They were called pupil-teachers and some went on to qualify as full time teachers later.

Discipline was very firm, with the cane often excessively used, especially in boys' schools. Pupils at elementary schools mostly sat at long desks, the girls wearing white pinafores over their frocks, and much of the learning was by rote. Tables up to twelve times were often recited daily, until at last they were memorised. Learning poetry and large sections of the Bible by heart was also common. Singing was taught by tonic solfa. Skipping and playing with balls were popular playground activities, and physical exercises were done in the hall, but organised games did not play a large part in the elementary schools. .

Then in 1902 free places to grammar schools were introduced for brighter children who could not afford the fees. However, even by 1914 there were only 70,000 free secondary school places in the whole country, so there was fierce competition. In London children aged eleven plus took the Junior County examination and new schools were opened to give welcome opportunities to girls. Children of the wealthy had a governess at home until the age of eight, when they were sent to boarding preparatory schools. At the age of thirteen they would proceed to a public school, and from thence many went on to university.

In 1900 only 20,000 students attended university, and very few of those were girls, but in 1907 the Imperial College of Science was built as part of London University, and new universities were founded at Birmingham, Leeds, Sheffield, Bristol and Liverpool. These universities were more accessible to the middle classes (and even some of the working class) than Oxford and Cam-bridge, but it was still difficult to find sufficient finances to cover all expenses.

With the outbreak of the First World War, education was dis-rupted for many pupils. Some of the school buildings were taken over for use by the army, often leaving the children to share another school part time, some attending in the mornings, the others in the afternoons. In London and the south-east, as well as the eastern coastal towns, air-raids also caused disruption.

Equipment in school was poor compared with today's standards, and the rapid price increases during the war meant there was even less money to spend on books and paper. Chalk and slates were used for younger children. Although infant schools were usually co-educational, this was not so for older children at junior and secondary schools.

Independent boarding schools were affected by the shortage of food and they and public schools had to accept women teachers. The OTC's at schools provided many of the officers who volunteered at the outbreak of war and they bore the brunt of fatalities. Of the 5650 Old Etonians who went on active service, 1157 were killed and 1467 wounded; they were also awarded many honours, including 13 VC's, 584 DSO's and 744 MC's. Other schools suffered similar losses and acknowledgement.

The school Hilda Morgan attended when she was four or five was quite new, having been built only in 1912. Before she retired she became Headmistress of the Infants' department.

Hilda Gibb, Fairy Queen.
St. Michael's Church of England School Playground,
Southfields, London SW18. c 1916.

I went to St. Michael's Church of England School. Miss Ashley, the Headmistress, we called 'Governess'. She sat at a desk on a dais in the centre of one side of the assembly hall, where she could oversee each classroom. One teacher I remember was a Miss Kathleen Chilcott, who taught the babies' class. She must have been very young herself then. Later we became great friends as Miss Ashley had moved to Allfarthing Lane school and Kathleen had joined her staff. I had been awarded a Student Teachership there for a year before being old enough to enter Training College.

Kathleen was a marvellous story-teller: most of them were originals, I'm sure. She loved dancing too, and asked her class to imagine themselves in a field of flowers and as they moved to music to sing:

> *One, two, three, pick it up,*
> *Put it in your basket,*
> *One, two three, smell it,*
> *Put it right in.*

A Mid-Summer Night's Dream in the garden of the house next door to 39 Balvernie Grove, London SW18, where Hilda Gibbs grew up. (Mrs. Morgan).
Hilda as Puck.

I certainly learned much from her approach to children, and when I qualified I was put on the 'List of First Appointments', which was fortunate for me as jobs were very scarce.

At home we wrote on wood-framed slates, with a special slate pencil, but at school we had boards and chalk. We learned to read phonetically. I remember being bothered by trying to pronounce final 'e's'.

Number was demonstrated on a bead frame, a clever device of wires on a square frame and coloured beads which could be slid along from behind a piece of board.

Of course we progressed to paper and pencil, and then to real ink in little pots that fitted into holes in our double desks. The ink monitor filled the pots from a little white enamel can with a spout like a watering can. Mother wasn't pleased when I was ink monitor for quite a lot appeared on my clothes!

Mrs. Kathleen Hogg (née Robinson) spent her early years in London but now enjoys retirement at the bracing seaside resort of Cromer. She was happy at school.

I escaped by a hairsbreadth being born in a hansom cab on 10 July 1908. My mother would tell with vivid detail how the cabbie managed to deposit her at the Kennington hospital with barely minutes to spare.

I continued to be in a hurry to get on with life! I accompanied my mother when she took my older sister to begin school at the statutory age of five years. When the time came to leave I refused to go home, and although I was only a few months past three years of age, it was finally decided that I might stay on at school. The teacher asked me my name and I replied solemnly, 'Kathleen Mabel get-under-the-table'. The teacher said, equally solemnly, that it was rather a large mouthful and she would call me Mabel. So I went through all my elementary schooldays as Mabel, and it was only when I went away to Christ's Hospital in September 1919 with a scholarship that I was able to change to my first name, Kathleen, much to my relief.

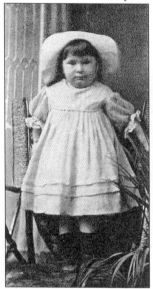

Winnie Robinson aged 1 year 10 months.

Kathleen Hogg (née Robinson) as May Queen at school in 1916.

It was not long after I joined the school that the same teacher decided to launch a campaign against nail-biting. She threatened to dip the next bitten nail in the red ink-well on her desk. Much to her dismay I, the baby of the class, was the next culprit! However, she stuck to her threat and I was mortified by having a bright red finger for the rest of the day. She was very apologetic to my mother, who only said I should not have disobeyed. I don't know how the rest of the class reacted, but it certainly cured me of the habit, and I was never known to bite a nail again.

Apart from this little contretemps, I was totally happy at school. As well as the usual lessons, which enthralled me, I enjoyed physical training and games. When we were old enough, we were given balls of thick, brown wool, and shown how to make slippers to change into when we drilled and danced in the main school hall. We knitted a fairly wide length in 'one row plain, one row purl' and folded this cunningly, then stitched another length as a sole. Finally, we crocheted an edge round the ankle and threaded a length of wool through the holes and tied it firmly. Thus we were able to prance around with little noise.

As well as exercises, we learned country dances like *Gathering Peascods* and reels and a sword dance, which became my party piece for many years to come.

We had a hard netball court in the playground where we played matches against other local schools.

I have a happy memory of a school holiday, when about a dozen of us were strung out across a quiet country road, arm in arm, singing:

> *"There was an old man named Michael Finnigan,*
> *He grew whiskers on his chinegan;*
> *The wind came out and blew them in ag'n,*
> *Poor old Michael Finnegan Beginnegan."*

Suddenly we were brought to a halt by what seemed like thousands of tiny frogs, about the size of a child's thumb, swarming across the road from one shallow brook to another on the opposite side. Imagine the carnage if this happened nowadays, with a stream of traffic in both directions!

Kathleen Robinson with her parents and older sister Winnie. 1914.

We used to go to the local swimming baths, where we soon learned to swim like fishes, and in due course were awarded our life-saving certificates.

When my father returned from the war, he took us for mixed bathing. This was allowed one evening each week and to get in one had to be accompanied by a member of the opposite sex, Our party was made up of my father, my sister, myself and a young boy-friend. There were changing cubicles along either side, and to observe the proprieties curtains were stretched the whole length of the bath, separating males from females while changing!

Cyril Davies' schooldays were affected by the outbreak of the First World War.

My early schooldays occurred at an eventful time, as war was declared with calamitous effects. It was a small one run by the School Board for London and was adjacent to the *Pavilion* cinema in Clapham High Street. There were no sirens or police cars touring around in those days. What I do remember is gripping my mother's hand as I accompanied her to help carry the shopping. A policeman with a flat cap, no helmet, came cycling along the curbside shouting out, 'Take cover. Take cover', and on his back was a piece of white cardboard about one foot square, with an improvised piece of string around his throat to represent a handle for this card. On it was hastily scrawled the words, 'Take cover. Air raid.' At the same time he rang his bicycle bell continuously. Young mothers gathered up their children as there was no time to lose, and directed them into adjacent shops, doorways, basements or anywhere that would provide some cover.

My arm was nearly pulled out of its socket by Mother, who was seeking cover for us, whilst I was gaping into the air to see what was coming over. Uncannily it did, because we had hardly reached the foot of some basement steps when to my mystification I saw droning about a hundred feet up, following the tramline course, a grey fabric-covered dirigible, which was a Zeppelin. It seemed only a few seconds before there was a terrific bang. They had dropped a bomb on to Clapham Road Station, some hundred yards ahead of us. As it proceeded towards Stockwell, I remember Mother cuffing my ear to get a move on towards our home.

When I left school I was coached privately and then eventually obtained a job at a solicitor's office at Bloomsbury off High Holborn. From there I moved to a clerical position in Cornwall, where I now live.

By the time Bill Hogg attended primary school, the First World War had begun.

I went to Hitherford Road school at Streatham Hill when I was five. We had rocking horses and a train, and there was a dolls house for the girls. We used slates and chalk for writing when I was older. On Armistice Day, 11 November 1918, we had a holiday.

Later I won a scholarship to Alleyns School, which was the Junior section of Dulwich College.

Doris Thorneloe enjoyed Sunday school, but was not so happy when she had to begin day school in Addiscombe, Croydon.

On Mondays Mother went to a Women's meeting at church and I went into the crêche, where we were looked after by a kindly lady. There were several other children and some toys. I also went to the Infants' Sunday School, which was a very gentle, caring kind of affair, with only a small number of children.

There came the day in 1919 when I had to start day school. I was coached up to this idea, but when it came time for Mother to leave me there, I was overwhelmed by the mass of children, the size of the place, and the organised atmosphere. Our garden backed on to the railway, and across the railway were the school playgrounds and then the school, so that it was very near home. Mother promised to wave at playtime. However, I cried on and off all the first two days, and I was put at the back of the class with a box of beads to play with. It was a shock to the system to have to sit in a desk for such long periods as, apart from drill lessons and playtime out in the playground, we had to sit still

Mother used to knit a lot of jumpers, and I think it was just about this time that cardigans first appeared. Also a pattern came out of a child's complete dress, which she knitted for me. Apparently this was quite a novel idea. I wore the dress to school and my teacher commented on it. When I said that Mother had knitted it, I was sent all round the school to show it to the other teachers, who duly admired it. It was about this time that my mother daringly had her hair bobbed. Women and girls wore hats out-of-doors, so it was not terribly noticeable, but my grandmother and aunts were simply appalled and ashamed of her. The new fashion had not really got down to our level of society. By the time everyone was catching on, many saucy postcards were appearing in the shops - 'Will you have it bobbed or shingled?' (with a little bit of real hair stuck on a funny old matron's head), and so on. Mother sent one or two of this kind of card to her family when they, too, succumbed to the bob..

Eileen Amsdon had to walk to school when she was small.

The first school I went to was nearly a mile away from my home in Chatham. There were no school dinners in those days so all the pupils had to go home after morning school and then return for the afternoon sessions.

When we moved to Dulwich Village, I went to Dulwich Hamlet school. As soon as all the pupils were in the hall in the morning, we had to stand and recite tables given us by the teacher on duty. We never forgot our tables, even when we were grown up!

I can't recall that I was a trial to my teachers at school, but I do remember an occasion when I was placed in the 'naughty girls' desk'. This was a desk with a seat behind the blackboard, where a naughty pupil was sent, with her back to the class teacher - an outsider. I found myself there once, and I don't know why, unless it was that I had been stupid. As it was not discovered until I was eleven that I had short sight. I wonder if I had misunderstood the writing on the blackboard. Anyway, there I was, and suddenly I discovered that I had one woollen stocking on inside out. Nylon stockings would not have been noticed, but there was a great difference with woolly stockings. I was more worried and upset about the one peculiar woolly stocking than I was about being in the 'naughty girl's seat.'

Dulwich Hamlet school was actually two buildings - one for girls and one for boys. The buildings were not connected and the playgrounds of each were separate from one another. The only way to get to one building from another was to go along the road.

Both the girls' and boys' sections had an Event - a play presented to the public. The girls always did a fairy story, but the boys tackled plays from Shakespeare. These were given in the village hall. I longed to be a chief character in the fairy play, but I was obviously not made in the heroine mould. However, I was once chosen to be 'Fairy Butterfly'. I had distinct ideas of how this fairy should be dressed - yards of gauze and vivid colours - but was very disappointed when my mother (backed up by a dress-maker friend) produced my costume. I had a plain white dress, and the only butterflies were small ones hanging diagonally from the waist to the hem. The wings were made of gauze, attached to my shoulders and wrists, so I had to be satisfied with that.

The boys once did *Julius Caesar*, and I remember discussing with friends how Caesar would be killed. Stabbed through the chest? It was really quite horrifyingly romantic, but, seeing Shakespeare, I was presented early with the delights of drama and theatre, which I still enjoy.

Special events were celebrated each year. In May we all went into the playground to dance round the maypole. The day never seemed to be a wet one. We also celebrated Empire Day in May. Again we all went into the playground to sing patriotic songs and dance country dances. I was very proud when one year I was asked to dance the Hornpipe on my own. (I was a proper show-off!).

Mr. Arthur G. Room now lives in Rustington, Sussex, but was brought up in Sutton, Surrey. He remembers school and the First World War.

I was born in 1903. I shall always recall the 4 August, 1914, when I was eleven. It was a Bank Holiday weekend, and the day war was declared. I went for my first country walk with my parents from Dorking to the Silent Pool at Albury, and loved it. After this I was taken on many country walks by my parents, who taught me to appreciate the countryside.

In the Spring of 1917 I went to the Sutton Secondary School for a two year period. At that time education was at a premium, with very little sport. Playing fields were turned into allotments in the 'Dig for Victory campaign. On a quiet summer's evening we could stand in the garden and hear the gunfire in France. Soldiers were billeted throughout the area. During the war I saw Croydon Aerodrome developed. It was within cycling distance of my home and I was lucky enough to see one of the first Handley Page 0400 bomber aircraft.

Between 1914 and 1920 I attended four different schools in three different areas! The first was a small private kindergarten in Wandsworth, London, where it was decided to send Jessie, two-and-a-half years older than me, when she was five. I wanted to go with her, and as Mother had a baby of a few months' old to care for, my parents thought it was a good idea. They assumed I would spend most of the time playing, but the Governess had other ideas. She thought I should be taught to write like the older children, and I was given a book with 'pothooks' to copy. Pothooks are like a 'b' left unclosed, and an 'n' with an elongated second stroke. We were told to practise at home, and I remember sitting on the floor doing pages and pages of pothooks. When my father came home and saw me, he decided that was most inappropriate for a two-and-a-half year old and so I did not go again.

Mother came to meet me with Kathleen in the pram that first morning, as I was only to be at school half-days. I thought that was most infradig and ran ahead on my own! A difficult child! Fortunately in those days there was little traffic on the roads as I had to cross two.

The next school was at Winchester, where we had moved to be near Father when he was in the barracks there. This was much larger, again a private school, and quite good I think. I was still under five and the only lessons I can remember were the French ones - le père, the father, la mère, the mother, learned by repetition. We also did colouring with chalks, which was fun.

When Father was moved to Bath, that meant another change of school. This time it was to the nearby Council school. A great change! I particularly remember the English lessons, the last period on a Friday. I suspect the teacher was busy adding up her registers, because for the last fifteen minutes we were told to learn part of Hiawatha. We could put up our hand when we knew it, and if we recited it correctly we were allowed to go home early. I found memorising easy and was always the first home! I enjoyed Hiawatha, as we also cut wigwams in coloured paper and pasted them on a piece of brown paper (no self-adhesive paper in those days!).

The Governess (the head teacher was always called governess in those days) took us for singing. She sat with her back to us whilst she played the piano, but every now and again she would look round to make sure we were behaving. She wore pince-nez, and her grey hair was combed back tight in a bun. What with that and her long black dress, I found her quite forbidding.

Arithmetic I always found easy, but not knitting! We had not not been taught to knit at home at that time, so it was quite new to me, though the other children seemed to be experts. We were meant to knit a square, which would eventually be folded to make

Swaffield School, London SW18.
Grace Solkhon = Horseman 1919.

a cap. I managed to increase a stitch at the end of each row, so produced a parallelogram!

The back garden of the house where we were living at that time led on to a sideway that also skirted one side of the playground. Instead of making a sandwich for us to take for elevenses, Mother did up a parcel and threw it over the school fence for us during the morning break. Much more exciting! There seemed to be a succession of epidemics - scarlet fever and diphtheria - whilst we were there, so the school was closed much of the time.

When the war ended in 1918, we were able to return to our own home in Wandsworth, London, although it was 1919 before we were settled there. That meant another new school, Swaffield in Wandsworth, where the teaching was excellent and I much enjoyed it.

Hannah Bruskin found that she was discriminated against at school because she was a Jew - the kind of attitude that was to lead to the vicious persecution of the Jews by Hitler years later.

When I began school we had one penny for pocket money. I always bought sweets. One very hot day our school was going on an outing. My father thought that I should have a hat to keep the sun off. We bought the hat but when we went to the school the coach had already gone, It was the only time that the school had an outing. When I got home I sat on the doorstep and cried all that day. It is something that I will never forget. Ever since then I have always been early if I have had to go anywhere.

I had some sad days at school, as well as some happy ones. For instance, I used to talk a lot during lessons so of course lost conduct marks. My teacher said that the girl who did not lose marks for a whole month would get a prize. I really tried hard and did not lose a single mark for the whole month. When I asked our teacher who won she said, "You don't think you did, do you?" What added to my disappointment was that the girl who sat next to me won. She normally lost just as many marks as I did, as she was as talkative as I was..

Another instance was when I got the cane for writing a note. My parents could not write English and it was one of our Jewish holidays. As they were religious they kept me home and told me to write the note. When the headmistress asked me about it, I explained that my parents did not write English. She did not believe me.

One day we had a competition for the most original sewing. Some girls hemmed towels, others did other everyday things. I tried to do something more unusual. I got a white straw hat and trimmed it with red ribbon. When it was finished I took it to school but when the teacher saw it she pulled the ribbon away, saying that the cotton showed. If I had used white cotton on the ribbon it would have shown, so when I sewed it on I made my stitches really small so that they did not show. The girl who won had just hemmed a towel.

There was another time that we had a competition for the girl who recited the best poetry. All the class voted for me but I did not get the prize then either, even though I was often asked to read aloud to the whole class. All these things happened because I am Jewish. My happy days were because I had a lot of very good friends of all nationalities. Those who are still alive are my friends to this day.

Attending school in Devon meant a long walk each day for Marion Yates.

I enjoyed school very much and got on well, but it was a long walk, three and a half miles to Dartmouth and then back again, except on a Friday afternoon. Then I was allowed out fifteen minutes early, as there were two lady farmers who had a large pony and trap. They went to Dartmouth on Fridays and would wait for me and give me a lift home. I thought that was marvellous.

We had a lot of music at school; I was always in the choir and was told I had a very good alto voice. I had a lady tutor who taught me to play the piano at home and this came in very useful later when I met the singer who was to be my husband (see *Growing Up In The Twenties*). I wasn't so keen on games but we all had to take part. Dancing, however, I enjoyed although they did not teach us much at school. I really learned to dance at Norton Parks, the big house near us. They had a staff of five or six girls and the master and mistress were very good to them. They engaged a ballroom dancing tutor and invited the young people from the surrounding farms to join them for lessons. They had a good ball-room and occasionally held small dances.

I remember the cook very well. She was Mrs. Snow, enormous but very kind. She loved Peter, the large bulldog, and he used to dribble and snuffle all round her. I was frightened to death of him in the early days and she said, "Just say Peter, Peter, and he will be all right." She opened the kitchen window and he liked to sit by it on a basket chair. My sister and I had to carry milk to Norton Parks on our way to school, but when she left school I had to go on my own and I was always happy when I saw the dog sitting in the chair. I left school before 1920 and helped on the farm.

Betty Bindloss remembers school as a happy place.

Almost my only recollection of life in Edgebaston, where I was born, is of the little school I went to nearby, kept by a Miss Griffiths whose skirts touched the ground, and where the ages of the pupils ranged from me, at four, to a big boy of fifteen.

When we moved to Newton Abbot, I had a long walk to school and back every day. We lived on Knowles Hill and the school, called Hillside, was on the opposite Wolborough Hill. The town lay in the valley between these hills, through which the River Lemon flowed. I used to be afraid of this walk at first, because at the main road in the valley a group of schoolboys from Kingsteignton, going to Newton secondary school, used to shout "Carrots" at me, laughing at my very bright red hair. I am afraid I used to shout back at them! However, we got used to each other.

School was a happy place., with small classes. I liked literature, history, dictation, spelling and scripture best. We learned lots of poems by heart and I have never forgotten them. We also memorised the Collects and many Psalms, too. Of course we also knew tables up to twelve times twelve in Arithmetic lessons.

I remember one year we 'did' Longfellow's *Hiawatha*, and not only learnt it entirely by heart, but acted it too. We made the Indian dresses and models of Indian villages, with wigwams and open fires. For a whole term we were steeped in America's Indian history! I made lifelong friends there, and naturally there were also some I did not like. To my shame I remember (with another ten-year-old) tying a girl by her plaits behind her back to her front gate, where her mother found her later. Great was the wrath of both our mothers!

I was sad when I was eleven that my day schooldays were over and I became a boarder at a school in Cornwall.

Maidie Stokes was unhappy in her second school at Cheltenham, where the discipline was very strict.

When I was four I went to a school on waste ground behind our house. I was only in the play group at first. It was very pleasant and I played with a bucket and spade in some sand. In the photograph I am sitting in centre front, in a navy frock with white buttons.

The next school was in Longmoor Lane, Fazakerley: we had moved to a better area to live. This school was dreadful! I was always put to sit by a dirty child and caught lice in my hair. I was regularly caned on the hand, arriving home in tears. In the photograph I am behind the notice in the centre front row.

Maidie Stokes - front, second from left.

Maidie Stokes - front row behind notice, aged 8-9.

Elsie Gomm found school at Upper Studley, Wiltshire, a mixed blessing.

When I first went to Newton Infants School we were allowed to take our own dolls and toys to school, but then I transferred to the Juniors where we sat in rows. We all had to walk to school, no buses or cars. I was good at English composition, grammar and dictation, but when it came to decimals, long division and fractions I was out of my depth - a real dunce! My parents could not help me as they left school early. I left in Standard 7.

Mrs. Dor Curgenven was fortunate in being able to attend the village school in Zelah, Cornwall.

I went to the high school in Zelah, the school on the top of the hill, when I was five until I was fourteen. Two teachers had to cope with all of us, somewhere between fifty and sixty pupils.

The school hours were between 9.0 am and 4 pm. The children who lived in the village had no problems, but many travelled on foot from outlying farms, two to three miles away. If it rained of course they got very wet, but there were two large stoves at the school and they dried off there. If they were extremely wet, they were lent some clothes which were kept at the school, to allow them to dry off.

The infants up to the age of about seven had a separate small room under the care of a mistress. The older children up to fourteen were divided into classes according to age under the Headmaster, all on his own, and there were quite a large number of them. It was co-educational, with boys and girls mixed, and they shared a desk. Mainly we were taught the three 'Rs', plus Geography, History, and some Religious Instruction. There was always a hymn to start the morning, and classes of sewing for the girls and woodwork for the boys; also some art classes for those who liked the subject.

Children who came from the farms brought their lunch with them, but the teachers made sure they had hot drinks of whatever they liked. Those who lived locally were able to go home. We also stopped mid-morning for break with hot and cold milk provided. Although we were mixed in school when we got into the playground that was strictly divided, with a wall built between the girls and boys. Each section had its own little set of toilets at the end of the playground. The boys kicked a ball around and the girls played hopscotch, hoops, skipping, tag - all the usual games, but there were no organised games like football.

At home we played board games like Snakes and Ladders or Draughts, and 'I Spy'. Boys enjoyed sticking things on to cardboard - they cut out pictures or coloured shapes to make up patterns, something like collage today. The girls knitted and sewed things for their own use. My mother usually sent me and my two brothers off to bed at 8 pm, so that she could have some time to herself, but even so she had to get our clothing ready for the next day. There was not much leisure in those days.

Mrs. Lily Barry was born in July 1903 and is now living in Liverpool.

When I was at school in 1914 the First World War had begun. Most of the teachers were kind, but strict. However, a Miss Crease was really cruel. She pushed a girl to the Headmistress and took no notice when her long plait was caught in the dividing screen separating the two class-rooms. Because she answered back she hit this same girl with a splintered cane, cutting her arm.

We must have looked sights in sewing lessons as we had to wear aprons and mob caps. We patched the sacks used for horses' fodder. We were also taught to read and write on slates, and to do sums. The tables from 2 times to 12 times we learned in a singsong manner.

The toilets were across the playground and it could be very cold in winter, with the water frozen in the pipes.

William Paterson had a head start when he began school.

I started school in 1916, but before that my parents had taught me the alphabet and two- and three-letter words. Counting the number of poultry we had I found easy, and also the number of cattle we wintered for the neighbouring farmer. After six months at school I was pushed forward a term and again a year later, due, I suppose, to my age and prowess.

School dress was a Norfolk knickerbocker suit and gutty collar, which was sponged and dried every morning. Footwear was tacketed leather boots and clogs. For inclement weather we had leather leggings, sou'wester and oilskin coats. The short route to school was approximately three miles over moorland, but in bad weather we had to take a detour via a neighbouring farm cart-track to the village. This took about an hour-and-a-quarter to walk. During the winter months country children were allowed to leave school at 3.0 pm.

Pocket money during my school days was usually a modest penny, but it was sufficient to buy sugarally and other liquorice sweets. School holidays were spent at home. There were no outings apart from treks into town.

In the autumn of 1918 came the terrible 'flu epidemic and all the schools in the area were closed for a few weeks. Two of my class-mates died. I contracted pleurisy, was poulticed day and night at home, and made a full recovery.

On the day the schools re-opened our headmaster, a Mr. Gordon, gathered all the classes into the school hall and announced the war had ended on the eleventh hour of the eleventh day of the eleventh month of 1918. (Those words I still remember!). After prayer and thanksgiving we were sent home.

Schooling as remembered in Scotland by Jessie Young in the early days of this century.

We had to begin school at five years of age, but as there were no nursery schools in those days small children from the age of three were allowed to sit with an older sister, provided they behaved themselves. I did just that, as mother then knew where her small offspring was for an hour or so.

Beginning school at five years was not so difficult then, but we soon appreciated that we were there to learn. The playground was outside, not in the class-room. As well as sitting still we had to fold our arms unless we needed them to write on a slate with a screechy pencil. Counting with coloured balls was interesting, and saying poems after the teacher and singing made a welcome change, too. Sport was not in our curriculum, but we had drill for half-an-hour each week all through my school days. There was enough work to keep us going and then homework every evening. We sat round the table with an oil lamp burning - electricity was very much a thing of the future.

As our village grew, a new school was built, a higher grade school, which accommodated children from surrounding villages after primary stage. We were fortunate in having such a good school on our doorstep, where foreign languages and science were taught as well as other subjects.

School days finished at the age of fourteen in Hopeman, though a very few went on to further education in the nearest town of Elgin. My youngest brother, the last of us eight children, went there and then on to Edinburgh where he became a solicitor., The majority of boys followed their fathers and went to sea. Careers for girls did not seem important: they helped in the home until they were married, just as their mothers had done before them.

Joyce Booth is now living in Ruislip, Middlesex, but was born in Glasgow. She benefited by beginning her education at a good school there.

My father had a modern outlook on education, so I was sent in 1917 to the up-to-date kindergarten at the Glasgow High School for Girls. We sat in small chairs at low tables, dressed in little green overalls, and listened to stories of Adam and Eve, and Noah and the Flood. I knew about the Flood because granny's books were all stained with water! When it came to the scary bits of Goldilocks and of the Three Little Piggies, I put my hands over my ears. We wove strips of coloured paper and made table mats of rope and raffia. I liked that. Soon we learned the phonetic alphabet and read how 'the cat sat on the mat'. There was a play shop where we spent and learned to count pennies, halfpennies and farthings, and weigh ounces. Reading and counting came so easily to us that I do not remember actually learning. Granny did not hold with new ideas so made me practise on a slate, with a squeaky slate-pencil. (She had signed her marriage certificate with a cross!). Mid-morning we had a glass of hot milk, brought up from the big school, with a skin on top.

At first parents took us to and from school, but soon we made friends and were able to walk the mile home on our own, except when a sailor uncle was attending a course on anti-submarine warfare at the School of Art opposite, and he escorted me.

Before we progressed to real books, we were taught how to handle them. No scribbling, licking pages, or turning down corners; never spill liquids or ill-treat them in any way. One, *The Children Of Odin*, was about Norse mythology and *The Story Porch* had wonderful stories and poems. It had a frontispiece of *Wynken, Blynken And Nod* that was so beautiful I only looked at it on special days! I saw it again years later. It was crude and badly out of register, but to me it had been a Botticelli!

One day we were shepherded into the little front garden to see an aeroplane fly overhead. On another we had to bring exposed negative plates to look out of the window at the eclipse of the sun - hardly a wise procedure

My reports were good, but when teacher read out the results of our first examination, my name was first. Such shame and humiliation! I did not realise that, although Class 1 was the lowest class, first in this context meant that I was top of the class! No wonder that on one of my reports was written 'Joyce must be more alert!'

Elspeth Burns enjoyed her school days.

My sister and I first went to a small local school, called Selma House in Falkirk, run by a Miss Menzies. She had a fox terrier called 'Z', as that is the letter you do not sound in 'Menzies!'.

One very frosty winter the canal was frozen and we all skated. We had half holidays from school to enjoy the very cold spell. My father said that was not what he paid fees for!

Later, we both went to St. Margaret's School at Palmont. This was a boarding and day school for girls.

When I left school I worked part time with my father, who was an Insurance Broker, while my sister, Margaret, went to the Northern Censorship during the war, then moved to Imperial College, South Kensington, in her beloved London.

Mary Blott's education began at Hampton Court.

There was a small school for children in the Palace, and a few extra from outside, with two teachers, who were very strict. My brother took me when I was four, and it was definitely the three 'R's' - reading, writing, arithmetic. There were no play schools in those days but we had a very good grounding before I was old enough to join a grammar school.

There were excellent schools in Kingston, Tiffins in Surrey, but as we were living in Middlesex, my nearest was Twickenham. I travelled by tram in winter and cycled nine miles in summer, through Bushey Park, Teddington, Strawberry Hill, to Twickenham County School for Girls and I was there throughout the 1914-1918 war. My memory of school dinners is of macaroni cheese, with white blancmange and a blob of yellow jam, or pink with red jam; vegetable stew with a dumpling; cress salad with half a boiled egg; and, very occasionally, a suety pudding and watery custard.

As I was cycling to and fro, Mother always made sure I had half-a-crown (2/6d) in my pocket. Food was short and food rationing slow in starting, so I joined any food queue on my travels. I never knew what I was queuing for: it might be half a pound of butter, a pound of sugar and, one day, I got a packet of Quaker Oats - that was really something!

Winifred Chandler is among the few girls at the beginning of the century who had the opportunity of being educated at a High School in London.

When I was five years old I started school at the Board School, conveniently situated exactly opposite our house, on the other side of the road. However, in spite of its proximity I was always escorted by Leila, our maid, on account of the danger from the horse driven traffic of that day - motor cars were only just coming into service.

School began at 9 am and at ten minutes to the hour we were summoned there by the harsh clanging of the school bell ('the first') and at 9 am 'the second' was rung - sending all the laggards scampering to get there before they got into trouble! Amongst the children there was much poverty and neglect, and nothing was done about it, but I remember my mother asking the headmistress to put me among the 'clean ones'. A sad reflection of the times. The girls all wore white pinafores. Mine was always trimmed with lace; most others were plain!

My education began with a slate pencil and slate, on which I was to do 'pot hooks and hangers' - the preliminary to writing. When I had mastered the art I was promoted to a lined exercise book and a lead pencil - the lines to enable me to keep my writing straight.

I was also taught to knit by a child two years my senior who, when I said "I can't do it" translated my words to the teacher as "I shan't......", for which crime I was made to stand on the form for all to see my shame. Young as I was, I resented the injustice of it and promptly made up my mind to hate school!

However, when I won a scholarship to Tottenham High School for Girls, all this was changed. I enjoyed the enlarged curriculum with French, German, Mathematics, Science, Cookery and Art as well as English. I had to travel on two trams to reach the school, costing 1d. each, so my mother gave me 4d. for the fares. I walked part of the way and so saved 2d. as extra pocket money. On Wednesday afternoons we often met the crowds who had been watching a football match waiting at the bus stop. We children did not have a chance!

I loved sport, netball, tennis and cricket, and probably indulged in it to the detriment of my education. There was no coaching so the standard of performance was not of a very high order. For tennis no special dress was required, and I remember my sister being photographed wearing a white blouse with a high collar and a long dark skirt down to her ankles and (to show she was sporty) holding a tennis racquet against her front!

Isobel Wookey was something of a tomboy whilst at school. Unusual in those days!

I attended Wellingborough High School for Girls and was nearly expelled for doing a cartwheel down 'the walks' and showing my knickers to the highly delighted boys of Wellingborough public school, which was directly opposite, in London Road. Also I did a handstand and was reported to Miss M. Tinkler, the Headmistress, who asked me "Why did you do that, Isobel?" "Because I wanted to see what a car looked like upside-down!"

On Saturdays my brother and I both paid sixpence a week to hire a bicycle. We also went to the 'flicks' (cinema) on Saturday mornings, sitting in the flea-pit at the Silver Cinema, eating pomegranates with a pin. It cost threepence to go skating in those days.

School was a happy time for May Goodman.

I won a scholarship to a grammar school when I was eleven years old. School days for me were happy ones. Classes were large, the teaching excellent, and there was much discipline which in turn caused us to respect our teachers. Even so long ago teachers took our work home to mark and there were no demonstrations or strikes. We had lovely prizes, some of which I still have today - real treasures - in which no-one else is interested.

I would have liked to train to become a teacher, but unfortunately my parents were not wealthy and, as far as I know, there were no grants attached to the scholarship, so it was decided they could not afford to keep me at school for the length of time the training would take.

Eventually I went to a commercial college for business training and secured a position with Thomas Cook & Son at their head office in Mayfair, London, and was there until I married.

School days for Jenny Hogg were disrupted by Zeppelin raids.

I did not go to school until I was six, when I went to Clement Danes Girls' School. In 1916 Zeppelins bombed our school overnight, but the boys' school was only slightly damaged. Then I went to the City of London Girls' School, where there were thirty-two classes up to 6A.

In the end the air raids got so bad that an uncle, a widower, at West Drayton invited me and my mother to stay there. I went to school at Uxbridge by train. On Armistice Day we were sent home from school for a special holiday. The porter on the station had a key and he opened all the slot machines and gave chocolate and sweets to the children.

Mrs. Nancy Ramsey (née Paterson) is now living in Hitchin, Hertfordshire, but her early years were spent in South West London.

I was admitted as a pupil at Clapham County Secondary School (known to my generation as Broomwood, after the road in which it was situated) in September, 1911. My parents paid 23s.4d. per term for school fees. There had been some difficulty about my admission, as the minimum age of entry to London County Council Secondary Schools was then ten years: I would not reach that age until the end of October, but some special pleading by Miss Stoker, the Headmistress, eventually prevailed.

Looking back, I imagine my mother must have been the type of parent who is the bane of school authorities, for I remember that she insisted that I should wear brown boots, instead of the regulation black. Nor would she allow me to wear the hard straw hat that was then de rigeur, but insisted on a panama. I was placed in Form 1C, in charge of Miss G. Dulais Davies. I made rather a bad start, for having been called Nancy all my life, I decided that at my new school I was to be called by my baptismal name of Annie. However, at the end of the first week Miss Davies asked me if I had not some other name by which I was commonly called, as I had not responded when addressed by members of the staff as Annie! I reverted to Nancy, by which name I was known throughout my school career.

Of the lessons in 1C, I remember French with Mlle. Pigneguy; English dictation with Miss Pope. which had to be written down in phonetic script; and ancient Greek and Roman history with Miss Davies, who dramatised many of the events so that we could act them.

The following September I went into 1B, where Miss Isaacson, who taught nature study, was our form mistress. Alas! at Christmas she left to get married and on the last morning of term the whole form was in floods of tears. A few weeks later some of us experienced some consolation as we witnessed the ceremony at St. Clement Dane's Church in The Strand. On that dreadful morning I was escorted home, both of us still weeping, by a form-mate, Doris Miles, who sadly died a few years later of TB.

The following term we had a temporary teacher, Miss Bray, as form mistress. She in turn was replaced by Miss Howlett, but during that term Miss Isaacson, now Mrs. Wilson, came back to the school to give us a lantern lecture on Egypt, where she had spent her honeymoon.

Meanwhile a group of us had been very busy out of school rehearsing some scenes from *Romeo and Juliet* (I was Friar Laurence), which were performed at the house of my friend Madge Parkin to welcome her mother back after a long spell in hospital. Both Mrs. Wilson and Miss Howlett accepted invitations to be present.

It was around 1912 that the Thornton Estate (Alfriston, Muncaster, Canford and Bowood roads, also that portion of the West Side of Clapham Common from which they run) was built. Wisley Road came a little later on, but the few houses on Broomwood Road between the school and Wisley Road must date from the mid- or late-twenties.

Each year, at the end of the Christmas term, there was the prizegiving, and at Easter the school concert, for both of which events we all had to wear white dresses. In the summer there was a dramatic performance, which usually consisted of a number of short items including one in French and possibly one in German. I think it was when I was in 1B that I was a hydrogen atom, clad in a diaphanous pale blue garment, in a play written by Miss Hughes, the chemistry mistress. I do not remember a full-length play ever being performed, nor do I remember these dramatic performances in my later years at school. Possibly, the First World War put a stop to them.

My next year in 2B is, for some reason, a complete blank in my mind, but I do remember my form-mistress in 3B, Miss Bradfield who taught mathematics. She was exceedingly kind to me early in the Summer term, when my favourite uncle was killed. She left at the end of that term to take up nursing; the next we heard of her she was at Etretat, presumably at the base hospital. I often wonder what she did after the war.

In September 1915 I found myself in form 4A, with Miss G.D.. Davies again as form-mistress. One thing which has always remained in my mind about that form is that it contained no fewer than eight Winnies! The highlight of that year was the celebration of the tercentenary of Shakespeare's death on 23 April 1916. There were no lessons that day, but the whole school assembled in the hall, where each form performed either scenes or songs from his plays. Our form did two scenes from *As You Like It*, in which I was the melancholy Jacques. I remember being somewhat indignant at being told to omit the line 'In fair round belly with fat capon lined', as it was not deemed quite nice for a schoolgirl to say! I regarded this as an affront to Shakespeare! The day was marred by a nasty accident when 6A was performing the scene from *Love's Labour Lost* in which Berowne hides in a tree. The step-ladder on which Berowne, played by Eileen Whitehead, was standing, collapsed and Eileen fell, breaking an arm.

During the previous week, our form had been set the task of writing an essay or sonnet, or drawing a picture, depicting some aspect of the Bard, and on the great day the best efforts were displayed in the hall. My sonnet was chosen for this honour and was afterwards printed in the school magazine.

There were no O or A levels in those days, of course, and while those girls who intended entering the Civil Service went into 5B, those of us who were promoted to 5A had no public exams to work for, except for the possible few who took the Oxford Senior Locals.

Our form-mistress was Miss Elliot, who taught Geography and English. It was 1916 to 1917, and sometimes she dictated wartime cookery recipes to us. She was short and fiery-tempered, and did not hesitate to lash us with her tongue, but woe betide anybody who ventured to attack her form!

The following year in 6B we took the General Schools examination, from which one could qualify for London matriculation. Our form-mistress was Miss Thomas, the senior mistress, who taught botany. She was known, of course, as Tommy.

On Empire Day, 24 May 1918, a party from Broomwood was included in the thousand-strong choir of London schoolgirls and boys, who sang *Land Of Hope And Glory*, accompanied by the massed bands of the Brigade of Guards, together with the orchestras of the Royal Academy of Music, the Royal College of Music and the Guildhall School of Music, at the Royal Albert Hall, in a concert given before Their Majesties King George V and Queen Mary, and Her Royal Highness Princess Mary. We had to attend a rehearsal the previous day at the Royal Academy. On the great day itself at one point in the programme we were allowed to leave our seats on the platform and wander round the corridors. Some of us lost our way back, opened a likely-looking door, and were unceremoniously shooed out. I have often wondered whether we had tried to enter the Royal Box!

My last two years, 1918-1920, were spent in 6A, where our form-mistress was Miss Case, 'Casus', formidable elderly lady with a limp, who proved to be not so formidable when we got to know her. She taught Latin.

Our form-room had been the secretary's office, situated between the Headmistress's and the lower staff-rooms. Its great attraction was that it had an open fire, and we used to spend the last two periods on Friday afternoons sitting round the fire, together with Miss Case, discussing all kinds of subjects - early forerunner of the present-day current affairs classes, I suppose. On one occasion Miss Case was absent and the discussion degenerated into a game of *Truth*. Somebody, I think it was Hilda Sinclair, when it was my turn to be told the truth, accused me of being vain. Indignantly, I replied that I had nothing to be vain about, unless it were my nose and ankles!

During our time in 6A Miss Case invited us all to tea at her flat overlooking Barnes Common. She was a charming hostess and entertained us with fascinating tales of her activities as a militant suffragette, in the course of which she had obtained her limp. I also remember her asking me to compose the music to a school song, the words to be written by one of the other girls. Alas, this never materialised!

11 November, 1918! The signing of the Armistice, which ended the fighting in the First World War, occurred during my first term in 6A and we were given a half-holiday. This event was later celebrated by two fancy-dress dances at the school, one for sixth formers and one run by the Quondam (Old Girls) Club, to which sixth formers were invited. These were all-female affairs. It would have been unthinkable to admit male partners!

I do not remember much about lessons in 6A. Miss McQueen's successor, Miss Devonshire, was anxious that we should develop the authentic French intonation, and urged us to practise it. This a group of us did during one hilarious free period in the school library, completely forgetting that it was directly above Miss Stoker's room. She was NOT amused!

Members of 6A were allowed to spend free periods in the library, but I do not recollect that there were any books there that would have been of any help to our work. Apart from that, each form went to the library once a fortnight to borrow two books each - one story and one study. Examples of the story books: those by Louisa M. Alcott (not only the series about the March family): a similar series set in Australia; and some of the Talbot Maines Reed Boys' school stories (eg The Fifth Form at St. Dominics).

Hilda Sinclair and I were the only two who took German, and my most vivid memory of those lessons is of Hilda and Miss Dallas arguing the respective merits of Mary, Queen of Scots, and of Elizabeth, in many periods when we were reading Schiller's *Maria Stuart*. Miss Dallas was the only member of staff who regularly wore her gown in class, and it was always slipping down her back, followed by her hair, which she wore in a bun on the nape of her neck.

One day I had been doing private tudy, when three or four members of the form who had been doing gym, from which I was excused, joined me and Hilda told me that Miss Dallas wanted to see me. Muttering something not very complimentary to that lady, I went in search of her, and found the room where she was teaching.

"Yes, Nancy?"

"Hilda told me you wished to see me, Miss Dallas."

There were a few seconds' silence, then we both (and the form) realised the date - 1 April! Miss Dallas was very sporting about it and certainly did not hold it against either of us, for she subsequently invited us both to tea at her club in the West End.

I do not remember many school outings - visits to the Houses of Parliament and the Tower of London, organised by Miss Parker, the history mistress whilst in 2B; later a visit to the physic gardens in Chelsea. That is all.

I remember three school societies. Firstly, the working party, to which I belonged for several years. We used to meet after school once a fortnight, when we sewed or knitted various garments; these were later distributed to some charity. During the course of the meetings, those of us who fancied our talents entertained the rest by playing the piano, singing or reciting. Secondly, there was the 'Deutsches Verein', of which I remember only one meeting, and I also have a vague memory of a debating society.

Other members of staff whom I remember are Miss Corbett, who was Miss Elliot's cousin and also taught geography; Miss Wightman, geography and scripture; Miss Podzus, history and needlework. I remember the latter had a lisp and on one occasion was heard to remark very indignantly to one girl, "My name's not Pudzthuth, it'th Podzthuth!" Miss Craig and Miss Hedgeland taught art and needlework; Miss Rowe, needlework and cookery; Miss Ellis, Physics; Miss Barrenger, singing. The latter once tried to make some of us write out the word 'wind' a thousand times for giving it a long 'i' when it was not meant to rhyme with another word such as 'kind'. Miss Williams married during the war and was allowed to come back as Mrs. Rees, something unheard of in those days. Miss Baker taught me the piano and Miss Landon who, whenever I ventured an answer in a maths lesson, invariably replied, "True, but not useful!" She was one of many members of staff who tried in vain to improve my handwriting. One other memory of Miss Landon is connected with the fact that in those days left-handedness was frowned upon. I was not exactly left-handed, but certain things I did and do instinctively right-handed; others left-handed. Tennis was one of the latter, and Miss Landon would come along and tell me to hold my racquet in my right hand., I would obey, but before the ball reached me, it was back in my left hand. Nor must I forget Miss Herring, the gym mistress who, when I first had my hair bobbed, exclaimed "Nancy! Whatever have you done with all those lovely curls?"

At Easter, 1919, Miss Stoker left to get married and was followed as Headmistress by Miss Jones. By that time I was school pianist, playing the hymn every morning. I remember Miss Jones wanted to vary the procedure by having a psalm on some days. This idea was quickly abandoned, whether on account of my incompetence I shall never know. Miss Jones also persuaded some of us to try for University of London Inter-collegiate scholarships and herself gave us special tuition in English. I am afraid I was not successful, but Hilda Sinclair obtained one and, I think, Faith Dew. So ended nine happy years!

Hilary Hellicar had the benefit of being educated at home up to the age of nine.

I was admitted to Clapham County Secondary School at the age of nine, although ten was the official starting age. I was amazed at how little the other girls, who had been at the national schools for some years, knew. I easily came top of the class and realised how lucky I had been to have teaching at home by my father. He gave my sister and me lessons each morning and some corrections every evening. But the other girls were much more at home with the teeming numbers at school, which I found overpowering at first.

The first form of ten year olds were taught Greek history by a very confident and effective mistress, Miss Dulais Davies, who made us act historic events in the class-room. A Polish mistress, Miss Podzus, taught us history and constantly tried to gain our sympathy for the plight of Poland. German was taught to girls in the higher forms, but there seemed no reaction against the speaking of German. We were made aware of the war, though, by our form mistress, Mrs. Williams, wife of an army officer, who collected money from the children to buy cigarettes for the troops. This was soon stopped by the Headmistress, Miss Stoker, who was probably more concerned about the collecting of money from children than the encouraging of smoking. There were meetings after school lessons to knit scarves and socks for soldiers. My parents also took us to Westminster Hospital, which was given over to the care of the war wounded. We gave the soldiers cigarettes and bars of chocolate.

There was a party at the school to celebrate peace in 1918, but there was not much spirit of festivity because so many families had lost their menfolk. There was no day off, probably because being wartime the mothers of many children worked and could not keep them at home. The same situation probably accounted for the lack of holidays generally. On religious festivals, such as Ascension Day and Ash Wednesday, parents would send a written note to claim a child's absence in order to attend church.

In 1918 Miss E.A. Jones, a distinguished classical scholar, became Headmistress. She was ambitious for her pupils and later told me she was sorry I was going to marry a clergyman, then added: "but perhaps he will become a bishop." He didn't, but her regard for him grew to such an extent that she asked for him to take her funeral, which he did in the sixties.

The First World War had begun before Gervas Clay went to his first prep school.

When I went to my prep school on the Hampshire coast in 1916, for the first time in history the majority of staff were women, because most of the masters had gone to the war. Those who remained were not physically fit to fight. I remember one master, an Australian who had been invalided out of the Forces and became a master. When he wrote with a chalk on the blackboard he would pause every now and again to bite off a piece of chalk and eat it!

In those days there were normally no restaurant cars on trains, so if you were going on a long journey, as I was when I went back to school, a hamper containing food for lunch would be ordered by telephone. When we had eaten the contents, the hamper was left on the train.

At school we were taken on walks along the beach. We were told by the headmaster not to touch or try to pick up anything made of metal, because it might be part of a mine. On one occasion we found a large collection of tin plates which had been washed up from a sunken ship: we had great fun skimming them back on to the sea!

All day long, day after day, aeroplanes would be flying over the school, as new pilots learned how to manage them before going out to the Front.

There was a Convalescent Home for soldiers near my school, and my friends and I would go and beg cigarette cards from the 'men in blue', usually inveterate smokers!

We used to visit the Convalescent Home and go to the hall to give a Show to the wounded soldiers. Most of it was a Concert and I well remember how difficult it was to sing, as the atmosphere was dense with cigarette smoke. This was in the days before wireless or television so people made their own entertainments.

The general attitude at school was that we must grow up quickly so that we could go and fight for our country. On several occasions boys were taken out of the class I was in, to be told of the death of their father or brother.

Wartime food was not very generous. We were allowed two slices of bread a day, usually divided into quarter-pieces. Most of us were used to eating white bread at home, but at school the bread was almost entirely brown. We used to queue up to go into the dining hall for tea, and we rushed to the nearest piled-up plate of bread to see if by chance there was a piece of white bread that had been left over from what the masters and mistresses had been eating. Butter varied between cocoa butter and potato butter. Chocolates and sweets were very scarce; we were allowed a ration of one chocolate a week, given to us on Sunday evening when the headmaster's wife was reading a book to us. To make the chocolate last as long as possible, it was customary to eat it off a pin, sucking it pinful by pinful until it was all gone.

I have a clear memory of Armistice Day 1918. We were in class when the headmaster walked in and announced that the Armistice had been declared and that the War was over. Everybody jumped up and waved their arms in excitement. The boy next to me had been sharpening a pencil at that moment, and in his enthusiasm he threw up his arms in the air and cut one of my fingers to the bone with the knife he was carrying. So I can boast that I have an Armistice Day scar!

Mr. Derek Kelsey now lives in London, but his early years were spent in Hertfordshire, from whence his father commuted daily to work in the City of London.

I was born in 1907 and went to my first boarding school outside Southampton early in 1918. One term we were told that a Zeppelin had gone over Southampton the night before, but that no bombs had been dropped. We felt at war, little knowing!

My brother was born in 1909. We had wonderful parents. Our father had no inherited wealth, but through his ability and hard work we were able to afford a parlour-maid, cook and odd job gardener; all of them happy in their work.

My parents came to see me once a term by train via London; only the very rich had cars and chauffeurs in those days.

After three terms I went to a proper preparatory school, where I was very happy and learnt how to play cricket, if little else. The food at both schools was poor and negligible in quantity during the First World War.

Holidays were taken in England by the seaside, sand castles and all that: the summers always seemed to be fine and sunny. Whilst living comfortably but without today's luxuries, bicycling, climbing trees, exploring woods were heaven, then the gift of a .410 shotgun was sheer bliss.

Some distance from our house ran the London Midland and Scottish main line and I well remember during school holidays in 1918 seeing trains with Red Cross markings on them going north to hospitals with the wounded. I was told that there must have been heavy casualties in Flanders when many trains were seen. As a young boy I could not understand the enormity of what was going on across the Channel. How fortunate I was to have such a lovely, carefree youth, which I can look back on now aged over eighty.

Kenneth Jones was fortunate that his home was next to Alleyn's school, which he attended in Dulwich. From there he was able to progress to Christ's Hospital, Horsham.

I first attended Alleyn's school, Dulwich, in 1912, where the fees were £4.00 a term. It was there I heard the news of Kitchener's death by drowning in the North Sea. Later I heard the newspaper boys shouting the news of the Jutland Battle.

At Alleyn's I sat the Christ's Hospital endowed schools' examination and later heard that I had passed. I was admitted in

"Maine", Christ's Hospital, West Horsham.

Kenneth Jones was in Maine B house.

September 1916. We were marched from the station to the Dining Hall to get our House clothes. I shall never forget the strange smell at Hall of 'kiff' (house tea).

I was put into Maine B. The Captain of the house was Morris. He left to join the army and was killed within three months, in France. My pocket money was increased at Dulwich from a penny to sixpence a week. I bought a penny pot of jam. With free coupons from the Home and Colonial Stores I was able to get Southey's *Life Of Nelson*.

I was put on the Classics side at CH and was useless, so changed to German on the Modern aide. At that time the Head Master was Dr. Upcott. He was keen on skating and when the doctor's lake froze we skated there or on Warnham Lake, near the school at Horsham.

I joined the Natural History Society. Maine B master, Mr. White, took us on walks around Horsham. He gave a penny for the first wild flower found and a penny for the first bird's nest.

For reading, we had *Chums* and the *Boys Own Paper*. My brother had bound volumes of the latter from 1900; in most of them were excellent photographs of CH - playing pitches, steeple chase, etc., taken by the house master of Coleridge A - a science master known as GANOT, because he was always referring to this science reference book.

While there was a good library at CH, it seemed to be little used. I went in to see the old copies of the *Strand Magazine* and *Illustrated London Magazine*. The former had Sherlock Holmes stories illustrated by the father of my friend, Jack Paget, in Barnes A, CH. As well as magazines, boys read books by Henty; naval books on sea battles, *Three Midshipmen/Lieutenants/Captains/Admirals;* books by Jane Grey and Gene Stratton Porter, *Freckles* and *A Girl Of The Limberlost.*

On Sundays we went for walks to the country around the school, and on whole holidays to big houses with grounds, such as Leonards Lea. We called at the latter house wanting to see the Wallabies and Beaver Dam. Lady Loder sent her butler to take us round the estate.

We went on the river at Pulborough, getting the train from Christ's Hospital station, and then found we had got into a 'Ladies only' carriage by mistake. When we reached the river we had a bathe, without costumes. We dived for the reeds when along came a boat with a master and his daughter in it. I had six of the best - and deserved it!

We had long weekly runs; one was to Tower Hill, near Denne Park, Horsham, and back to CH. The longest run was to Barnes Green and back. On one occasion we got into trouble by hitching a ride on a milk float at Southwater!

The swimming baths were over by the CH station. Non-swimmers were taught to swim by a master holding a pole with a loop over the end round the learner's body. The swimming sports had an event where competitors swam lengths of the bath wearing a Housie cost. Non-swimmers had to learn to swim two lengths, then five, to earn points for their House.

When old enough, boys joined the Officers' Training Corps. As a swab (fag), I had to clean my own buttons and boots and also those of my platoon commander - a Grecian.

Library Christ's Hospital, Horsham.

The beds at CH were fitted with boards, with fringes. If you were unlucky, someone arranged them so that they all fell out when you got into bed.

The classes at school were very good. We had an excellent geography master, T.K.M.0 Booth., The French master, Mons. Bué, was also excellent and gave me a lasting love of the language. One of his relations wrote the *Bué French Text Book*. In French and German lessons we had Dent's book, with pictures of the four seasons on the wall. All the lessons in French and German were based on objects shown in the pictures.

We had interesting history lessons with Mr. Dale, who was said to be a fierce master, but we enjoyed his tales of the Battle of Omdurnan, etc. He also coached the 1st Rugby XV.

The art school at CH must be one of the finest in any school. Mr. Rigby and his assistant took drawing and painting, and had a separate room for sculpting. I was hopeless at all three and was given a book on architecture to study instead. The art teaching must have been good, as Maine B produced well-known artists such as Pip Youngman Carter and Ashley Havinden, whose commercial advertisements for Bird's Custard were seen on many hoardings - the Birds were in squares and cubes.

I left Christ's Hospital in 1921 and worked at Lloyds Bank for forty-three years.

Laying tables for Dinner. Christ's Hospital, Horsham.

Mrs. Margery Clow (née Tagg) was born in the Islington area of north London. She, too, knew what it meant to lose a father when she was young. However, in spite of that she had the opportunity of a good education.

I was born on 31 December, 1906. My father had a little second-hand furniture business in Blackstock Road, but unfortunately he died on 27 December 1911, shortly before my fifth birthday. There were four of us children, and then a fifth was born six months after my father's death. In those days there was little provision for widows, and after a few months my mother decided she could not cope with all of us.

My grandfather and a great friend of his, Mr. H.M. Hyndman (a socialist and a publisher) subscribed to one of the Shaftesbury schools and managed to get places for my sister and myself at Royston and my eldest brother at Twickenham.

The schools were run like public schools, and we were taught to behave like young ladies (and the boys like young gentlemen).

In the summer we wore blue and white striped linen dresses with a blue blazer. In the winter we had navy blue velour coats and hats to match. We always wore gloves. We had grace before our meals and grace afterwards; the background was very religious. In our dormitories there were texts all round the walls. If for some reason we misbehaved, we were sent to the dormitory and had to sit down and read these texts over and over again. Nothing else to do. I went to the school when I was nearly six and stayed there until I was ten years old.

We were taught to sew and darn, and once they said there would be a prize for the one who did the best darn. I had to darn the matron's stockings - a great big hole, I well remember. However, I did it so well I was given two sweets, and the privilege of darning matron's stockings thereafter! We learned arithmetic and poetry, and I was always having to stand up and recite.

We were taught the importance of saying 'Please' and 'Thank you' and deportment - how to walk correctly, with our feet turned a little way out. We enjoyed skipping and were taken out in the country lanes once or twice a week in the afternoons, and told what to look for in the hedgerows.

Elocution was another important subject. We had to sound our 'T's' - the 'T' amongst the consonants was the chief one when talking. We would not think of saying 'wa'er' for 'water.'

Christmas was the highlight of the year. They had a Christmas tree reaching from floor to ceiling and friends of the Shaftesbury Society came to hear us perform, and to watch us given all the gifts.

One Christmas morning somebody woke up early. It was dark but she woke all the dormitory up and we all had our toys out. We were thoroughly enjoying ourselves when suddenly the door opened and there was matron! "Everybody back in bed!" We were not allowed to open our toys until the bell went. We were punished, but not whacked.

A.J. Brown, an Old Colstonian, died in 1992 at the age of 101, but another O.C., George Moore, printed in Cribsheet 1993 (the Old Boys' magazine) the following account of his life as it was at Colston School, Bristol, from 1900 to 1905. Brown's three brothers also went to the school. He passed the entrance examination in 1899 and entered in January 1900.

I well remember that day my mother took me. When we arrived at the school there were about twenty boys there, each with a parent. We were a sorry looking lot! Some boys looked very much as if they were going to break down. We were marshalled by the Headmaster and another master. We were identified and then each given a number and that number was 35 and I held that for five years. The parents were then told they must go, and there were some very pathetic partings and a couple of boys broke down. I felt like it but I was brought up to believe that boys did not cry - only girls cried. Still, I was on the verge of tears. We were taken up to the top floor of the school to a dormitory and we were then allotted a bed in one big room: there were about ten beds down each side of the room and at one end were the windows and at the other was a bed by itself. We found out that that was for a prefect who would be responsible for the conduct in the bedroom. We were then taken downstairs and into the classrooms. There boys of ten years of age (I was one) were put in form 1 and those of eleven in form 2. We were each allotted a desk. We were told that that was our desk and no one would ever come to it without our permission or on the order of a master, and that we were never to go to any other boy's desk without his actual permission or the order of a master. They were ancient desks made of wood of about one inch thick, once polished but they had got worn over the years. There were initials carved all over them, but it was a very spacious desk. Under the flap we kept our books, our pens and some of our other things. Our personal belongings we felt were quite safe and throughout the years I was at the school there was only once a case of a boy stealing from another boy.

From there we were taken to the box room, outside of which were all our boxes. We helped each other to carry them into the box room and put them onto empty spaces on the shelves. There we were told to unlock our boxes and never to lock them, because to lock them was to imply that there were thieves about.

Later, much later, one boy complained that he had lost a shilling (a considerable sum in those days) out of his box. The school didn't half suffer for that! For two days we were not allowed to play games until the boy confessed. When he did so a dreadful scene followed, because he was publicly birched in front of the whole school. A shocking experience which I shall never forget and I never saw again, but I understand that public birching was fairly frequent in public schools in those days for serious offences.

After we got our boxes stored we were allowed out. A band of boys crowded round us and started telling us awful stories about the school in what was known as the game, stuffing the new boys. What they said was so fantastic that we soon realised that it was all fiction. We then, of course, became initiated into the school. For the first week we had tailors who came to measure us for our clothes, boot makers for our boots and hatters for our hats.

I had better now describe the general routine at the school. In the summer we were woken at 6.30am and in the winter at 7.00 by a large bell being rung outside each dormitory. We then went to a side room where there were the lavatories and numbered hooks on which our towels hung. There were also a number of basins filled with cold water. On several occasions in winter time we had to break the ice on the top of the water before we washed. This was put in the day before by the maids. We never saw them, nor were we expected to see them as we were not allowed into the dormitories in the daytime without special permission. When we had washed we made our beds and were then inspected by the prefect. When the prefect was satisfied the beds were made and we were dressed he gave the word and we descended to our classrooms.

The whole routine of the school was on a time basis. In summer, because we began half an hour earlier we had a lesson from about 7.30 to 7.50am: then we had a few minutes to ourselves. At 7.55am all the school gathered in the main hall and joined their tables. We then went into the chapel and took our normal places. At 8.00am the Headmaster came in and we started morning prayers. By 8.20 we were finished and filed out straight to the dining room. Breakfast was over at about 8.45am and we had to be at our desks by 9.00am for lessons. They lasted all the morning except for break between 10.45 and 11.00am. We finished morning lessons at 12.50pm. Dinner ended at 1.30pm and we were then possibly free until 3.00pm for more lessons on Monday, Tuesday, Thursday and Friday. During that time each boy was conditioned to have a hot bath. This was done by tables. The baths were in a very big room around which were two large calibre hot water and cold water pipes, which were attached to the baths. There were about thirty baths all around the room. The prefect saw that every boy had a bath and he didn't waste hot water and soap. It was supposed to take us twenty minutes or so and as soon as we had finished another table would be coming through.

We were free until 3.00pm, when we had to be at our desks for afternoon lessons. They lasted until 5.00pm when again we had an hour to ourselves until supper at 6.00pm. Then it was evening school from 7.00pm until 9.00pm. The master in charge of the prep. then read a short prayer and off to bed we would go.

When I was secretary at Colston School during the Thirties there was a timid knock on the study door one day. When the Headmaster said "Come in" a very small new boy entered and said shyly: "Please may I have my new boy's shilling?" Canon Millbourn, the Head, looked taken aback for a moment and then felt in his pocket, found a shilling and handed it to the boy. I wonder what the other boys thought!

Lady Helen Asquith's education in her early days was very varied, partly at home and partly at different schools.

My sister and I didn't go to a 'proper' school until about 1917. My mother's only sister was married to a delightful race horse trainer at Newmarket called George Lambton. She had a boy a little younger than me and a girl a little younger than my sister. It was a very nice house with a garden and paddock, on the edge of Newmarket Heath. My aunt was very good to us and we stayed there for two quite long periods in the spring of 1916 and 1917. While we were there we went to a very primitive but rather nice 'Dame's School' in Newmarket. It was attended mostly by the tradesmen's and grooms' children and the teaching was very limited but I learned some arithmetic and geography in the mornings I spent there. By then I could read easily and passionately enjoyed books. At home we used to play with bows and arrows and go for rides on the heath and visit my uncle's training stables at Lord Derby's Stanley House.

Having been homeless for a while, in the summer of 1917, my mother bought a less expensive house, still quite big, in Oxford Square, just off the Edgware Road. It overlooked gardens with plane trees and was very pleasant in summer. For a short time we went to an independent school in Lancaster Gate, very High Church, with a very good headmistress. We enjoyed it, or at least I did. We used to walk there every morning, about fifteen minutes' walk, picking up a very able contemporary friend on the way. I was in a form which I think was too old for me; I couldn't make head or tail of maths: fractions were absolute nonsense and worried me and the science was boring, but the Latin and English and History I very much enjoyed. The headmistress, who had written a textbook about the seventeenth century, gave us thrilling lessons about the reign of Charles 1. I was rather good at Latin because I had had Latin lessons from the age of about eight from my mother's father. My love of classics started then. My father and his father were both classical scholars, and my father had a wonderful classical library. We went to the Lancaster Gate school for about two years, 1917-1918, but in both years we missed all or most of the summer term as we went to the country or to the sea. I vividly remember the time of the Armistice and the great rejoicings when it was declared on November 11,1918

In the summer we went to Mells and my mother gave us lessons. One summer we had a French governess and we were very naughty and horrid to her. We quite liked having lessons with our mother. She had never been to school but she had had a governess who was more highly educated than most governesses in those days. She had been to Cambridge and got the equivalent of a degree. She had taught in a school and she gave my mother a good grounding in English Literature, History and German. She wasn't much good at Mathematics and knew nothing at all of Science. On the other hand, my mother was very interested in botany and wild flowers. We learned the names of flowers and birds from her and from our nurse from a very early age and we enjoyed that. Mother had a well known Botany by Bentham and Hooker, with lovely line drawings, and she used to paint in watercolours the ones that we found and write the English names in. Then in the summer of 1920, we had a very nice governess, a friend of my mother's own governess, a young woman, but I have lost track of her ever since. She was intelligent and cultivated and she liked water colour painting and took us sketching out of doors. She was very stimulating and companionable. She introduced us to Quennell's *'History of Everyday Things'*. which was quite a new idea at that time. Before that my history had come out of a delightful book called *'Our Island Story'* by Marshall from which I read a chapter to my nurse every day and I got a lasting grip of history from that. My mother made a list of kings with their dates, which again I learned without difficulty, up to the Georges. The latter part of history, after 1815, escaped me in all my school days. For mathematics when we were at Mells, we went to the village schoolmaster in the evenings and he taught us the old kind of elementary school arithmetic. It is quite out of date nowadays, but we enjoyed these lessons and I don't suppose they did us much harm. I think we were quite bright children.

After the war, in 1919 and 1920, we stopped going to the school in Lancaster Gate. For some time we spent three mornings a week with a very capable French governess whom we liked very much. We did all our lessons in French. Later we went to a class in the house of one of my mother's friends. There were three other girls of about our age and a very competent English teacher. I chiefly remember reading and acting Shakespeare plays with enjoyment, Henry 1V and Richard 11, but I think we must have done other subjects as well. In the afternoons we attended rather good classes in Art, Music and Dancing in various places in London. So it was a somewhat scrappy but quite effective all round education.

Mrs. Noreen Beaumont, now living in Southampton, has supplied letters and information about her parents, John and Norah O'Donoghue, and their school experience in Ireland.

When my father was eighty-five he wrote the following letter about his schooling. It is incomplete and does not describe the wounds he received in the war. He intended to ask for a war pension; instead he was awarded a Constant Attendance Allowance for his health and particularly his eyesight which was failing. His wife Norah had a full-time task caring for him.

John's parents, if they went to school, would be punished for speaking their native Irish language. A wooden board was hung around the neck and marks made upon this to record transgressions and fines imposed - very hard on a poor rural community. John, ironically enough, was rewarded for speaking in Irish.

John's parents spoke in Irish when they did not want the children to understand. However, he had a gift for language and he soon did understand and speak Irish! At school the teacher was taking a star pupil to a Feis (Arts Festival). He took John along too, and it was John who carried off the prizes!

My father often declaimed his prize poems to me, in a musical chanting with much variation in pace and volume. At a certain point in the recital he would stamp his foot and raise his arm in the air, while his eyes flashed with patriotic fire. He was defending the little green shamrock against the depredations of the great black crow, which was plundering the fields of Ireland. An Preahan Mor.

*Noreen Beaumont's father - John O'Donoghue's birthplace pictured in 1920.
(See school experience)*

The letter from John O'Donoghue - born 6 April 1893, Co Clare:

Low thatched cabin on lower side of mountain and bogland. Barefoot to Second School, which necessitated crossing the stream, which sometimes became a flowing river.

Teacher thought I had possibilities in Civil Service. Correspondence indicated 'possibilities' and he sent me to the first Boy Clerk exam, age sixteen to seventeen, at fifteen shillings a week in London. I was posted to the Board of Education, Charles Street, Whitehall, Welsh Regy. Whilst most of the Civil Servants in situ were naturally Welsh, it appears to have been 10 April 1910, Ascension Day and an Isle of Man national who took him to the RC Cathedral in Victoria Street.

Meanwhile Norah Hook, John's future wife was carrying off prizes at the Mount, the Quaker School in York, just as she had done at the village school at Acomb. She had excellent reports and references, grade B in Piano and passed the Senior Cambridge in 1913 in English, French, Maths, Geography and History, with Distinction in Drawing, when she was seventeen years old.

Nanette Hales was able to attend local private schools in America.

Until I was four I had a nurse, a beautiful Irish girl. She left when I went to kindergarten, which was just around the corner. I remember filling in the outline of a duck, with pure yellow colour from a little jar. The modelling clay was deliciously cool because it was kept under a damp cloth. One day we made feathered Indian head-dresses out of coloured paper.

At five I went to a little private school, also within walking distance, scuffing through the fallen gold and scarlet leaves in the fall.

Each autumn the school provided crisp new school books, with interesting pictures. The infants' teacher had a natural gift for making learning fun, games to teach spelling, things written on the blackboard in coloured chalks. For geography a map of Europe was rolled down. I could still draw that map, although I couldn't possibly draw a map of post-war or present Europe! In the fourth grade we did Greek history, Roman in the fifth, English in the sixth and, finally, American history.

When we moved to our new home in Portland it was necessary to cross the river by bridge to get to school, so we went by trolley car (tram) unless my mother took us in her electric automobile.

The school had been started by a group of parents who thought the state (called 'public' in America) school was too 'rough'. At that time there were not many black people in the New England States (the six states on the north-east seaboard), but there were many children of people who had just come from Italy, Ireland, Poland and so forth.

The school was purpose-built and had three attractive class rooms and three teachers, with about thirty-six pupils, mixed boys and girls. There was an assembly hall which was let out for local dances and theatricals. Every morning we first marched in there, two by two, to a Sousa march played on the His Master's Voice gramophone. Singing and saluting the American flag followed. "I pledge my allegiance to this flag, etc." My favourite songs for this were *Columbia The Gem Of The Ocean* and *America The Beautiful*. In a country with no monarchy and so many nationalities, I think saluting the flag was very useful, as giving a symbol to unite people.

There was just enough land in the back to run about in at recess time and/or play basketball. There was a bicycle shed and I remember two of the children rode to school on ponies and tied them up in the shed.

The only punishment was being sent out of the room. The first time this happened to me, I was so incensed that I walked out of the door and straight home where, instead of sympathy, I was rapidly bundled into the electric automobile and taken back to school by my mother!

3. OCCUPATION

The choice of occupation was limited, especially for women, but the building of the underground in London and provision of buses meant that men could travel easily to the city to work in the banks and other large institutions. However, often they worked in small, crowded offices under artificial light, adding up lengthy accounts without the aid of a calculator; writing and copying letters by hand.

Much changed during the war. As men were called up women were more and more in demand, both in factories, offices and teaching in schools. Nurses also were much in demand, as more and more wounded soldiers were returned to British hospitals. Many women had opportunities denied them in peace time, but even so many professions were still closed to them. Changes occurred only gradually, especially when the new universities were built, allowing girls as well as boys to achieve much higher qualifications.

Women doing men's work.

Teaching was among the few professions open to women before 1920 and Norah O'Donaghue did well to qualify.

Having secured her Leaving Certificate, Norah did not leave the classroom. Instead of sitting facing the blackboard, she stood up and turned her back to it, and began teaching. She had no formal training, though she did acknowledge help from the Headmaster.

In an application for a post at a much later date, she states 'I did not go to college. I studied for my Certificate Examination (Teacher's Certificate) during my first two years' teaching, passed, and was recognised from April 1917.

Norah's year was the last in which teachers were not required to attend a Training College.

At Castlegate Council School in York, where she was teaching full-time by day from August 1915 to 1920, she opened and organised an Evening Playcentre.

Norah had gained employment in a profession which offered to women, exceptionally, equal pay if not equal opportunity for promotion. By successfully gaining a post with the London County Council early in 1920, she ensured that she could continue earning her living even when she later married, something impossible in York. She spent the rest of her life in the classroom and when she retired at the age of sixty-five was a Deputy Head with the London County Council.

Winifred Chandler left school when she was sixteen and went on to Clark's College, where she studied for the Civil Service Examination.

I passed the Civil Service entry examination in 1916. Competition was fierce, and very few women qualified in those early days, so I was fortunate. I heard that there were five vacancies so applied and was given a place with the Ministry of Health, doing clerical work. I always used an ordinary pen, dipping it in the ink-well, although some people used a fountain pen. I earned £1. 7s. 6d a week: quite a large sum in those days!

Later I was promoted to be an Executive Officer, without taking the usual examination. I sat at the head of a table with six juniors under me, dealing with claims for sickness benefit. Many people subscribed to private societies, others became deposit contributors and paid 4d a week, to which the State added 5d. This was introduced in 1915 by Lloyd George. Any queries I could not deal with were passed to the Query Section; eventually I found myself working in that department and dealing with the problem cases.

I was based in various places - Acton, Old Street, Whitehall and Baker Street, travelling by Underground and changing at Piccadilly Circus.

During the lunch hour in the summer I would take sandwiches to watch a match like Gentlemen v. Players at Lord's cricket ground. This cost one shilling and allowed me to use the same ticket to return after work to watch the end of the day's play.

Margery Clow's widowed mother found that she had a gift with children and nursing. Later Margery was to find employment, too.

One day a young man who worked for a baker and lived across the road from us, became very ill with a flour-related illness, and my mother nursed him. When he died the doctor - Holliday - asked Mother to help with another patient, and the practice grew. She was called upon more and more to nurse people, and lay them out. Then she began helping the doctor with midwifery. In those days people rarely had their babies in the hospital. The doctor realised how good my mother was and kept recommending her from one to another, until she was quite well known in the district.

As we got older, she began to sleep in and be away for three weeks at a time, to look after patients. The money she earned was very useful, and I was capable enough to take over the housekeeping. I left school when I was fourteen, but in those days it was very difficult to find work. Then a girl who lived in my road who had gone to work at a laundry nearby, said they wanted somebody else. So I applied and they took me on.

I was paid about ten shillings a week. Men wore stiff collars and I had to put them on a round piece of metal, and then I had to use a hot iron to bend it double and shine it. One after the other all day. One day the boss came in. I looked up and he was watching me. He said "Buck up! Go quickly!" I thought he was lovely, so I worked very hard, polishing all these collars. I nearly wore them out - just because this man had spoken to me kindly.

Shortly before I left school, a law was brought in compelling children who left school at the age of fourteen to spend two half-days a week in further education. I was sent to Offord Road, Islington, every Tuesday and Thursday afternoon. The laundry had to give me time off. I don't know that I learned very much. We were all strangers to one another, from different quarters; girls and boys together, nobody with friends. Up to then I had been with girls only. Being with boys I was shy at first, then I was showing off. They put on charades, with a prize for the best boy or girl. Guess who got the funny part and won the prize?

With so many men killed and injured during the war, there were more vacancies for youngsters than in later years. Arthur Room was glad when he could begin work.

At last the grand day arrived when I left school and went to my first job of Junior Clerk (office boy!) with a firm of Quantity Surveyors in Queen Anne's Gate, London. I quickly learned that any form of ready reckoner was not allowed during the preparation of bills-of-quantities for the construction of docks for the Port of London Authority.

I travelled to London by steam train from Sutton and at lunch time enjoyed sandwiches in St. James' Park, weather permitting.

After school Elsie Gomm did not enjoy her first experience of working.

When I left school I first learned dressmaking. We used sewing machines to make dresses, costumes and skirts, but were not allowed to do the cutting. I did not like it and one day a friend I knew from school days met me and said "I have a job for you." The friend said she did not enjoy the work she was doing at a photographer's shop, and suggested I might like the job.

I applied and was taken on at a pound a week, rising to thirty shillings. I helped with developing and mounting the photographs, which were taken with an old fashioned camera with a hood. I was very happy there and was able to buy my own clothes and shoes with the money I earned.

Florence Slade was glad when the time came for her to leave the orphanage and live at home again.

It was good to be living with the family again after so many years. My mother always wore long, black dresses, which was common in that era when mourning often lasted a life time. Black dresses sweeping the ground were worn by Queen Victoria after Prince Albert died and she set the fashion.

My mother kept pigs and had about sixty on our allotment: they were killed by licence at a recognised slaughterhouse and then sold to a local butcher. One of my aunts had a restaurant in Regent Street and she came to collect vegetables from my mother's allotment.

My brothers Bill and George were in the war in France, and Alf in the Indian Army.

I started work as a canteen assistant with Didian Boutons, an engineering firm. It was there I met my husband.

4. CLASS DISTINCTIONS

At the beginning of the twentieth century there were wide differences between groups of people and the distribution of wealth was extremely unfair. In 1904 the total British income was £1,710,000,000. Of this 1,250,000 of the wealthiest group took more than a third; the middle group of 2,750,000 took about a seventh, leaving the 8,000,000 poorest people to share just £125,000,000. Many of the wealthy owned more than one house, while the poor were crowded into insanitary slums.

In 1912 David Lloyd George was the Liberal Chancellor of the Exchequer, and he introduced a bill giving State pensions to the elderly. This meant they at least had a small income of their own, although this did not prevent many of them spending their last years in the dreaded workhouse.

At the beginning of 1914 there were one and a quarter million people still working as servants, but all this was to change during the war. Never again would the wealthy be able to employ as many servants as they wished, and pay them paltry wages.

Wandsworth & Clapham Union Workhouse.

The war also changed the lives of many women. New opportunities opened up for them, as men were called up. They were especially useful in the munitions factories, but others took on work usually done by men, like driving trucks, delivering milk, bread and coal, or working on farms. For the first time in their lives they had money they could call their own, and although they worked long hours they could at least call their spare time their own, no longer at the beck and call of their masters. When they had proved their worth during the war, the Government could no longer refuse them the vote.

Class distinctions between men were also eroded. When officers and men were side by side in the trenches under shell fire, they could not stand on ceremony when they met again after demobilisation, and there developed real friendships between some of them.

Although Betty Bindloss found there were no class distinctions in Brownies and Guides, nor in the church, yet she realised this was not so in every day life.

Girls from the homes of railway men, clay workers, shop keepers, farmers and labourers, and children from what were called 'scattered homes' run by the County Council, were all friends together. Church life gave us dozens more friends of every 'class'. My mother had what were called two 'districts', parts of the Parish were she (and I) visited with the Church magazine, gifts of food at harvest and Christmas, and where newcomers were welcomed to the church. Religion meant much in our lives - we had family prayers before going to school and always church-going on a Sunday, dressed in clean clothes and a hat with elastic under the chin. My brothers wore sailor suits and hats.

We may not have been conscious of class distinctions, but we certainly noticed how ragged some children were, often bare-legged and barefooted, with rickets and thin bodies. There were tramps walking the roads and begging at homes for something to eat or money to help them live. At Christmas the children from our church used to visit the Workhouse or Institution, where elderly men and women were cared for, with presents and to sing carols. The women wore red shawls and the men red jackets, husbands and wives being divided into segmented wards.

Mr. Gervas Clay was born in 1907 and had a very interesting career in Northern Rhodesia, as recounted in *Growing Up In The Thirties*. His marriage to Betty Baden-Powell, younger daughter of Lord and Lady Baden-Powell, also added to his range of activities. He enjoyed the privileges of the middle class in those days.

One of my earliest recollections is of a fire in our nursery. My brother and I were having our bath when the nursemaid tried to blow out the spirit lamp that was cooking our supper. She blew so hard that the flames jumped out and caught light to the curtain. We were rushed out of the room and had to have porridge, which I hated, before going to sleep! Meanwhile the household rushed to help put out the fire. The cook arrived with her apron full of flour and threw handfuls of it on to the fire. The kitchen maid seized a block of rock salt from the kitchen, ran upstairs and threw it through the plate-glass window. Meanwhile my mother and the housemaid had run to the far end of the house where they got the fire extinguisher, very heavy, with which they struggled back and eventually put out the flames. It was the custom in our household that every morning, before breakfast, the servants would all come into the dining room with everybody in the house for daily Prayers, led by my father.

Before the First World War, I remember when my father went to London for the day from Burton-on-Trent, where we lived. He wore a morning coat and top hat; when he arrived at the station he was met by the stationmaster, similarly dressed, who escorted him to the train. This was because he was a director of Bass Ratcliffe & Gretton, the brewers, and was therefore an 'Important Personage'!

Every winter my parents gave a children's dance, in the drawing-room. This entailed taking out all the furniture, removing the carpet, and polishing the floor. Very often the children's dance would be followed the next evening by a servants' one. Many of the village children came outside the house to try and look in through the windows to watch us dancing.

When my younger brother and I were aged three and four and my mother had guests for tea, we were taken to the drawing-room door, which was opened by our nurse; we would then walk in, hand-in-hand, bow to the assembled company and go to stand by our mother's chair.

Every morning when we were getting up, we heard the sound of the horse pulling the milk cart, going 'clip-clop' very fast, as he trotted along the road past the house.

My first recollection of motor cars dates back to very early in my life, for my father had one of the very earliest cars. I went with him to visit my grandparents, some miles away in Staffordshire. I was very amused to find that he, too, had to be tied in with a strap across from one side of the car to the other, put there to prevent our falling out. Steep hills presented a real difficulty in those days, and on a number of occasions we failed to make the top of the hill and had to roll back and start again, with a good run at it. I remember seeing out chauffeur coming into the house to say goodbye before going off to join up in the First World War. He came back to us after the war and was with us for very many years.

I remember going with my mother in a hired carriage with a groom driving, to call on various friends when we were staying in the Isle of Man. She would leave cards, two from my father and one from herself, as was the custom in those days.

About 1910 there was an Air Show near our home. My father managed to get himself taken up for a flip; he sat in a basket, with his legs dangling in space. When he came down, his Irish mother-in-law walked up to him and said "If you'd been killed I would never have forgiven you!"

At the time of the coronation of King George V in 1911, my parents went up to London, and my brother and I were taken to the village cricket field, where I won a race for the Under-Fives. My grandmother presented me with a tiny silver cup, which I still have.

The newspapers we took were the *Morning Post* and *The Sphere*. I remember reading a headline and running upstairs to my parents shouting, "Brussels has fallen!" That must have been 20th August 1914, when I was seven.

Mary Blott, living at Hampton Court, was definitely aware of class distinctions.

I was brought up to respect all the old ladies in the Palace who lived in grace and favour apartments. In that era I think everyone more or less knew his place in society, respected and accepted it.

I went to Chapel Royal on Sundays, which was deadly. Pews were like horse boxes in those days and we each had our allotted place. I could not see over the top until I was about twelve; then it was at least a bit more interesting to be able to look at the elegant hats being worn by the ladies! We just accepted this: it was what we all had to do!

Many of the ladies, who were all widows, in the grace and favour apartments were not too well off, so they employed Irish cooks who enjoyed their tipple. Occasionally Father was called to help settle a dispute, when someone was abusive; he would see they packed their trunks and then put them on a train home.

Another lady took a fancy to my elder brother. She had a pedal harmonium in her apartment and taught him to play it. She left it to him in her will. She also wanted him to sing hymns with her; Mother had to rescue him - homework was a good excuse.

During the war Father used to send me round to take surplus fruit and vegetables to those he realised were not too well off.

Mr. Cyril Priestly was born in Lincoln and now lives in a nearby village. Like many other large families in those days, he knew what it was to be short of what nowadays we would call essentials.

I was born on 31st December 1913, the next to youngest of eight children. We lived in a small house, two up, two down, and we four youngest children slept in one bed, two at one end and two at the other. There was no such thing as a bathroom and just an outside toilet, with newspaper for a toilet roll. On wash days Mother would wear a man's cap as she scrubbed the soiled clothes before boiling them in the copper and putting them through the heavy wooden mangle. When we went to bed Mother took the warm shelf out of the oven, wrapped it in a blanket, and put it in the middle of the bed, so we all scrambled to get our feet on it to keep warm.

Unfortunately my father was a heavy drinker, which meant we children had to endure many hardships. Even in the winter when my father came home for his lunch break (he was a turner at Robey's engineering at Lincoln) those of us who were still at school were not allowed to stay in the house. First one of my sisters or I had to go to the corner shop (an off-licence) to fetch a pint of mild for my father to have with his dinner. Then we were sent out into the streets with a sandwich of bread and dripping until he had gone back to work.

Once a week one of us (and it usually seemed to be me!) had to take my father's suit, wrapped in newspaper, to the pawnbroker's, to borrow money to eke out the housekeeping. The money Dad earned did not go far between ten of us. When he got paid at the end of the week, we had to take the money to the pawnbroker again to redeem his suit. A self-defeating exercise!

Once a year, around Christmas time, the police organised a 'Robin dinner' for the poor children in Lincoln, and we were invited to a slap-up dinner at the Drill Hall. We were also given a pair of boots.

There was little money for entertainment, but I remember once my mother took me to a matinée at the picture house (cinema). I sat on her knee and watched Charlie Chaplin and a cowboy serial with William S. Hart.

One cold night when I was older I went out on my own, with a whip and top, and walked round the streets with it. I stopped at a sweet shop window and was gazing in, but had no money to spend. Then from behind me someone put a coin in my hand. I looked round and saw two elderly ladies, smiling kindly at me. I looked down and saw it was half-a-crown (2s 6d). I had never had so much money in my life. What should I do with it? I walked to Lincoln High Street to a toy shop, where I had looked longingly many a time at a box of lead soldiers, priced 2s. 6d.

I went into the shop and bought them, all beautifully wrapped up. When I arrived home I told Mum I wanted to go in the front room. There was no furniture, heating or paper on the walls, but I had a wonderful time unpacking the parcel and playing with the soldiers. Then there was a knock on the front door. It was the lady who had given me the half-a-crown. She said she wanted to speak to my mother. She explained she was very sorry but she had given me the 2s 6d in mistake for a penny, and she needed the money back. So I had to pack up my precious box of soldiers and take them back to the shop, and get the money. When I got home the lady was still waiting, and she gave me a penny. The saddest day of my young life!

There was some consolation though, for a neighbour made me a marble board. There were channels in the wood, with the numbers 1 to 10, and the idea was to roll the marbles to get the highest score.

Mr. Havre Brown spent his early years in Manchester, but is now living in Chichester, Sussex. Many children lost their fathers in the war; he was to lose his mother and grandfather through influenza, and also to experience some of the privations suffered by the poorer community in those days.

The house where I was born in Manchester was fairly large, with a white bay front. On the opposite side of the road was a row of shops and, according to my sister who was two years older than me, we did not seem to go short of food. My father we saw only occasionally, when he came home from the war.

In 1918, when I was only three, my mother and grandfather both died in the terrible influenza epidemic that swept the country. I myself also contracted it, with pneumonia, as I was told by my relatives, but fortunately I survived.

I remember seeing men returning home from the First World War with various limbs missing, which to me as a small child was very frightening.

We children, when not barefooted, wore clogs like the bulk of the people living in Manchester at that time. I shall always remember the click-clack sound as we walked along.

After my mother and grandfather died, my sister and I went to live with my grandmother. I shall never forget the daily visits to a soup kitchen, where for a halfpenny we received a bowl of horrible thick brown soup!

My grandmother could not cope with two young children, so when I was four years of age my sister and I were sent to live near Stourbridge with my aunt and uncle and their child. They were extremely kind, hard-working people. My uncle worked in a glass works, feeding the furnaces non-stop (except for lunch) for about ten hours a day. I used to take him his lunch there, wrapped in a large kerchief. The glass blowers occasionally made me small animals and Jacob's ladders, which I loved.

The house was a rented two bedroomed terraced property, with a cellar and a communal outside wash-house, and a water pump only - no taps or lighting. The communal toilet was situated at the far end of the garden, again without lighting.

The front room was only used on Sundays or very special occasions: the back room was the kitchen, living room and bathroom (tin bath in front of the fire on Friday evenings).

Cooking and lighting were by gas, which was supplied by putting pennies in the meter. The gas mantles for lighting were extremely fragile, and always went pop when lit. Great care had to be taken not to damage the mantle.

To wash up dirty crockery, cold water had to be collected from the wash-house pump, heated on the gas stove and transferred to a bowl.

The cellar was very cold, dark and damp, and was used to store food and for general storage.

Even though we never had much money, we were never short of food, because my aunt made her own bottled fruit, jam and chutneys, bread and cakes. These were delicious! My favourite treat was a thick slice of newly baked bread with beef dripping.

Neighbours shared allotment produce, often selling any surplus; others kept ferrets, and rabbits were always available. From nearby fields we used to collect dandelions and nettles, to make dandelion and nettle wine, which when bottled was stored in the cellar. We called this pop.

Gypsies were always calling with large baskets of blackberries and apples for sale, and occasionally a large rabbit.

Our annual holiday was to go fruit picking at Malvern. Several families went together; we slept in straw covered barns, and as children had a wonderful time. We went to the same farm every year. The farmer and his wife provided us with food, and before we returned home told us to take as much fruit as we could carry.

The type of games we played were marbles, whips and tops, and football. A local butcher gave us pigs' bladders, which we inflated to use as footballs; or if none were available we used a bundle of old rags, rolled and tied together. Our football pitch was the street.

Every Saturday evening, about 10.00 pm, we walked as a family about two miles to Brierley Hill market for the weekly bulk shopping. We took advantage of the cheap food which was auctioned off by the butchers, fishmongers and greengrocers. We then walked home again, to save a few more pennies. Sunday morning breakfast was always smoked haddock, purchased the previous night.

On Sundays we children attended the Wesleyan church service in the morning and the Methodist Sunday school in the afternoon. Our attendance was recorded by stamped cards, and for good attendance prizes of books were given annually. On Sunday evenings the whole family attended either the Wesleyan or Methodist church service.

Mrs. Ivy Ross is now living at Westcliff-on-Sea but spent her early years in Glasgow. She knew something of the suffering of the poor in those days.

I was born in Glasgow in 1906. My father was a stereotyper, so we did not suffer from the poverty that affected so many people around us.

In the slums the women could not afford prams, so they carried their babies in tartan shawls tied in a special way to leave the mother's hands free. If a woman lost her husband, there was no help from any quarter. My friend and her sister were put in an orphanage when she was six, after her father had died. Her mother was allowed to visit her only one afternoon each month. In the four years she was there, she never saw a cake. Breakfast porridge was always lumpy, but if it were not eaten it was brought back to be consumed at dinner time! Eventually her mother remarried and had two more babies, so my friend came home from the orphanage to look after the infants. This enabled her mother to go out to work. Aged eleven, my friend had no more schooling.

Keeping warm was always a problem and there was usually only the kitchen stove to cook on and provide heat. Coal was one shilling a bag, but it was possible to buy a few pounds' worth (by weight) in the local shop. It did not last long, but people were always scrounging for anything that would burn. Anyone who was lucky enough to live near a carpenter's shop could buy a bagful of shavings for a few pence. The nearby gas works were a wonderful place, and children could push an old pram and galvanised bath and ask for sixpenny worth of coke.

Some large families had to keep their children off school when there was not a decent pair of shoes for any of them. Trying to feed a brood of growing children was almost impossible. I knew a woman who used to take a pillow case to the baker to get it filled with stale bread for twopence. Hot water was poured on to the bread, pepper and salt stirred in, and that was dinner.

In Scotland there were plenty of coal pits, surrounded by high coal bings (heaps). It was possible, but not legal, to find plenty of pieces of coal around, but if caught stealing you would be fined in court.

In the Jewish quarter of the city, called the Gorbals, it was the custom for one woman to go round and collect a penny a week from every householder who could afford it. The money was then given to a desperate family.

An agricultural worker with a family of eight earned 12s 6d a week, with rent of 1s. 6d. It was possible to make a meal for six persons for $9\frac{1}{2}$d., but if there were no money in the house there was only the Relieving Officer. He also had care of the insane, which was so shameful.

In Scotland before 1920 there were not as many houses as tenements. A family of six would live in two rooms. There was a bed recess in each, and everything was stored underneath. The coal bunker was in the kitchen. If the coalman saw his notice in a window, he would climb three flights of stairs to carry the bag of coal and tip it in the bunker.

Every tenant had to wash down her part of the stairs each week. In some parts of the city it was the custom to decorate the edges of the close (entrance) with various patterns. This was said to be a relic from the past.

Mrs. Lily Barry, was born in 1903 and now lives in Liverpool. She describes what it was like to be poor and have to live in a workhouse.

When I was young and living in Northcote Road, Walton, Walton Hospital nearby was a Workhouse. One day we saw an old gentleman sitting outside, as it was his day out. The inmates were only allowed out once a month in those days. My father felt very sorry for him and brought him home; mother gave him meals and he stayed all day. After that he came each of his days out, and we children called him uncle Rigley. He had no relatives and made us his family. He was over eighty when he died and was buried in a pauper's grave. My father went to his funeral.

We were quite poor as my father was a docker and did not get much work. My mother was a dressmaker and she helped by making little pants out of old coats for sixpence, and a larger size for ninepence. She always felt sorry for people who were worse off that we were. In those days pensioners received only ten shillings a week.

Mr. Terence Frank Watkins was born in 1902 and has lived all his life in Newton Abbot, Devon, but he suffered much hardship in his early years. Then he had a happy married life, with five children. His wife has unfortunately died but one of his daughters comes regularly to help him.

My mother deserted me from birth, and that meant my early days began in what was known as 'scattered homes', so called because they were in various parts of the town. Single homes contained twelve children; double had twenty-four boys and twenty-four girls. In the home each boy had so much work to do before going off to school. At the age of five or six this would be something simple like polishing the stair rods. We arose at 6.30 am; then we had to make our beds, which were checked by the foster mother. We did jobs such as cleaning the bedrooms, stairs, and all the rooms of the house. We also had to polish our boots, which had hobnails to prevent them from wearing out too quickly.

We had three meals a day:

Breakfast - porridge. Dinner - Monday: soup, Tuesday: steam pudding, Wednesday, Thursday and Saturday: varied, Friday: fish, Sunday: roast.

We went to the local Highweek Infants and then Boys' schools from 9.00 am to 12.15 pm and 2.00 pm to 4.30 pm. If we were late we had a stroke of the cane from the Headmaster. There was no transport in the early days and we had to hurry to school by foot, then back home to dinner and again to school for the afternoon session, thence home again at 4.30 pm.

For part of my life until I was fourteen I was fostered out to a family (in those days people were paid for looking after unwanted children). I was never badly treated by them, but they were heavy drinkers and this made my life miserable. That is why I am now a teetotaller.

When I was fourteen I had to leave the home and go out to work. My first job was at a Market Garden in Torquay. They also kept four cows, which I had to fetch in every day for milking. The milk was taken into town by horse and trap. Machinery as we know it today was unheard of then. Digging the ground and tilling had to be done by manual labour. The first real fright I had was when I was picking brussel sprouts and suddenly realised I was on my own, with no-one to care about me.

When I was about eighteen I eventually got a job on the buses at 8d an hour. I had palled up with four other teenage boys and eventually found a lodging with some people who treated me as their own son. I stayed with them until I married at the age of thirty-two.

I saw my mother up to the time I was twelve years old; after that I heard nothing until I was over fifty years of age.

5. TRANSPORT, HOLIDAYS & OUTINGS

The early years of the twentieth century saw much progress in modes of transport. First there were the electric trams, but these were confined to the track fitted into roads, with over-head wires to provide the electricity, so did not have the versatility of the later buses. But they were cheap and envi-ronmentally friendly. Although fares were mostly a penny or less, in 1913 the total tramway receipts were fifteen and a half million pounds! There were still many horse drawn vehicles on the streets, which produced large quantities of dung. This could cause a health hazard, so it had to be cleared from the streets. Small boys could be seen with bucket and shovel collecting the manure and then trying to sell it to owners of nearby gardens. Horses on the streets persisted for some

Southsea. William and Etheline 'Horseman' with Arthur & Ken, Grace's Father and Mother-in-law.

Transport in the Edwardian period. Horse-drawn and motor-powered transport at Piccadilly Circus, 1910.

years, but gradually buses, cabs and cars superseded them. By 1913 there were three thousand motorised buses on the streets of London; the following year when war was declared horses were requisitioned. This was the death-knell of horse-drawn buses, though a few horses continued to be used for such things as the delivery of coal, milk, etc. Penny-farthing bicycles with the large front wheel and high seat were replaced by lower models with equal sized wheels but with no gears, and they were very heavy. It was a very popular means of transport and allowed people to explore the countryside at minimum expense. The long dresses of ladies proved a hazard and some of the bolder ones wore bloomer trousers, leading to the ditty:

> *Every morning on her bicycle*
> *Miss Piggywig goes out;*
> *She cuts a funny figure*
> *For she's getting rather stout.*
> *And all the children in the gutter*
> *(the saucy little mockers)*
> *Cry, 'Oh, come and have a look*
> *At Miss Piggywig's knickerbockers!*

It was during the first decade of the twentieth century that the underground system was built in London. At first they were steam trains, with all the attendant problems of smoke and grit, but they were replaced by new electric systems in 1906. Gradually they were extended far out into what were then rural places, like Ealing and Golders Green. In the early days passengers had to climb and descend many stairs to and from the platforms, but in 1911 the first moving-staircase (escalator) was introduced at Earls Court and gradually throughout the system.

The railways were still cheap and popular, and many an infatuated young lad would hang around railway stations checking the numbers of the enormous steam engines. They looked invincible, but the rail strike of 1911, especially as it was during the holiday season, made the owners of cars realise they had an alternative means of transport. From then on the decline of the railways began, as they gave place to cars and coaches (or charabancs, as they were known in those days).

It was in 1895 that the earliest motor-cars appeared in Britain. They were mostly made in Germany or France and resembled horse-drawn traps. In those days the speed limit was 4 m.p.h. and the car had to be preceded by a man with a red flag. Even in 1903 the speed limit was only 20 m.p.h., and at this time number plates were introduced so that offending motorists could be identified. By 1908 there were great improvements - that year the 'Silver Ghost' car manufactured by C. S. Rolls and Henry Royce won the Tourist Trophy event in the Isle of Man.

These cars were expensive and only the wealthy could afford them, but in 1908 the mass produced Model T Ford at £133 arrived in England, to be followed in 1912 by William Morris' cheap cars. Previously he had made bicycles. These early carts had no roof or windscreen, so drivers and their passengers had to wear goggles and masks, with fur-lined leather coats to protect them from the weather as there were no hoods. Cloth caps with earflaps were worn, with veils for the ladies. Motorists brought new prosperity to the country inns, and the poor state of many roads was evident. Tarmac surfacing proved very successful in London and was then introduced elsewhere: a great improvement on muddy, rutty roads. However, it was flying that was to have the greatest impact, both in peace and in war. Hot air balloons gave way to airships, which were steerable, and in 1908 the first British Military airship was seen in London. In Germany the Zeppelin was developing rapidly, and later was to cause considerable damage to London during the First World War. It was in 1903 that a flimsy aeroplane made its first flight in America, but it was not until 1908, when the Wright brothers demonstrated their aeroplane at Le Mans, that the 'plane was taken seriously. The following year Louis Bleriot flew across the Channel from France, and at last the British took the development seriously. If it could be used in peace, so it could be in war. In 1912 the Royal Flying Corps was formed, and although in 1914 they had only sixty-three machines, the British were to produce some of the finest fighting aircraft.

Mr. Cyril Davies was born in the Clapham area of London in 1905. He became a policeman and later had the interesting task of being a bodyguard to Winston Churchill. He has some unusual memories of transport when he was five years old.

My earliest recollection is of holding my older brother's hand when he took me to the south side of Clapham Common. I was fascinated as we stood outside the Post Office and watched a man from the local Tramway's depot standing at the curbside, as he pulled a huge lever towards himself. Then we saw a tram start up at his signal and turn right towards Cedars Road and on to Lavender Hill, en route for Clapham Junction and the terminal at Kings Road, Chelsea.

There were no traffic signals to stop and start in those days of 1910, and in my little mind I marvelled at the speed and dexterity with which this operation was carried out. The position was the same in reverse for the return journey.

On the other side of this busy road, called the Pavement, there was much traffic - motor buses, horses and carts, and men pushing produce in barrows, who invariably paused en route to their destination either at Clapham Junction or Peckham Rye. At this time my brother and I witnessed the introduction of the 'steam bus', as it was called. Thomas Tilling introduced it to outwit the London General Omnibus Company, who were operating the same route as they. Until that time they had had no opposition. Of course it was thrilling for us two to stand outside the bakery and confectionery shop called Carpenter and Co. and watch.

The previous General Omnibus had filled up with passengers, but their journey to Brixton and Camberwell was marred because they were filled to capacity, leaving a cluster of irritated passengers on the footway. However, only a few minutes elapsed before, from the bend which was by the roadside at Clapham Parish Church (that accommodated the local duckling population), a strident hissing rent the air. There was a cloud of steam as Thomas Tilling's bus appeared and stopped alongside the footway, which was used as an improvised bus stop. As it came to a halt, red hot ashes from a container beneath the propelling section of the bus fell into the roadway. They were promptly kicked into the gutter, either by prospective passengers or passers-by. When the conductor of the bus saw that he was full of passengers, he shot his arm across the entrance of the platform and, after calling out "Full up; full up!" he rang the stop/start bell and the bus proceeded forward, past the dear old stone clock, which stood outside at the triangular piece of garden and forecourt provided by the local Council. Having edged safely across the road leading to Clapham Park Road and Acre Lane and Brixton Town Hall, we walked home from there, which took about half-an-hour.

As we were walking down Clapham High Street for home, my brother jerked me to a halt, as from a distance we could hear the clanging of a fire engine. There we stood, awaiting the arrival of the engine. Soon it came into sight and there we stood watching with envy the magnificent fire engine, drawn by two lovely horses. Their manes were flying in the air, and driver and crew were still fastening their uniforms and donning their helmets, as those lovely creatures galloped down the road to the seat of the fire. All the thoroughfare was lined with people, who had stopped to gasp at the wonderful spectacle before them. This special event of my early life so impressed me that I remember it very clearly as though it occurred only yesterday. Never to be seen again!

Kenneth Jones' family were great walkers and they went on many outings.

Each weekend we enjoyed walks to various places, including Ruskin Manor, Herne Hill Park, Dulwich Picture Gallery and Dulwich Park. There was boating in the summer and skating in the winter on Park Lake. We met Sir Hiram Maxim, inventor of the machine gun, whilst walking near Dulwich College. The tea merchants Hornimans left their house and grounds to form the museum, which we visited, as well as Crystal Palace. Grandma from Carew Hill took us to see the circus. We also went to the Camberwell Green Hippodrome at Camberwell, where we saw Charlie Chaplin on stage in *Mumming Birds.*

When trams were extended through Dulwich to Forest Hill and Greenwich, we visited the latter on Bank holidays. We also visited my maternal Grandfather at Forest Hill, and went to Brixton and Tooting to see other relatives. Another visit was to Grandma from Carew Hill, who was then living at Durdham Down, Bristol.

Father took me to London to see the King of Portugal drive past. He was assassinated the following week in Portugal. The *Daily Mail* put through the letter box of our house in Dulwich stated that King Edward VII had died. Father went to London to see his funeral. A lady next to him said, "I wonder how our good king is looking today!"

In 1914 we walked and bussed to the Thames to watch the boat race. Cambridge won.

For summer holidays we went to Leigh-on-Sea and Herne Bay. When we went to Leigh-on-Sea in 1911 we stayed in digs near the station. On the beach was a large vessel used as a club. If the weather were hot, we sat in its shade, made sand castles or bathed. My legs got sunburnt and an Italian girl playmate said "Your legs are ruined." When it got too hot we went to fields near Hadleigh Castle (painted by Constable) and looked over the cockle sheds below.

At Herne Bay in 1916 we again stayed in digs. During the black-out we went to the Pavilion Theatre on the nearby grassy slopes. In the day we went to Reculver Church, a ruin. On one occasion my father and I walked to Margate via Reculver and along the beach at Birchington. After Reculver we sat on the sand eating our sandwiches. All of a sudden there were squirts of sand around us: we found we were at the back of a rifle range!

We read in the newspaper that an ammunition dump had exploded near Aldershot. My brother was there serving in the Rifle Brigade, but we later heard he was safe. One morning, while bathing, puffs of smoke appeared above Margate. We found it was a German air raid: one machine which was brought down had a German in it who was only seventeen. Sometimes a local squadron appeared and dive-bombed the Pavilion on the pier. One plane crashed into the sand.

At the Pavilion where a concert was held, I heard Dame Clara Butt and her husband sing *Land of Hope and Glory*. At the end of the pier there was an exhibition of high diving each day. The diver climbed up, wearing a cat's head, as an advertisement for *Black Cat Cigarettes*.

The McJollity Boys' Pierrots gave an afternoon show on Herne Bay front. They were shown in an episode of *Upstairs, Downstairs*, on ITV.

Mrs. Daphne Rayner enjoyed various outings with her parents, using different forms of transport, when she was young.

I was born during the First World War. We lived in a small flat near Bishop's Park, London. My father was not in the army as he had a weak heart following rheumatic fever as a child. On Sunday mornings he used to take me to feed the ducks and very often we went to a small garage he had under railway arches, where he kept his Red Indian motorbicycle and sidecar. Once I was dressed in a white coat my mother had made me and got a lot of oil on it. My father tried unsuccessfully to remove it with petrol and my mother was very cross when we returned home for Sunday lunch!

In the afternoons we all went into the country, my mother nursing me in the sidecar! But sometimes her friend Jean came as well and then Mother would sit on the pillion and Jean would nurse me. After that my father bought another motorbike with a larger sidecar that had two partitions. That meant two extra passengers could be taken out as well as the family.

We went to Thames Ditton in the summer and then went on the river in a punt. My father and his friend Billy did the punt-

Daphne Rayner with her mother.

ing, whilst I had a small paddle. I was very nervous when we had to go in the locks with other larger boats, and I preferred it when the punt was transferred on rollers and we walked.

All along Fulham Palace Road there were trams; noisy monsters which ran on rails and we had to walk out into the middle of the road to board them. Often they held up the traffic, which was allowed to pass either side of them. Finally my father was able to sell the motorbike and sidecar and buy a secondhand car, a Rustin Hornsby, at Pevensey Bay, near Eastbourne, where we were staying for our summer holiday. The first drive he took us was up Beachy Head. No driving tests in those days!

When Father had to return to London on business, my mother, Grandmother and I would go out in a pony and trap. It was not wise to rustle a sweet bag, as the pony would stop until he had been given a sweet! If we came to a hill we all had to get out and walk to make it easier for him!

We continued for many years to stay at Pevensey Bay for holidays. People did not stay in hotels so often in those days, but took rooms. At first we stayed at Richmond House. This was a large double-fronted house, which was let off as apartments to families. We each had our own sitting room on the ground floor, and bedrooms upstairs. There was gas lighting in the sitting rooms, but we had candles to go upstairs to the bedrooms. Halfway up the stairs there were cases filled with stuffed birds, and the owls' eyes used to shine in the candlelight and frighten me. My granny always took me up to bed and shared a room with me.

There was a woman called Mrs. Akhurst who did all the cooking and cleaning, brought us up hot water for washing, and emptied the chamber pots! She lived in another small terraced house, with her husband and two children. I realise now how hard she must have worked.

My father's friend, Billy, played cricket and we went to the ground at Battersea Park to watch him. My mother and his wife used to do the teas. Later on when I went to the Froebel School, which was co-education, we all played cricket together.

I can just remember my grandfather taking me to Harrod's to see Father Christmas. This must have been in 1919, shortly before he died. One of my friends said she didn't believe in Father Christmas and I said, "I do, 'cos I've seen him at Harrod's". A good advertisement for the famous store!

One of Eileen Amsdon's outings had a dramatic ending.

Once when Auntie Lou was staying with us, Mother planned an outing. I was in my auntie's charge, whilst Mother had Betty. As soon as the tram came to our stop, everyone rushed to board it. In the confusion I was parted from my aunt. The tram started and I was left standing in the road. I can still see myself running, chasing the tram, with tears cascading down my face, and shrieking "Mummy! Mummy!" Passers-by tried to stop me, but I eluded them and still ran on. Presently my mother spotted my aunt, alone. "Where's Eileen?" "I thought she was with you" my aunt replied. "Stop the tram!" Mother yelled - and the tram stopped. My mother climbed out to see a woe-begone, tear-stained little creature still pounding along the tram-lines. Who got blamed? I did - for letting go of my aunt's hand!

I enjoyed Dulwich when we went to live in that area. It was a leafy village, with many places to visit - the park, the picture gallery and the cemetery. I loved to walk round the graves on a Sunday, looking at the flowers. The park had a lake and I learned to row there. My first boyfriend taught me. I fell in once and he just laughed. That finished him!

In the holidays I went by tram or bus to London to visit the Tate Gallery, which was free. I had to take my sister, of course. We had not heard of child-snatching then, and I don't think we were warned about talking to strange men either.

While at Dulwich we spent Christmas with my relatives in Camberwell. Grandma and Pa lived at the top of the house in three rooms. Dinner for the eleven of us was served downstairs, in what was normally a doctor's surgery. Then we all went upstairs to the big sitting room for the rest of the day. We made our own entertainment. My cousin Madge played the piano; then Tommy accompanied Madge while she sang. Next Tommy had a piano solo. Doug played the violin, with Madge as accompanist. I recited long, heroic poems. Then my father and my uncle sang. Oh, those lovely sentimental, melodic songs! *The Trumpeter, I Hear You Calling Me, I Passed By Your Window,* and *Friend Of Mine.*

My family went to the seaside every year. I liked the concert parties on the sands, particularly as they often invited children to come on stage and sing. I longed to sing and had practised at home with '*Ours Is A Nice House, Ours Is*' and '*I'm Forever Blowing Bubbles*', but somehow I never got picked.

Hilda Morgan's family enjoyed many holidays and outings.

The earliest holidays I recall were spent in the country, staying with relatives. We travelled by train and were met at the station by someone with a pony and trap, or simply an open farm cart and horse. A large trunk contained all the family clothes: no suit cases then.

When war broke out we were in Hampshire with Aunt Nell, one of Father's sisters. There I saw aeroplanes for the first time. They appeared to me, aged five, to be desirable toys. I thought 'If only I had a long stick, such as my mother's clothes' prop, I could hook one down!'

A clothes' prop was a long, thin branch of six feet or more, with all side shoots cut off except at the tip, which was left as a Y shape. This held up a line of washing at the centre, so that sheets would not dangle on the ground or blow against the fence or house wall.

I little thought I would ever fly in a plane or that my sons and grandsons would frequently fly around the world.

I think the war must have curtailed our holidays, but I remember daily picnics on Wimbledon Common, where my father buried his primus stove to save transporting it every time! Sometimes we went to Richmond Park, which meant a long walk for short legs, but they were always ready to run and play in the bracken. Once mother made a rabbit pie for us; it had to share the pushchair with baby Brenda.

During the war when Grace Knight's father was serving in France, her mother, who was terrified by the bombs in London, took the family to Halstead, Essex. There they enjoyed all the delights of living in the country, far away from the air-raids. She describes a family picnic.

Mum and Aunt Grace, being Londoners, were very nervous of the animals you expect to find in the countryside. They would go miles out of their way to avoid any possible encounter with cows, horses, even sheep! Before venturing into a field they would reconnoitre thoroughly to ascertain whether there were any animals about. There was a lovely field in Colchester Road which was a favourite for afternoon picnics. It was especially inviting, with lush grass, a profusion of wild flowers, and a wonderful great tree in the middle of this large field. There had never been any animals there to deter Mum and Auntie, and we came to regard it as 'our field'. On hot, sunny days the rugs would be spread out in the shade of the tree with the baby twins placed on them to play with their toys, while we older children went exploring for anything we could find - flowers, butterflies, snails. We would return and enjoy the food and drink and stay until Mum said "Time to go".

It was always so idyllic - nothing ever spoiled it - that is, until one terrifying afternoon! We were there, everything as before, babies on rugs, picnic things at the ready. We children were already wandering off, when a scream sent us running back to the tree where Mum and Auntie were frantically gathering up everything - babies, picnic, rugs in an agony of desperation to get out of the field before a herd of cows, which had been driven in the gate at the far end of the field, could reach us. By the time the babies were in their prams and we had reached the gate, the herd was quite close. The two ladies were almost hysterical and in such a state of panic that they had to rest by the side of the road to recover. From the other side of the gate the cows gazed at us so benignly and then continued with their grazing quite unperturbed by our presence that I burst out laughing to think that we had been afraid of them. Even Mum and Auntie joined in the laughter, but we never went to that field again.

Outings for Margery Clow when she was young meant going on foot to Hampstead Heath.

We lived in Hanley Road, which runs from Stroud Green to Hornsey Road. In our summer holidays we walked from there right up to the Archway, round the back of Archway and across Dartmouth Park Hill to where fields began. Then we walked across the fields to Hampstead. We took a bottle of water and some sandwiches with us. When we reached the corner of our road there was a public house. We drank the water and then knocked at the side door of the pub and asked if they could re-fill our bottle. There was a housekeeper and she filled it for us, until she tumbled to it that there was something wrong - all these children needing water. So then she said she would box our ears if we didn't go off, so we had no more water.

We went on via the three Highgate ponds, one for men's swimming and later one for women. Then higher up the hill and across to the 'Spaniards' public house, and down the other side, where we picked the blackberries that grew there. We roamed the whole day with just a couple of sandwiches and a bottle of water. We would refill the bottle here and there from fountains, then back home to a good wash by Mother, then bed.

Once a year, around 1st September, a fair was held at Barnet. It was a famous fair and everybody who could get there, went. It was held in fields at the foot of the hill. It was a horse fair, and people came buying and selling horses. In addition there were roundabouts and swings, and other entertainments. We travelled by tram and invariably I was sick. Other children were also affected as the trams swayed so. We had to hang over the side of the tram.

Although we had no money to spend we had a lovely time running around. We enjoyed the music and all the people. Then we climbed to the top of High Barnet, again more fields than houses. We went along the top of High Barnet High Street, past some very big houses, and there were some little cottages down the side. One of us wanted to 'spend a penny', so my mother knocked at this cottage to ask if it could be allowed. Very kindly the lady let us go down her garden. It was one of the old lavatories with a hole, with a scrubbed wooden seat and a bucket beneath. We all used it. She was such a nice person and asked my mother if she would like a cup of tea. She gave us each a cup of tea and a homemade cake.

Mother had a great love of the country and wild flowers, and she shared it with us. Because she had no meals to prepare or housework to do when we were evacuated to Winchester and then Bath during the war, she was able to devote much more time to us. We had wonderful outings to the Downs at Winchester, with the baby in the wheelchair. On the way we always stopped to feed the donkey!

She taught us the names of all the wild flowers, and had her own pressed flower collection, which we were allowed to look at. She loved the scent of honeysuckle and white violets, which grew in abundance on the more sheltered parts of the Downs. When we explored the wood, we collected dry timber and were thrilled when she kindled a fire and sometimes boiled a kettle on it. Other days we went by the river near St. Catherine's Hill, carrying our fishing nets, and had great fun trying (unsuccessfully) to catch the tiddlers. Again I can remember the sweet scent of mint and meadowsweet, and the beautiful blue forget-me-nots. At that time there was a wire strung across the river with a basket on it. We could order snacks which we paid for and then they were delivered across the river to us. Much more exciting than going to a shop!

We also had some very happy times at Bath. Again Mother was free to take us for excursions, and very often we took a picnic and explored further afield. Paddly Woods was a very special place, as for the first time we saw yellow irises growing wild by the edge of a pond. It was a very hot day and on the way we stopped to drink from a little stream that was bubbling from the bank. No ill effects.

The first seaside Holiday I remember was when we went to Bognor during the early days of the war. Unfortunately we all developed whooping cough whilst we were there, so had to be

taken to part of the beach far away from other children. One of my vivid recollections of that holiday is when Mother had to return home to London on urgent business, and left us in charge of the owner of the house where we were staying. She was not used to children, and insisted on sitting in the room with us after we had been put to bed. For some reason we all got the giggles, which made her very cross. Kathleen, still very small, said: "I've only got one leg and I'll get out of bed and throw the covers at you!" We were all very relieved when Mother returned. Apparently she was told I was the ringleader!

Mrs Grace Allott   Mrs Jessie Solkhon with Jessie
Mr. Percy Allott   1909.

Grace   Father holding Kathleen   Jessie 1919

The Asquith family enjoyed some enchanting holidays, mostly in Devon and Cornwall.

In 1919 my mother took a bungalow in Cornwall, a place called Polurian near Mullion in the Lizard Peninsula. Last time I was in Cornwall, I went to see the big hotel on the cliffs above it which still exists. The place was just a little hamlet and the bungalow was quite primitive with an earth closet and a little garden, about half a mile from the sea. We walked down a beautiful track bordered with honeysuckle and roses to a nice little semi-private cove, which was intoxicating. Then sometimes we walked along the cliffs with my mother to Kynance Cove near the Lizard, which is a great beauty spot with serpentine rocks, or we went bicycling over the Goonhilly Downs. Friends used to come down occasionally to see my mother and stay at the Polurian Hotel. That was a lovely holiday.

The next year we went to a place called Polzeath near Padstow, which was also rather fun. We had a little house there where the sea ran right past us, with a fine headland, Pentire Head, opposite.

We travelled by car from Mells. There was a kind of estate car belonging to my grandparents' agent, and his chauffeur drove us down from Mells to Cornwall. The first time we stopped for the night on the way at the Two Bridges Hotel on Dartmoor. The second year we stayed with a friend of my mother's at Hartland Abbey between Clovelly and Bude and both those were rather wonderful experiences. It was trying being cooped up in the car; on the other hard, we greatly enjoyed the narrow flowery lanes full of wild roses and honeysuckle. I suppose we came back the same way, but I remember the outward journeys rather than the return ones.

In 1921 my mother and a cousin who, like her, had been widowed earlier in the war, and a third friend who was called Goonie Churchill, sister-in-law to Winston and married to his elder brother, all had a holiday together. They took a house called Menabilly, near Fowey which, much later, belonged to Daphne du Maurier and was the scene of some of her books. In our time, it was a large bare house, full of portraits of former owners, set among rather neglected lawns and woods which were full of blue hydrangeas and ended in a great row of cedars. A cool shady path led down to the semi-private cove where we bathed and played and kept a small sailing boat. It was an exceptionally hot summer, so we spent the whole day out of doors except during lessons and we even slept out on a great pile of hay in a field near the house overlooking the sea. It was an enchanting and memorable summer which lasted all through May, June and July.

Each of the mothers had small children about my brother's age, so there were several little boys aged five, six and seven, and my sister and myself who were 11 and 12. We had the same delightful governess who had taught us the year before and she somehow managed to teach us all. We had lessons in the great big library full of delightful books.

This was the last time for many years that we were able to combine education with spending all the summer months in the country.

Transport in Zelah was somewhat primitive when Dor Curgenven was young.

Once a week, and occasionally twice, two horse-drawn wagonettes came from Fiddlers Green and Newlyn East: they travelled to Truro and back, taking a full day for the return journey. When the horses reached Truro they were given corn and water, then back up Kenwyn Hill, when the heavier men got out and walked to make life easier for the horses. They were driven by Mr. J. Gray and Mr. Benetto. Some years later Mr Gray's son had a bus named 'Fearnot'. That was different! We had a lot of laughs, especially when it wouldn't go and we had to get out and push.

People got around mainly on bicycles, but there were a few road horses and carts, and the well-to-do might have a pony and trap; however, if you lived away from the village there was only the bus.

The road in the village was unmade, but it was looked after very carefully. The men were designated to clear it on a Saturday with hooks and rakes, to make sure it was raked and cleaned. Nothing much changed until the First World War. Then the Americans sent in armoured troops to England and some were stationed here in Cornwall. They wanted to modernise things, but they couldn't do much about the village as there were houses both sides of the road. On the outskirts they widened it and improved it; then during one night they knocked down two cottages to widen the road, which did not go down very well with the villagers. They were the first people to suggest a bypass in 1915: it took until the end of the eighties to get it!

Holidays were a pleasant time for Winifred Chandler.

In August we spent a fortnight by the sea, generally in a boarding house at Hastings on the South Coast Mother tried to keep our departure secret from my sister, as she go so excited each time she had a bilious attack. However, the large tin trunk that contained all our luggage had to be ready and collected by Carter Paterson a few days before we left, and there was no hiding that!

Every morning before breakfast we went down to the beach, where Billy Welch and his son auctioned the small fish (plaice, dabs) from the night's catch. We could get seven for sixpence, which our good-natured landlady would fry for our breakfast - yummy!

The rest of our time was spent mostly paddling and making sand castles, but on one occasion we went for a bathe. For this purpose we were not allowed the modern scanty attire, but made to wear a home-made bathing costume of thick material (no see-through!), which reached to our ankles and wrists, and had frills. Moreover, to preserve our modesty, instead of undressing in the warm sunshine, we were obliged to use a cold, draughty bathing machine which was particularly uncomfortable when we were wet after the return journey from the sea. I never tried the experiment again!

Christmas was great, and I remember well the occasion when my father, who had more ingenuity than money, borrowed a sheet, a large ball of string and some dark green velvet, and created a spider's web with a fat, sinister looking spider in the middle and all the presents caught in the web.

Like most children, we hung up our stockings at the end of the bed on Christmas eve, and were delighted when we found an apple, orange, nuts and a sugar mouse. No expensive toys in those days!

We always had books for Christmas presents, and discovered that our parents hid them on top of the wardrobe in their bedroom. If they were out in the evening, my brother would climb up and get them down. He had *The Boys' Own Annual*, and my sister *The Girls Own Annual*, and I had one more suitable to my age group.

On Boxing Day, we went to see one of our uncles, whom we called our 'rich uncle'. He had seven children and also invited Auntie Kate and her seven offspring. All we children were sent up to the nursery with a packet of wafers. When the rich uncle visited us at home he asked "Do you like sweets?" Naturally we said "Yes", so he took us to a shop where we were allowed to choose something we liked. When we arrived home they were all put on a tray and soon disappeared!

Marjorie Davies has some happy memories of holidays with her grandparents.

Christmases at Ansley Hall were particularly memorable. Santa came down the chimney and left a pillowcase full of presents at my bedside. Another Christmas memory is of being taken to see Wee Georgie Wood in the pantomime *Mother Goose* at the Birmingham Theatre Royal, as we were on the bus route to Birmingham. In summertime Grandpa would take me to the gardens with him and I remember the luscious black grapes in the vinery and the warm fire in the potting-shed, where the boiler heated the pipes to the greenhouses. There were cats and kittens there, too, to keep the mice down. On one of our Ansley visits I was taken seriously ill with measles and sadly most of my little play-fellows there contracted from me the germ I must have carried from Brailsford. I recall feeling so ill I wanted to die. Measles was very serious in those days.

On Saturday nights we all travelled into Nuneaton by bus to go shopping, mainly in the street market, as there were no shops at the Hall. Sometimes, as a special treat, one of my aunties would take me to see Charlie Chaplin or maybe Jackie Coogan or Mary Pickford at the old silent movies. I sometimes think that was how I became an early reader, for I managed to follow the sub-titles at an early age.

Summers always seemed very hot and winters very cold, snow being quite commonplace.

The next decade in my life brought school, which I detested, and my halcyon days were sadly over except for the holidays, but the memories will always remain.

Mrs. Mary Horseman is now living at Henbury, Bristol. She describes transport in the Bristol area before 1920.

We lived outside Bristol, about two miles from the Centre and a mile from the shops. There was terrific excitement when they began bringing a bus across the Downs, $1^1/2$d. for adults and 1d for children. Before that we had to walk across the Downs and then get a tram into Bristol. Bristol Tramway Company did not like this competition and quickly started up a rival service. So for a time two buses came out at once, each trying to collect the other's clientéle. Eventually they settled their differences and came to a fixed alternative timetable.

When I was three years old I went to a Montessori school, which I much enjoyed. We had to sort out colours and do up buttons and laces. I learned to read quite easily. I had a tricycle to ride up and down the pavement or to the local shops with our nanny. I did not have a bicycle until I was ten, so the tricycle must have been quite a large one. My grandpa was an MP and he had

Gordon Lodge - Mary Horseman (née Gardener) front left.

a car with a chauffeur. Both my aunts drove and one had a two-seater AC. It was a great treat to be taken out in it, firmly strapped into the dickey seat.

Elspeth Burns remembers some very happy holidays in her childhood.

We loved to go to Arran for holidays. It is a Hebridean island which, somehow, has slipped into the Clyde. We usually went to Whiting Bay - or Brodick - and it was there I learned to swim in the sea when I was five. Mother stood on the shore with a 'chitterybite'.

Many afternoons we took picnic teas with us and walked up Glen Rosa and sat by the Rosa Burn; later sometimes walking up to the top of the glen. Arran was a lovely place for walks - up the String road or Glen Sannox, or sometimes we would take the ferry round to Lamlash, with tea in Fuller's tea-room, then the lovely walk home to Brodick. This was one of the best walks on the island.

The 'castle children', the two sons and two daughters of the Duke of Montrose, were at that time usually on holiday in Brodick Castle and with friends put on very good performances in the Brodick village hall. The Duchess was gathering funds for the Arran Hospital - now at Lamlash.

They were happy, happy days; cousins and school friends came to stay with us. Many families rented the same houses year after year for holidays. It was always a sad day when we boarded the dear old ferry *Glen Sannox* or *Atlanta* for home and the next term at school ahead!

Mrs. Elsie Paget, who was born in 1907, describes some of the magical experiences she had on the Isle of Islay where she lived when she was young.

Sometimes on waking up, perhaps in the night but more often in the early morning, it is there - the sound of the tide. Our house stood high, slightly sheltered from the south-west wind by the rocky hill from which it had been built. The rock face, soft browns and greys, caught the daylight warmly even when no sun shone. We looked down first on a grassy slope, then the roofs of two small rows of houses, and on to the distillery building roofs. A hairpin road descended to these buildings and thence to the pier, which was wide enough to accommodate a good-sized cargo ship, but jutted out only about twenty-five yards into the sea. The slope into the sea and its continued steepness was thrilling.

Deeper and deeper it went with darkening greenness, yet with a clarity revealing beautiful seaweeds, gently waving; so deep that large cargo vessels only needed space to turn.

That was the small but important village of Caol Ila; a distillery was built there largely because of the purity of the water, which was the chief need. A burn flowed down from a loch high in hills a mile off and wandered through a marsh. There were banks of heather, clusters of irises (yellow flags) rushes and bracken. Then, at the steep slope among cliffs, it became a lovely waterfall and was captured by the distillery for its use.

Caol Kyle, Strait or Sound (they each mean a passage between islands) sometimes varying in width and direction, was always used by twice-daily tides and the ocean's playground: eight hours north, slack, and eight hours south. The slack still, quiet, no movement, a gentle slackening, then still. Later a gentle movement the opposite way, strengthening until the fast tide flowed.

Knowledge of the tides and their behaviour in the great variety of patterns of islands and rocks was a science all kinds of people needed to study and respect. I can scarcely remember any deaths from drowning among our fishermen, local people or the shipping around our coast in the twenty-seven years this beautiful island was our home. The four years of the First World War are not included, of course: that was quite different.

Children were brought up to respect the sea and the land as it slopes increasingly towards it, ending suddenly in sheer cliffs. A beautiful coast with cliffs, beaches, sand and pebble; joints jutting out to sea; hazel trees holding rock and soil together, making cliff paths possible and safer; small bays with one or two houses and, of course, small boats.

The Sound varies in width from one mile or more to half-a-mile, where a ferry boat can cross from Port Askaig (named after a Norwegian Chief) to Jura, quite a different island. There, there are fewer rocks and cliffs, a smoother coastline with at one point almost perpendicular cliffs, very even, shapely and regular, down which flow sudden waterfalls when it rains heavily. On a quiet day, with no wind, we could from Islay hear these individual waterfalls, each with its own 'voice' of falling water. To me it was like many voices in a choir. In my young days I had never heard a human choir, but this was a good introduction. In the Autumn this lovely sound was often added to by the almost musical roar of the rivalry among the stag population.

Most of the year Jura is charmingly purple with heather. There are three beautiful mountains, Ben More (big), Ben Gorm (blue) and Ben Cruachan (rocky). These three names are repeated in many areas of Scotland. Near these waterfall cliffs was a favourite bay of my brother, Don. He was strong and clever at managing Dad's little boat whether rowing, sculling or sailing, and sometimes he would ask me to go out with him.

It must have been early summer of 1914, before we had any inkling of the approaching war. School holidays were in June, when the weather was often good, and one morning Don suggested we went over to this bay, put down the anchor and read our books. It was a perfect day, calm, sunny and still, with the musical murmurings of the tide. With strong strokes he rowed over to almost opposite our Caol Lila home. Incidentally, our quiet, thoughtful Dad kept binoculars near his desk so that he could see much of the opposite Jura coast.

It was a south flowing tide, so Don, soon after rowing out into it, began to head slightly north to counteract the powerful pull of the tide. Crossing over, from midway we could see the lovely coasts to north and south of Jura, with its shapely volcanic mountains.

The little bay Don and I liked was deep green and clear, and in shallower water sapphire and turquoise. Don let down the small anchor while still rowing gently. It settled on some stony seaweed spot. That was just right to make it easy to haul up again when he moved the boat in the opposite direction. The land was in many-coloured greenery, and a little river flowed into the sea past the inland gamekeeper's house. There seemed to be no-one about: he and his son were probably miles off, and mother and daughter busy on their little farm.

Don took out his Boys' Own Paper, and I my book of fairy tales. It was summery, quiet and beautiful. Don was in the stern of the boat, I in the bow. A memory of peace and happiness. Everything was very still, very enjoyable. I became aware, with no sound at all, that someone was interested in something. A few inches from my right elbow. Yes, there was somebody there.

A lovely sleek, beautifully shaped little head and two golden-brown eyes were gazing intently into my book as I leaned on the gunwale close to the water. A beautiful young seal, probably a 'teenager', who did so want to see my book. Little bright eyes were looking interestedly, small flippers working to keep the head in a position to see better. What are those marks on the pages? What are the colours? What is she concentrating on? He wasn't a bit interested in me: it was the book I was holding.

I gasped with a delighted laugh; Don looked up and came forward. Before you could say 'look', he was gone, a sudden turn and nothing left but gently swirling water. It might have been a little lady or gentleman, but we said 'he' because of the courageous curiosity and delightful determination to find out.

Rudyard Kiping in his Rikkitikkitavi story states that all little mongooses are filled with curiosity. Mother encourages this. Her advice is always 'Run and find out'. Maybe both creatures are equally capable of disappearing in no time if necessary. Mother and Dad, both lovers of nature, were delighted when we told them. It reminded us of Isaiah 11:9. 'They will neither harm nor destroy on all my holy mountain, for the earth will be full of the knowledge of the Lord as the waters cover the sea'.

There was another special expedition, one quiet day in early summer, carefully chosen by Dad for a trip on one of his free days. We rowed along on a south flowing tide, which would later slow Into slack tide. Then it would be still for a while before beginning its eight hours of flowing north; then we would return. Mother and Dad loved all the wildlife, especially the birds. It may be that Dad had noticed a golden eagle on some rare occasion when we had taken our little boat so far south along our shores or the Sound of Islay. Old enough to give Dad some help with the rowing, I must have been aged eleven or twelve. We landed on the shore where a small river flowed into the sea. Mother and I turned the stones there, to see if we could find any little eels on their way inland.

Dad, who had been gone for a little while, came and said, "Would you like to see a little golden eagle?" We were surprised, but Dad had a way of examining a situation and thinking all round it before asking if we would like to do something. I was sure it would be safe for the little eagle, as well as us. He had watched mother eagle circling over the beautiful ravine down which the little river flowed in lively hops and skips, and small falls. She had then flown quickly away inland.

Mother was a little anxious and preferred to stay on the beach. I was on tip-toe. "Come then," said Dad, and to Mother, "We won't be long". Mother looked at the sky inland, but I was sure Dad would time it perfectly.

We went quietly up the watercourse, whose little stray strands of falling water fell musically over smooth stone. Up towards the steeper slopes we saw the higher parts of the ravine opening further and further skyward.

Dad whispered, "We won't break any more twigs than we can help, so as to be as quiet as possible". Dad helped to find firm little footholds in the climb and grasp tree roots or any small firm branches. He gently led me up, watching the positions of my footholds. It was a lovely feeling of adventure, *safe* adventure!

I don't remember his exact words, only a few like, "Yes, that's right", "hold on", "very quiet". We came to perhaps a one-yard high rock, jutting outwards, flat on top like a shelf, behind which was more rock rising high. What a safe place! Then we saw the nest, the baby eagle's home. It looked at us, standing, but did not move. Dad made a few gentle soothing sounds - sounds he had long ago made to encourage me when frightened. He had whispered on the way up, "We don't want to frighten it, so we won't touch it or move at all - just look". Wise words.

It looked at Dad. I wonder, yes, perhaps it enjoyed the very gentle reassuring sounds he made. It was *so* lovely, I was spellbound and couldn't have moved if I'd tried. About the size of a gosling still at the fluffy stage, or two or three times that of a duckling before wing and tail tips had grown much, it stood there without moving, quite unabashed and unafraid of being looked

Pales - The ancient rocks tell to the fast flowing tide.

at, standing firmly on two little legs, hidden by the bright covering of golden fluff. The beautiful head of silky golden down and
two lovely large eyes, golden and yellow, which were not at all
alarmed, was an unforgettable picture.

Perhaps its majestic ancestry, its powerful wing span over great
heights and vast distances, were all there contained in that beautiful little form.

Dad said softly, "Now we'll go". Very quietly, slowly and carefully, we descended. I can't remember much about returning: it
was like having had a glimpse of another world.

As we came out of the ravine Dad said, "She will know that we
have been there, but when she has examined everything I don't
think she will be worried. Down on the beach he was watching
the sky. We found Mother sitting just above the high tide line on
some small rocks among clumps, or pincushions, of thrift, mostly
pink. Glad to see us back, she was delighted to hear all about it.

Then Dad said, "She has returned". I don't remember whether
he saw her drop from the sky above the nest or, making a bee-line
from inland, shoot straight in. Dad said, "We need not tell anyone
on the island about this." We solemnly and happily agreed.

Joyce Booth had some delightful holidays in her childhood. One she calls 'Doon the Watter'.

Fuchsia hedges and paths of wet pebbles always remind me of
holidays on the Clyde Coast. There was a ritual to be observed:
a trip to the selected resort to look for a house to let, with the
children in tow. My cousins and I soon tired of looking at flats
and cottages and set up a whine: "I want a spade; I want a pail.
When are we going to the seaside?" We usually had to be content
with an ice-cream cornet and a stick of rock before we caught the
early boat home.

The coast hamper was packed with domestic napery and necessities for anything needed for a fortnight, or a longer two
months' stay if the men folk were coming down at weekends. It
was sent on in advance. On the great day the horse-drawn cab
would take us to the station with our personal luggage and my
dolls' trunk. Then the train would deposit us at Wemyse Bay.
Such a pretty station, with baskets of geraniums hanging from the
glass roof of the covered walk that led to the pier. Then the rush
of salty air, screeching seagulls and the waiting boat. Someone
on board would be shouting "Kirn, Dunoon, Innellan, Rothesay,
an' roon the Kyles"; then we walked unsteadily up the swaying
gang plank.

The paddles started to turn, water churned, seagulls followed
us and porpoises leapt out of the water. My mother, who had

been known to feel squeamish even in dry dock, would begin to look green, while we were taken to look at the great engines turning the paddles. A small orchestra appeared with harp, harmonium and fiddle: a pleasant sound over the waves. Before we arrived at the pier a man came round with a bag to collect money for the players. Stewards, mostly university students earning a few shillings, would help us to disembark. The holiday had begun!

Canvas shoes with rope soles were a must, and stockingette bathing costumes, navy or black with a yellow trim, designed to conceal any hint of human form underneath. We changed into them in a bathing machine. The water was so cold it took our breath away and when we came out it needed a lot of hard rubbing to stop our teeth chattering. When paddling with petticoats tucked into drawers we always managed to get wet! The seaside was not all that they said it would be, yet our mothers met old friends and we made new ones, ate lots of *real* ice cream, and came home happy with seaweed, shells, pebbles and midge bites, thinking how wonderful it had been.

A holiday in Dumfries was different. The sun always shone on the honeysuckle and wild roses in the hedgerows, and there were buttercups and daisies to gather in the fields. Always we lodged with Miss Irving in Maxwelltown, as my father had done when he had been on tour. Miss Irving had cats - not that I ever saw them, but in the evening she would call them in the garden: "Wee Puss, Old Puss, Big Puss". They never had any other names. Mostly she sat in her kitchen with a bible on her knee praying for rain!

Miss Irving

She had two permanent boarders, young girls acting as post women instead of the men who had been called up. Sugar was rationed, but there was a special allocation for jam making to people who grew soft fruit. One day the girls told her than an inspector was in the area to check its use. In a panic Miss Irving stewed pounds of rhubarb (without sugar!) and filled all the jam jars she could find. The contents of her press looked impressive. There never had been an inspector!

Joyce Booth   *Nettie*

I went for walks with my father. We picked wild flowers and looked them up in *Wild Flowers Shown to the Children,* and stopped at farms on the way home for a glass of milk, warm from the cow. My father was a vegetarian, so Miss Irving was sure I was half starved and gave me bowls of broth from the big pot that hung from a hook over the kitchen fire. She also gave me a bowl of soapy water and a clay pipe, and showed me how to blow bubbles that floated far away over the green and into the garden. Sometimes she would tell of her days in the service of the Duke of Buccleuch and how she would hide her pretty bonnet in the meat-safe for when she went courting. One day the butcher delivered poor quality meat so when she heard him coming on his next visit she threw it at him, with a piece of her mind. Only it wasn't the butcher but the young master looking for a snack! I loved her dearly and wrote to her till she died.

My cousins came to Dumfries too - their father was a native. We waded across the Nith at low tide and ran back over the suspension bridge. We stood on the bridge when the girls from the mill came out, and it shook with the vibration of their clogs! We played with a little boy called Jackie, who would walk barefoot, but put his boots on to cross the river! He gave us rides on his buggy, and when asked which little girl he liked best would say without hesitation, "The yin wi' the currls". A lady sat by the river every day and talked to us; then she would suddenly get up saying, "I must go to the station to meet my man". He never came, and never would come. There was a war on.

Once I went with my cousins to visit their great-grandmother, she whose property was blocking the progress of a new bridge. It was a dark room with every item of furniture covered with plush and velvet drapes. On one little table was an arrangement of wax flowers under a tall glass dome: on another exotic birds and butterflies, while she sat like Whistler's mother in the window.

There was so much to do and see in Dumfries, from the little mouse on Burn's statue to the lovely countryside beyond, and an unusual view from the camera obscura. "Look!" cried the 'yin wi' the currls'. "There's my daddy going into Johnny Biggars (the pub.)!

Mary Blott was able to experience the fun of a holiday in Paris with friends.

I left school when I was seventeen and went on to Pitman's Business College for a year, doing shorthand, typing, book-keeping and French. I found it all rather boring and wanted something with more movement and variety, so I never used any of it. Instead I got into the Telephone Service, where there was plenty of variety. I also played tennis for the exchange, as I loved sport. I was a telephonist at Central Exchange in the City, just off St. Paul's Churchyard, a very busy and a very happy one. I made good friends there and after about a year some suggested a holiday in Paris. We were allowed a holiday in February. My five friends were about four years older than me, so had a week due, but I only had four days, so I asked for leave without pay. The powers that be had never heard of such a request, so 'No' was the answer. Nevertheless I took it (and nearly got the sack!). We each had £10.00 for everything. I was young and innocent and hadn't a clue what I was in for. I think probably I was invited because I was the last to leave school and had a good smattering of French.

Fortunately the rate of exchange was so much in our favour that we did everything we wanted. We arrived in Paris at 4.00 am, after a dreadful crossing from Newhaven to Dieppe. On arrival at the station we took a taxi to a hotel somebody had recommended. We arrived there about half-an-hour later, only to find when we arose next morning that we were right opposite the station where we had arrived. Obviously we were greenhorns! but we sure did Paris on that £10.00. We went to the opera, the Moulin Rouge, Versailles, Follies Bergère, Eiffel Tower - the lot. We also had good meals out. France was at its lowest ebb after the war, so we each bought a silk frock and presents to take home!!

Holidays in the wide open spaces of America offered opportunities not available to those living in England, and Nanette Hales had some very interesting experiences.

Our summer holidays were divided between the two sides of the family. In July my mother and sister and I went to grandfather's summer cottage on Lake Ontario (near Rochester). The lake had a stony beech and interesting driftwood from wrecks. Huge thunderstorms swept across the lake. It was called 'Eagle Bluff' because an American eagle was thought to nest there. A flagpole stood near the edge and when our boy cousins were there they raised and lowered the flag each day! Back from the shore was a farm which grandfather owned. It was a hundred acres of peach orchards and wheat, with just a few cows and pigs and chickens. The cows had names like Daisy and Buttercup. We would walk up each evening and watch the milk go through the separator, then carry it back in tins with handles. We were allowed to ride on the hay wagons, pulled by horses, who had once been the carriage horses. We could jump down from a ladder on to the hay in the barn loft, the barn being built on the American plan.

In August my father, who loved 'the woods' would join us and we would go to an island on a lake in the Addirondock Mountains (Upper New York State). It was a sort of hotel club and the people there were almost all family relatives and friends. There were individual cabins with sitting rooms, with fire places for log fires, but a central dining room. People would come into breakfast with trout they had just caught. My paternal grandmother was a keen fisherman. She was a plump little person with a neat knot of grey hair on top of her head; she always dressed in voluminous black skirts, even for fishing. There were, of course, row boats and canoes, and the groceries and the post were delivered by motor boat. There was a tennis court and an assembly room where they did amateur dramatics and had dances. There was a wonderful pervading scent of balsam among the evergreen trees, there being many balsam trees.

6. RECREATION

In Edwardian times, it was the wealthy who were able to indulge in a wide range of entertainments not accessible to the working class. The theatre was a social event; the men wore evening dress, with stiff collar, white waistcoat and tails in the stalls and dress-circle, and the women elegant, expensive evening gowns. Other classes queued for cheap seats in the pit and gallery, but for many including servants even this was an impossibility. *The Merry Widow* ran for two years, and musical comedies like *Our Miss Gibbs, The Quaker Girl* and *The Chocolate Soldier* were very popular. American revues, like *Hello Ragtime,* brought new dances such as the turkey trot as well as new music:

> *Everybody's doing it.*
> *Doing what? The turkey trot!*
> *See that ragtime couple over there*
> *Watch them throw their shoulders in the air!"*

Harry Lauder.

Sir Henry Irving was still performing in plays by Shakespeare and there were productions of plays by Bernard Shaw, Galsworthy, J. M. Barrie and Ibsen. There were also good plays produced in the provincial theatres.

Music-halls had spread throughout the country. In the West End there were the Alhambra, Empire, Tivoli and London Pavilion, all around Piccadilly Circus, but elsewhere there were hippodromes, coliseums and empires. The popular stars like Marie Lloyd, Harry Lauder and George Robey could earn £1,000 a week by going from hall to hall by cab. The programmes contained sen-

Marie Lloyd.

timental or comic songs male or female impersonators, and sometimes conjurers and performing animals. Some also added short moving pictures at the end of the programme. Films had been pioneered by the Frenchman, Louis Lumière, and first appeared in London in 1896. By 1910 the film was ousting the music hall. It had the great advantage that it was cheap enough for the poorer section of society to enjoy.

By 1914 there were about 4,000 'picture palaces' showing black and white films to the accompaniment of a piano or sometimes an orchestra. Early films included *The Great Train Robbery (1903),*

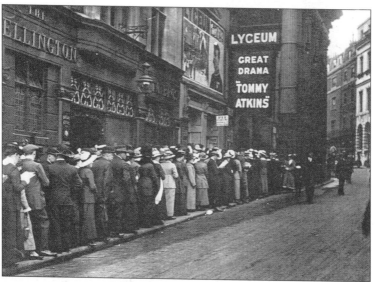

Queues outside a cinema showing a war film in 1916.

Charlie Chaplin in the film 'Shoulder Arms'.

Christmas Carol and *David Copperfield*. Charlie Chaplin was to delight many with his comedies, particularly so during the First World War. During the war, wartime films were popular, many of them glorifying the actions of the British, although there was the occasional documentary.

The Factory Act of 1867 included a free Saturday afternoon for factory workers, leading to new opportunities for them to take part in sport. The Football Association, the County Cricket Championship and the Rugby Union were all established in 1873. At the Crystal Palace Cup final in 1901 there were 110,820 spectators from all parts of the country. Football was most enthusiastically played in the Midlands and the North East, which soon produced successful professional teams. In the summer it was cricket, and Jack Hobbs is still remembered as an outstanding batsman from those days. There were local clubs based on towns, villages, churches, factories and schools. Crowds lined the banks of the Thames for the Oxford and Cambridge Boat Race, everyone sporting their chosen colour.

For the wealthy there were the traditional sports of hunting, fishing, shooting, racing, boxing and cricket. To these was added golfing, as golf courses were laid out on unprofitable heathlands.

Ballroom dancing was popular: it included the old fashioned waltz as well as quadrilles; *'Sir Roger de Coverly'* was very popular, and also the *'Gay Gordons'*. The ragtime craze began a revolution of popular music and songs after 1912, and new dances were introduced. Nearly every family boasted a piano, and there was much home entertainment - singing, reciting, and dancing. Country dancing witnessed a revival. There were various clubs connected with political parties, or swimming and other groups, but it was the Boys Brigade and later Scouts and Guides that attracted most of the young people.

Nancy Ramsey, who was born on 29th October 1901, came from a musical family and was able to enjoy entertainments of many different kinds.

My father was an orchestral flautist. He was one of the sons of a former army bandmaster, Kneller Hall trained, who, when he had served his time, was put on the reserve in what was then known as the Militia, and sent up to Scarborough to live. He was a clarinet player and he obtained work in one of the orchestras in a theatre there. The orchestras were a permanent fixture, but they had different visiting theatrical companies each week. On one occasion the play which came demanded the presence of a flautist and there was no flautist in the orchestra. My father was then nine years old, but my grandfather had been teaching him the flute and he took him along on the Monday. He became the flautist in the theatre orchestra, and so his theatrical career began. When he left school he was training to be an accountant, but he soon gave that up for music. In those days most musicians were not trained in colleges as so many are nowadays.

He first went up to London shortly before my birth. In the mornings he went to the Musicians' Association in the West End and would stay there in the club house, hoping that somebody would come along and say that there was a vacancy for a flautist in such and such a theatre. Or a flautist who was playing in one of the theatres might be off ill for a few days, or want a deputy for some reason, then if my father were on the spot 'Oh, you can go and do that', and he would get paid for the number of performances for which he played. They played an overture and also music between the acts.

My father, besides playing in theatres, played in symphony orchestras, and he did gramophone recording, which was then developing. During the London season he played after the theatre at society balls and even at functions at Buckingham Palace, probably disguised as a Ruritanian bandsman!

The music hall was still flourishing at the beginning of the twentieth century, but it was to fall a victim to the silent cinema towards the end of the first decade. Nevertheless, during those first ten years there were many famous music halls. In the West End of London the Empire, Leicester Square, and the Tivoli in the Strand were among the most famous. There were also local ones in the suburbs and in the provincial cities. Well known stars would travel from one music hall to another, perhaps appearing in three or four in the same evening, and they did two houses a night. Names that I remember are Marie Lloyd, Vesta Tilley, Florrie Forde, Albert Chevalier, Dan Leno and Little Titch. The songs they sang were whistled by all the newspaper boys and errand boys on their bicycles.

In the second decade of the century, the cinema (pictures) became more and more popular. I can remember in Clapham Junction there were at least three, one half way along St John's Road, the main shopping street in the Junction, one just round the corner opposite the entrance to the railway station, and yet another nearby.

Ownership of a piano was the symbol that a family really belonged to the rapidly growing middle class. Family entertainment was mostly home-based and to a large extent centre round the piano. Daughters were taught to play the piano and possibly had singing and elocution lessons. The whole family would gather round the piano and play and sing in the evenings. They also played cards and board games together.

The West End of London contained very many theatres. The great theatre streets were, as now, Shaftesbury Avenue and Charing Cross Road, but I am sure there were more theatres there in my childhood and early teens than there are today, and certainly there were more in the Strand. I believe the Strand, the Adelphi and the Vaudeville still exist, but I remember when the old Gaiety still stood on the island at the entrance to the Aldwych. But the theatres then were very different from what they are today. The early years of this century were the great hey day of the actor manager, when you would associate one theatre with a certain manager. Most of them were what were known as matinée idols. The last one really to be designated by such a name was Gerald du Maurier, who was still holding his audiences in the Twenties. Then there was Cyril Maude, who reigned for many years at the Playhouse, which is now, I believe, a recording studio for the BBC. That, of course, is right down at the Embankment end of Northumberland Avenue, right off the usual ground of theatre land. The Old Vic was famous, both under Lilian Baylis and under her aunt, who really opened it as a place of good, cheap entertainment for the poor people of the district.

There were performances of Shakespeare's plays but also on Thursday and Saturday nights (and I think every other Saturday Matinée) there was a grand opera accompanied by an orchestra of about twelve players, under the baton of Mr. Charles Corri. My father, whatever else he was doing, whatever other theatre he was playing in, would put a deputy in his place and go to the Old Vic for those performances. When I was twelve or thirteen he would take me on a Saturday afternoon to the matinées, and I would sit in the orchestra pit next to Madame Van Eyck, the Dutch pianist. I can remember to this day the first three operas I ever heard, in the order in which I heard them. There was Faust, Carmen and Don Giovanni; I also remember one very shaming day when I was playing with a string of beads I was wearing when, at a very quiet passage during the opera, the string broke and these beads plopped one by one on the wooden floor. Those were performances my father would not miss. Even when, during the latter part of the war, he was called up under what was known as the 'Derby scheme', he was in the Pay Corps at Woolwich, but was allowed to live at home, he was put on night duty. On the Thursday and the Saturday, he put in his appearance in the orchestra at the Old Vic before going on to do his night duty at Woolwich, sorting out soldiers' problems over their pay.

Apart from the West End, most of the suburbs had their own theatres, as did most towns of any size in the provinces. Some cities such as Birmingham and Liverpool had their own repertory theatres, but most of them relied on touring companies. Some of these were very good, but the quality varied with the size of the city or town and the amount of money they could offer the company for performing.

In those days every theatre had its own orchestra, as I know because of my father's involvement.

In addition to the music hall and the theatre there were concerts, with the two great concert halls in London. The Queen's Hall was unfortunately bombed during the Second World War but was the home of the Promenade concerts from their inception until that time. Then they moved to the Albert Hall. There were other smaller halls as well, which were more suitable for soloists, singers or small groups of instruments.

Gramophone and phonograph recordings also contributed to home entertainment. In the very early years it was the phonograph with its cylindrical records, but that was being replaced by the gramophone, with its flat discs. These were very different from today's records and only played for a very short time. I remember the excitement when the Marathon record company, for which my father recorded with an orchestra (usually accompanying some singer), devised a record which played for four minutes! That was really a long time in those days. The most famous record company was His Master's Voice, with the advertisement of the little black and white terrier sitting up beside a gramophone horn, listening to His Master's Voice. All these gramophones had to be wound up mechanically; there was no electric reproduction in those days, but nevertheless they did play a great part in home entertainment.

Many children, especially the girls, went to dancing classes. I remember going to classes where we learned the waltz, the valeta, the barn dance, the military two step and square dances such as the Lancers, the Quadrille and the Waltz Cotillion. The last two were dying out by the time I learned them, but the Lancers really lived on into the Twenties. Towards the end of the First World War and just after, there were subscription dances at the Town Hall in Wandsworth and the Battersea Town Hall, run by volunteers. I know one or two I attended in Wandsworth were run by the Primrose League. Unfortunately, when I was old enough to go to such dances there was a great shortage of male partners, owing to the ravages of the war, so you would see many girls dancing together.

A popular hobby was collecting, especially the collection of cigarette cards. Others collected Goss china, with the arms of various seaside places and other notable tourist attractions painted on them. Then there were the postcard albums. These linked up with the theatre, because during the early years of the century there were postcards of famous actresses, particularly of the Gaiety girls, people like Ellaline Terriss, Marie Studholme, Edna May and many, many others. All the young ladies used to collect these.

The Bindloss family enjoyed a variety of games and entertainments, all home-produced.

Family life was happy, with many great aunts and uncles surrounding us, two gardens to enjoy, a nursery with a rocking horse and a dolls' house, books and comics like *Tiger Tim* and *Rainbow*. The boys had scooters and a tricycle; we had pigeons and rabbits to look after and there were trees to climb. We made Christmas presents for all our relations. We had dolls and animals and a pogo stick, skipping ropes and hoops.

There were children's parties with games like 'Oranges and Lemons' or 'Here we come gathering Nuts in May', or 'Lucy Locket lost her pocket'. There were expeditions to pick blackberries, and on Good Friday we went in a cab to woods where primroses grew in masses, ready for decorating the church for Easter.

There were Pantomimes to enjoy in the winter holidays - not only professional ones at Torquay and Exeter, but several wonderful ones by Mrs. Pocock, the rector's wife, who lived on Wolborough Hill with my family. She used all the children possible of their school friends for the pantomimes. These were most imaginative, full of fairies, giants, goblins, ice maidens and always a prince and princess, around whom a pantomime story was woven. Mothers and aunts made the costumes and the town's dressmakers helped where necessary. Songs were learnt and the script made word perfect; an orchestra of violins and piano got together and the Newton Pantomime entertained the town each Christmas holiday for some years.

From being perhaps a cloud or a shadow, dressed in yards of floating muslin, at the age of six or seven we graduated to being a courtier at a ball, doing a minuet with some fair maiden, to having a slightly larger part saying a few words by the time we were ten.

We were never bored, and we were energetic. We learned to use roller skates and small bicycles: we rode endlessly round flower beds in the lawn and we slept out under a pine tree on fine nights in summer. On wet days we read or painted. We took *Little Folks* magazine, where there was always the latest chapter of a serial to look forward to, and a wonderful Canadian magazine called *St. Nicholas*, full of adventure stories of life in the wilds, with moose, and bears and snowstorms.

Games of various kinds were enjoyed by Catherine Field's family.

During the war I spent much of my spare time knitting socks for the soldiers, but my father played games like Ludo, draughts, and Snakes and Ladders with us. However, anything to do with cards was taboo, and he had an abhorrence of strong drink: he was a teetotaller.

Dad, being a carpenter, made me a marvellous doll's house. There was a front door on a hinge, and when you opened it you saw a beautiful staircase leading to a landing and the upstairs bedrooms. Each door had a lovely little handle that you turned. I was able to buy furniture in Woolworths, but he made an overmantel for the fireplace and bay windows, glass with wooden frames. Sadly my brother Bob decided to try out his new hammer on the windows, and broke them. In the loft of the dolls house was a bicycle bell, with string to the front door, and a ring to pull.

We all had a lovely time playing with it, but when Margey developed TB my father was so upset he broke it up. He may have thought that it was infected with the germ and this had caused the illness. So one day I returned home from Sunday school to find it shattered. I knew how upset he was so just had to accept it. I was sixteen by then.

There were many simple games that delighted Grace Knight and many other children when they were young.

Children at play in the street in the early part of the twentieth century provided interest and colour to the otherwise quiet scene. They amused themselves at very little cost, pocket money (if any) being no more than a penny or two per week.

When spring arrived and the outdoors beckoned, the first pastime would be the whip and top. The wooden top with a metal tip was spun on the ground and whipped along with a cord tied to a short stick, the aim being to propel the top great distances and outdo each other.

Hoops (metal ones for the boys, wooden ones for the girls) usually followed the whip and top season. Hoops were simply bowled along with the boy or girl running alongside and giving it a whack with a stick to keep it going, sometimes racing each other.

Skipping ropes lasted the whole of the outdoor season. It was mostly a girls' hobby and they made up rhymes while skipping. One I remember went:

> *Rosy apple marmalade tart,*
> *Tell me the name of your sweetheart;*
> *A..B..C..D..*

and so on until the rope stopped and the letter arrived at indicated the initial of the girl's admirer.

Marbles also had a long season and was played much as it is now, the difference being in the marbles themselves. Most modern ones are very crude compared with those of our day. The ordinary marbles were brightly coloured, with a marbled effect. The 'glassies' were lovely, being of clear crystal glass, with whirls of different colours inside, as delicate as the filaments in an electric light bulb.

One of our more bizarre pastimes was 'Cherry-hogs and screws'. When we had gathered a full bag of cherry-hogs (cherry stones) and acquired (probably from Dad's tool-box) several good specimens of screws (shiny and in top condition) of several sizes from about one to three inches, the procedure was thus:

You sat on the pavement with your back against the fence or wall, then you spread out your legs and arranged your screws in the ground in front of you. Your opponent, with his cherry-hogs crouched by the kerb and aimed them one at a time at the screws. Those he knocked down he kept, ready for his turn at being the screw displayer.

The satisfying thing about this game was that nobody really lost - you either won screws or cherry-hogs!

Hopscotch was as popular then as it is now; there were two layouts, one of squares and numbers and one in a sort of snail-shell pattern. We had 'lucky' stones or bits of slate to throw on to the numbers in the squares: these we kept specially for the game. Grown-ups frowned on this game because of the mess it made on the pavement!

Cricket could be played quite safely in the street, the danger of being knocked down by a motor vehicle being almost non-existent. The wicket was usually a lamp-post, or sometimes a 'stink-pipe', which was a long pipe rising out of the ground from the underground drains and sewers to carry away noxious odours. The game was mostly played by boys but girls were sometimes allowed to play if the boys considered their game was good enough. Great fun!

The children in Jessie Young's family provided their own entertainments.

There was a shortage of everything, but we children did not miss the luxury of toys as we did not have any bought for us. We made or invented all our playthings. A skipping rope had no handles or bells - just a piece of clothes-line kept us happy. Dolls were home-made, with buttons for eyes, usually a padded stocking, but with an old cast-off dress of baby's was quite cuddly. Only daughters in small families possessed dolls' prams, and even rubber balls cost money, so we made a firm wool one, which of course would not bounce, but it was a ball to throw and pleased us.

A great aunt once gave me a dolly. I thought it was beautifuly, with a wax face and such a pretty hat. I took it to bed with me and in the morning found my dolly's face had melted and was flat. I must have loved her too much! The family roared with laughter, but my heart was temporarily broken. So I was back to my stocking dolly again.

Being one of a large family, I grew up knowing I had to watch my p's and q's; no showing off was tolerated nor bragging. I was often told "And who do you think you are?" Not by our parents, but by the next in command - big brothers or sisters. We were a happy lot on the whole and had some cheerful gatherings round the fire on a winter evening, laughing until we were tired. Although I was the youngest of four girls I did not have to wear hand-me-downs - the sister one step older was such a tomboy that her clothes were unusable by the time she had grown out of them. If there were a jagged edge to a desk in school, or an unguarded nail, she found it, so triangular apertures appeared often in her clothes. In fact, I was rather fortunate in being well-dressed when the older children left the nest for various reasons, and mother had a little more money.

With no radio and certainly no television in the early years, we provided all our own recreation. Books, of course, were the most important, but we also played games like Ludo, Snakes and Ladders and Draughts. We used playing cards, too, not only for games like Snap and Beat Your Neighbour Out-of-doors, but also for building into a pyramid. Not easy, especially if someone accidentally pushed the table and they all collapsed.

Other interests were silkworms, provided by our school. It was fascinating to watch them build their cocoons, but we did not succeed in unwinding the silk. I think we hoped the eggs would hatch, so left them undisturbed, but I don't remember seeing any. Kathleen, when she was two, liked picking up worms and putting them in her pocket. It was not until she was about to wash the garment that Mother discovered them!

At one time Father was asked to mind a canary and a goldfinch, whilst the owner went on holiday. They were attractive to watch and listen to, but I could not feel happy about them shut up in a cage. Another day Father arrived home with two young puppies he had been asked to look after whilst a friend went on holiday. They looked very endearing but we were not so happy when they snapped at our ankles. One of them got caught up in the treadle of the sewing machine and had to be rescued.

When we were at Bath we had our own pet dog Barlow, a lovely Airdale. He was so gentle that he would carry one of the new laid eggs from one end of the garden to the house, and then place it on the draining board, perfectly whole. Sadly, one day when we were preparing to take him for a walk he accidentally knocked Kathleen down in the road, not far from an approaching cart and horse. She was not injured, but Father decided it was not safe for us to keep him, especially as another baby was on the way. As he was serving in the army he was not often around to help. He found a good home for him some miles away, but we were all in tears when he left. It was even worse when the following week he appeared on the doorstep, having found his own way back to us. But he had to go back to his new home. More tears.

In the summer we enjoyed outdoor games. Bouncing a ball was popular, as we recited rhymes like:

> *One, two, three O'Leary,*
> *I spy sister Mary*
> *Sitting on a lump of jelly*
> *Eating bread and treacle.*

On the last word of the first three lines we bounced the ball under our right leg, but when we reached the last line we bounced it very hard so that it went up high enough for us to catch. There were many similar ones, sometimes involving bouncing the ball against a wall.

There were also rhymes for skipping, which sometimes included a 'pepper', when we skipped doubly quickly, and sometimes 'bumps', when we turned the rope twice to one jump. We also enjoyed using a long rope, stretched across the road (possible in those days of little traffic, and nothing fast like cars), then a group of us followed the leader jumping through the rope and queuing up on the other side for a return. There were many variations of this. Summer was also a time for hoop, but I always envied the boys who had metal hoops whilst we girls had to be content with wooden ones, which did not seem to go nearly as quickly or make such an enticing noise! Marbles and conkers provided other entertainment, and at certain times of the year children would make a grotto in the street, using moss and flowers and anything else they could find, then badgering passers-by for a 'penny for the grotto'. Near November 5th a grotesque guy would be wheeled in a pram round the streets or station outside a shop with a similar cry 'Penny for the guy'. Then the money was spent on fireworks, but they were very simple ones compared with those of today.

David Leach enjoyed games with his Japanese friends and also holidays with his family.

Our close neighbours were very friendly and I enjoyed playing with their two sons and daughter. Their house was bigger than ours and had a large lawn, where with their help I learned to ride a tricycle and later a bicycle. We were very close friends and Japanese became my first language. When I was about four and five I went with them to a Japanese kindergarten. I was the only foreigner and sang Japanese with them. The Japanese esteemed children far more than Western countries do, and I was always treated very well.

Whilst we were in China in 1915 a young Chinese servant, Jung Hai, was detailed to look after me and he invented some wonderful games. With my wooden bricks he built a castle at one end of the cobbled courtyard, and in it he esconsed the emperor (a doll). Junghai and I were armed with more bricks which we threw from the other end of the courtyard, trying to dislodge the emperor. Whoever did, won. Another time Junghai took me to the Peking wall.

In 1915 my sister, Eleanor, was born in Peking. She had a pram on high wheels, which I proudly wheeled round the courtyard,

Junghai the Chinese boy with David Leach in courtyard.

but unfortunately I managed to tip it up and Eleanor fell out, bruising herself. I was in disgrace!

During the summer holidays we rented a house on the Chinese Coast. We spent much time on the beach. Father made a junk and filled it with fire crackers. He attached a fuse and pushed it out to sea. The crackers went off about 60ft. from the beach. It was great fun. One day he asked Wong, our chief servant, to hire donkeys for rides. Hundreds of them arrived, the owners all clamouring for custom. Wong had a long bamboo pole and he lashed it about to try to drive them away.

During the summer holidays 1917-18 my parents rented a house in the mountainous part near Karuiwizawa in Japan. This was a large European structure. There were vicious thunderstorms and I remember hiding under the bed with my young brother. One day my father took me for a long climb up the Asamayama mountain. It was too much for me and I had to lie down half way up to recover, though I was quite proud of my achievement. My parents both enjoyed mountaineering, as did the English missionary Dr. Speckman, who lectured in English at Kelley College. Many Christians were keen on mountaineering.

One day I was cutting brambles with a sickle and cut my foot badly. I still have the scar. I did not learn to be more careful and another time cut my shin.

7. HEALTH AND SEX

One of the main killer diseases at the beginning of the twentieth century was consumption, pulmonary tuberculosis, and there was no known cure except fresh air. Windows were kept open day and night in all weathers and schools were bitterly cold as there was no central heating. The first sign of the disease was loss of weight, so to be fat was to be healthy. Children were weighed regularly at school, and big babies were desirable. Children were fed on suet puddings, dumplings and fatty foods, and they were encouraged to eat every scrap of fat on their meat. Scarlet fever was also often serious and most children who developed it were sent to the fever hospital. I remember my mother saying she had it as a child and was isolated in hospital for six weeks, separated entirely from her family. She lost all her hair. Outbreaks of diphtheria were quite common, and many children died from it. Poliomyelitis also claimed many victims, and rheumatic fever led to heart and other conditions. With no antibiotics and little known about immunisation, doctors had few of the drugs available nowadays. Vaccination against smallpox proved very efficacious, but the scabs were often very large and left scars for life. Poor diet affected those on low incomes, especially during the First World War, but, for those who could afford it, food was much more healthy and appetizing than nowadays.

Head lice were common and the 'nit nurse' examined the hair of each pupil of primary schools every term. Anyone found infested had to have a special shampoo and then the hair combed with a special comb with very close teeth to get rid of the eggs. Ringworm also was quite common and was treated later with x-rays. This caused the hair to fall out and it often grew again curly.

There were various superstitions, such as crossing your fingers if a hearse passed by, and holding your breath when passing a dust cart (but as the contents were uncovered, the stench made that desirable in any case).

There was no sex education from school and little from parents, and there were many myths about menstrual periods. You must not wash you hair or take a bath, or get your feet wet; no running or taking part in gymnastics or games. Sitting on the radiators or wet grass or cold stone meant it would be impossible to have babies. Sanitary towels had not been invented in the earlier years, so 'nappies' were used and then washed.

Teachers taught children to keep themselves covered when undressing if it was necessary to share a cubicle with another girl at the swimming baths.

Sex outside marriage was taboo, and anyone with an illegitimate child was ostracised. The child also was often affected, and there was no state support.

Catherine Field describes how the scourge of tuberculosis affected her family.

I was born in London on St Patrick's day in 1903, the eldest in a family of five, and we moved to East Ham when I was quite small. I was eleven when we moved again, this time to Southall, where we had a three-bedroomed house. My parents and the babies had one room, Bob and Lesley another, and we girls the third. There I went to the elementary school and left when I was fourteen. To earn some money I looked after a little boy, living in, but after two years I had to return home to take care of the family. Tuberculosis had struck them. My brother, Norman, only four years old, was the youngest and the first to be affected. His childhood memories are mainly of the sanatorium. He was well looked after and had schooling there, but when he returned home after two or three years he could not remember me: he thought I was his Mum.

Meanwhile my mother also had contracted TB and was in a sanatorium; Jessie died very quickly of it. Margey, another sister, was sent to Truro Cripples hospital, as the disease had affected her spine. She recovered eventually and lived until she was about forty. Bob and I, the two oldest, and my father were the only members of the family to escape TB, possible because there was more food around when we were young, before the outbreak of the First World War. My mother died when I was eighteen and I was left to bring up the family.

Yet in spite of all the pain, we were a happy family, played and worked well together.

Kathleen Hogg writes of health care when she was young.

In order to reach the Natural History Museum at South Kensington, we had to pass the Brompton Chest Hospital in Fulham Road, where beyond an expanse of lawn we saw the patients in their beds pulled out on to the ward balconies, whatever the weather, their bright red bed covers making a cheerful picture.

The hospitals were all voluntarily supported in those days, as there was no National Health Service. Day patients would put their contributions into the collecting boxes; in-patients went to the Lady Almoner's office at the end of their stay, and paid whatever it was agreed they could afford. The hospitals all set themselves targets for their collections, and we took a great interest in the wooden structure erected in the grounds of St. George's Hospital at Hyde Park Corner, with the total aimed at emblazoned at the top, and the figures on the way up showing how much had been collected.

My mother had certain nursing skills and was able to cope with our childish complaints without recourse to the local GP. In face, neighbours came to her for advice, and usually she was able to help them and save a doctor's fee.

There is no doubt Mother often had a struggle to make ends meet, especially during the war and when my father was ill for three months with pneumonia and pleurisy. There was no National Health Service for her to turn to, and the doctor's visits and medicines had to be paid for week after week. Yet she managed to keep her anxieties from us children, and somehow we were kept well fed, well clothed and, above all, contented.

Ivy Ross knew that many people could not afford doctors before 1920, although her family was more fortunate.

Doctors were a luxury few could afford. Our doctor had his shop in our street. In the window were two very large coloured bottles - one green and one red. We would jump up and down outside, declaring that the tiny figures we saw were the doctor's supply of babies! Patients sat in the front shop and the doctor dispensed the medicine in his surgery at the back. The thought of caster oil and cascara still makes me heave!

My friend was always boasting about the fact that she had her tonsils out on the kitchen table at home by her doctor.

I still remember the day my mother took me to the Royal Infirmary for a tonsillectomy. When my name was called, you took off your dress and shoes, and were helped on to a table before a mask was put over your face for the anaesthetic to be administered. When I came round Mother was holding a basin in front of me, as were several others around the room. Still feeling groggy I had to go home in the tramcar. Someone asked my mother if I had been to the dentist. I just reached home in time before I was violently sick.

Mrs. Joan Partrides (née Naidley) shares some of her mother's potent home-made recipes for sicknesses.

For a bad cold, the treatment was lemon, honey and whisky in hot water, taken in bed after a hot bath, with a hot water bottle to hug. I think it was safer to take it in bed as the patient might not be capable of getting into it afterwards!

COUGH MIXTURE (called by us Witch's brew)

> *2 pennyworth Ether*
> *2 pennyworth Laudanum*
> *2 pennyworth peppermint*
> *2 pennyworth aniseed*
> *2 pennyworth Spanish liquorice stick*
> *1 lb black treacle.*

Cut up Spanish liquorice stick, put it in a pan with treacle, pour over one pint water, simmer and stir to dissolve the liquorice. When cool, add other ingredients. Take a tablespoonful several times a day or night, when the cough is troublesome.

FOR CONSTIPATION

> *1 pint bottle Gin*
> *1 dram Heira Picra*
> *1 dram rhubarb*
> *1 dram Jalap*
> *1 dram ground ginger*
> *1 dram saffron (finely chopped)*

Put all dry ingredients into the bottle of Gin and shake well before taking. Drink half a wine glassful first thing in the morning on an empty stomach for three mornings, then rest for three; until you have had nine doses altogether. Rest a few weeks then repeat same as before. If it acts too freely on the bowels, take a smaller dose.

Mary Blott's family were not plagued by some of the sicknesses suffered by other people in the early days of the twentieth century.

My family kept mostly healthy. As far as I remember, the standard 'white' bread was grey, unbleached and unadulterated. My father had a very big garden (I suppose today one would call it an allotment) and grew all the fruit and vegetables in season that we needed. A cartload of horse manure used to be delivered every Good Friday, and everything was organically grown.

I am told I was banished one day whilst the family doctor took out my younger brother's tonsils on the kitchen table. When I was quite small, the family had to move out whilst the house was fumigated, as my elder brother was in hospital with diphtheria, during an epidemic of the disease.

A Lady Creighton (widow of the late Bishop of London) came to live in the Palace. Mother used to dress me in sailor suits (quite fashionable in those days). My brother had developed ringworm and at that time I had long curls. Mother, fearing I might catch it, cut my hair short. That Sunday Mother was not there, so Father sent me to our pew in church alone. Presently the door opened and Lady Creighton, who was a very big woman, came in, saw me and said, "Little boys should take their hats off in church, now take it off and remember in future." Apparently I caused quite an upset as I shouted, "I'm not a little boy. I'm a little girl." I roared and was taken home.

Mrs. Cleone Heath, now living near Kingsbridge, Devon, describes life in a doctor's house at Walton-on-the-Hill, in Surrey, before 1920.

My father was a doctor and before the introduction of the National Health Service, a doctor's family was very much involved in his work. His patients came to his private house.

Two rooms were given up for the practice, one as a consulting room off the hall and connecting with another large one, as a wait-

The doctor's house, built in 1912, at Walton-on-Thames.
The Nanny with his children.

159

ing room. In between these was the dispensary, a little room where the doctor made up his own medicines. 'Private' patients came to the front door and were brought straight through the hall into the consulting room. The 'Panel' patients came down the patients' path through a separate gate, into the waiting room, where they sat around on hard chairs. As children, whenever we had to go through to fetch something, we were always extremely polite and compassionate to these people who were 'Daddy's patients' - a very special and important race, different from other people. When gypsies came to him from Epsom at Derby time they were given cups of tea: I remember being very interested that they preferred to drink from the saucer rather than the cup!

In the days before the NHS, my father made his own charging system. At that time when there was a particularly large gap between the rich and poor, he charged the impoverished as little as possible, while giving them as much care and attention as he did to the better off. The latter could make up the difference by paying him higher fees, because they were more able to afford them.

The telephone was constantly ringing from patients needing a visit in their own homes. My father would leave a list of his intended visits; messages had to be passed on to him at one of these houses to catch him on his round. They were usually phoned through by one of the maids, but if they were not available at the time, one of the family would have to do so. When domestic staff became less available, the doctor's wife was tied to the phone.

My brother, who is older than me, remembers that the main illnesses at that time were scarlet fever, measles, poliomyelitis, pulmonary tuberculosis and diphtheria. When it was necessary for patients to get to hospital they were taken by horse-drawn ambulance. Hospitals at that time were very different from today, and it was customary for operations to be performed in a private house. Our nursery was at times turned into an operating theatre. The place was scrubbed and clean dust sheets hung over the furniture. I, myself, had my tonsils and adenoids removed on the nursery table by an ENT surgeon. My father had previously driven me round to the fishmonger to get some ice for me to suck after the operation.

The doctor made up his medicines himself, putting them usually in bottles with tablespoon doses marked off by ridges on the glass. The bottles were corked, labelled and expertly wrapped in shiny white paper, which was sealed with a dab of hot sealing wax melted over a little methylated spirit lamp. On one occasion my father had to mix up something for some poor old soul, for whom he was particularly sorry, so he decided to make the medicine taste nice. The patient came back and said, "Doctor, I know mistakes can occur, but did you forget to put the medicine in?" So he had to make it taste horrible for her to feel that it was doing her good.

Later on he was able to change to giving his prescriptions to the chemist to make up. This he did by telephoning from his upright telephone, with the earpiece which hung from a hook on the instrument. He was always anxious not to be kept waiting (no direct dialling in those days), and if the telephone exchange did not answer at once there was much rattling of this hook to attract the operator's attention. Growing up in a doctor's house, with a caring and compassionate attitude engendered by such contact with the sick and suffering from an early age, must have made a very deep impression. Three of his five children (and even his grandchildren) entered the medical and allied professions.

Doctors had much more time for their patients in Dor Thorneloe's young days.

When we were ill, the doctor called and, even with a slight problem like German measles, he would say when he left "Very well, Mother. I'll look in again in a couple of days." It amazed me as a tiny tot that the doctor called Mummy 'Mother', and it would amaze me still more now if a doctor mentioned calling in again! I twice had a bad throat and then a covered cart called and the driver came in to 'take a swab'. He put something down my throat and presumably took a little scrape (swab), perhaps to be tested for diphtheria. I imagine that doctors had to report bad throats and this was the result. Nothing ever came of my swabs, I am glad to say.

Many children had adenoid and tonsil operations. I was taken to a London hospital and had adenoids removed: I came home again the same day.

Small children wore combinations, which were detestable garments made of a speckly cream wool fabric, buttoned down the front. They had a slit at the back for convenience and no doubt were difficult for a small girl to manage. Bloomers topped these.

I was given Parish's Food as a tonic. This was inclined to make your teeth black, so strict brushing had to follow. Many other children were given Virol each day - probably these supplements were necessary because of wartime diet. I recollect that the whole family used the same tin of Gibbs' toothpaste (pink and flat, like a tin of shoe polish). It must have cost only a few coppers.

The range of children's toys was quite small. We had Ludo, Snakes and Ladders, Draughts and Snap cards. I had two or three dolls, a dolls' pram and later a scooter and a wooden hoop to bowl along. Boys had iron hoops and a hook with which to bowl them, and they also had roller skates.

Ringworm was quite a common disease in the early part of the twentieth century, and Margery Clow contracted it whilst at school.

Somehow or other ringworm affected the school. Nearly every child developed it. In those days they cured it with x-rays, so we all went in turn to the Cambridge Hospital with one of the nurses. Our hair was washed every day in some special solution: then we had to have our heads shaved, and lie on a table. We were told not to move at all, then the machine was switched on. Unfortunately something tickled my nose and I sneezed; the top of my head was burnt. When I returned to school I was put in the Infirmary on my own, waiting for my head to heal. They brought me cups of cocoa, with milk that seemed to be curdled. I could not bear it in my mouth so opened the window and tipped the dregs outside. Unfortunately there was an iron staircase (fire escape) outside the window and all the muck rebounded and splashed on the window below. I got into trouble for that! They said, "Have you been throwing your cocoa out of the window?" "No!" I said. I'm certain I would have had a good whacking if I had not been in the Infirmary, because I did not tell the truth.

When my hair grew again it was very frizzy, with tight curls. We had been given half combs to put in front of our hair, from ear to ear. They broke very easily and Matron said, "The first child to break her comb will be punished and made an example of." My hair was frizzy and tight, and the very first time I put the comb into my hair it broke in the middle, so I had a piece either side under control, and a huge lump of hair sticking up in the middle, full of frizz. Everybody was laughing at me!

When we went into our dinner we had to pass the matron. She took one look at me and said, "Margery Tagg, after dinner I want you!", and I knew I was for it. I was sent to the bathroom, and if you were sent there you knew you were going to be punished. They kept you waiting quite a long time, then they pulled your knickers down, made you bend over the bath and hit you with a slipper. It could be quite painful. They mended the comb by putting one piece over the other and binding it round with cotton. This made the comb short and my hair stuck out at the sides.

Noreen Beaumont describes her mother's varied experiences of sickness, dating and sex.

Norah had a good contralto voice and she joined with a soprano of her own age to sing at concerts for the troops in church halls and the like in York, which was a garrison town. She was twenty years old when John was billeted there in 1916. They met, not in a church hall but in a street in York. Their paths crossed, they eyed each other, stopped and spoke. It was ten years later they were to marry, but Norah kept him out of her bed until her wedding night.

Her singing friend, who also loved a soldier, came to grief. She was not married when brought to childbirth. I picture a candlelit room in a cottage, the window well blacked out against Zeppelin raids, the door shut to exclude innocent children and nosy neighbours. Her mother, who was acting midwife to the village mothers, was not too dismayed when she delivered her daughter's two babies, for twins ran in her family. What she did not realise was that a third infant remained in her daughter's womb. After the death of her friend, Norah refused to sing any more to the troops.

John wrote in 1917 to Norah from St. Peter's Ward, Mater Hospital, Eccles Street, Dublin:

"Just to let you know I have arrived at the above hospital wounded in the right arm, back and head. Unfortunately my right arm had had a hard knock - fractured in two places - which necessitates my using the left..."

Norah risked crossing the Irish sea to visit him. From the deck she saw a line of foam approaching, narrowly missing the ship, and continue away into the distance. A deckhand confirmed her suspicions that it was a torpedo, but added "Don't tell the other passengers, they might not be as brave as you."

There is a curious lack of reference to the visit in John's letters. Had he been warned to be discreet? Only in one sentence is there a clue.

"Your 'holidays' will now be over" he writes on 20th August 1917. *So perhaps you will find time to write.."* He stresses 'holidays' because she has spent them not at Colwyn Bay or even Holyhead, but at Kingstown with him. *"Some place, Kingstown"*, he adds, Mischievously. Yes, indeed. Norah was twenty-one years old, a school teacher, living at home.

One 4th September John wrote:

...The wound is still open and arm in gigantic splint so although I can trot about I am not so very comfortable.

I have had a letter from poor old Gillies and notice that he has gone over to France to fill my place. I wonder how long before I shall relieve him.

And on 6th September:

...Can you tell me if they have weeded out any more men from the APC or are they keeping only (C2?) men? If I get marked in a lower category than A1 (which is now likely) I shall probably be sent back to APC if I can't get my final ticket. It would be strange if they sent me back to York as unfit! Would you mind? By the way, our Regiment have been terribly cut up since I left them at Messines. The Sgt. Major told me I would be recommended for something I don't know what nor do I care. He was killed the following day. I don't want their medals. I want my arm better. It is so slow. Over three months ago and still much the same...

John was discharged in consequence of being no longer fit for war after serving four years 82 days with the colours.

Mr. J. H. Langley-Jones was confined to a hospital whilst still a young man.

When I was first wounded in 1918 I was taken to the Canadian General Hospital in France. The consultant said, "I am afraid I must advise you to have your leg amputated. It will be two inches shorter than the other when it is healed." My reply was. "No jolly fear! I came to France with two legs and I'm going back with two."

After I developed gangrene in my leg the treatment was quite grim. There were no antibiotics and sterilising facilities were very primitive. I had about thirty clips on one side of my leg and thirty on the other. Every morning these had to be removed and then replaced, so that the wound could be cleaned and a new dressing applied. The Matron gave me a pillow and told me to bite it when the pain was too severe. Therapy was elementary! There was a bicycle fastened to the floor on which to practise, with a gadget graded 1 to 4. They also had a rowing boat with loaded oars, and you rowed it to strengthen your arms and spine. They also used electrical impulses to help restore mobility.

Much of the ligaments and muscle in my leg had been destroyed, but through determined exercise I regained much of the strength in it. In later years, however, I had some problems.

Dr. Marie Stopes (1880-1958) will be remembered for bringing birth control into the open and making it available to poor people. For many men sex at the beginning of the twentieth century was one of their few pleasures, and they were quite unable to support properly their many offspring, leading to premature death and other deprivations.

Marie Stopes was a brilliant student, both at school and university, and took her final Bsc examination with honours in both botany and geology, after only two years at London University College. She had had a very close relationship with her father, and after he died of cancer in December 1902 she decided to go to Munich, where she continued her studies at the Botanical Institute. She became the first woman to achieve a doctorate in Botany and was the first woman to be appointed junior lecturer and demonstrator in botany at Manchester University.

She was outstanding in her academic achievements, but her private life was less successful. Her first marriage ended in divorce on the grounds of her husband's inability to consummate the marriage. Marie Stopes considered that her marriage had been doomed because of her ignorance of sexual matters and she determined to try to prevent others from falling into the same trap, so in March 1918 she published her first book *Married Love,* although at that time she herself was still without sexual experience. Notwithstanding, many people considered her an expert on sexual matters and consulted her accordingly.

Her lack of first hand knowledge was remedied in May that year, when she married again. It was after that that her second book *Wise Parenthood* was published, giving a clear guide to contraceptive methods.

We three Solkhon sisters contracted the usual childish ailments of measles, mumps, whooping cough and chicken pox, but suffered no serious ill effects. There was no vaccination except for smallpox, and measles in particular could be quite severe. Scarlet fever was another serious illness, and I remember Mother telling us that she had to stay in a fever hospital for six weeks when she developed it as a teenager. They were allowed no visits from their parents in those days, and I used to dread the possibility of catching scarlet fever and being sent away to hospital. She lost all her hair and when it grew again it was black, instead of fair!

It was when we went to live in Bath during the First World War that we had other problems. Both head lice and ringworm were prevalent in the local school, and Jessie and Kathleen contracted the latter. The treatment made their hair fall out, causing much embarrassment, so they wore caps until it grew again. After that they had their hair bobbed and I was very envious. Mine was quite long and fair in those days and if we were going to a party or something special Mother would 'curl' it before I went to bed. First she washed it, then whilst it was still damp she took long, narrow strips of cloth and wound one end with strands of hair

round the other piece, finishing with a knot. They were most uncomfortable to sleep on and I would much have preferred to have a bob, but it did look quite pretty when it was brushed out the following morning. The school was closed for several months because there were epidemics of diphtheria and scarlet fever. We did not mind that!

It was when we returned to London that the real problems began. We were thirsty after the long journey and Kathleen ran into the kitchen before Mother could stop her and drank some of the water. The house had been empty for some time and Mother would not let the rest of us have a drink until she had turned the tap full on for some time. The damage was done however, and Kathleen developed typhoid fever. In those days before antibiotics, starving the patient was the only cure. She was very ill and Mother was having to cope on her own with Jessie, nine, me barely seven and Jack just a toddler, as well as nursing Kathleen (five). She had always been 'Daddy's girl' and pined for him, so as the war was over by then the Army granted him compassionate leave from Italy, where he was stationed. Kathleen made a good recovery once he returned, and still remembers him saying "If you don't eat something, there will be nothing but your eyebrows lying on the pillow!"

Poliomyelitis was another dreaded disease and the two sons of a neighbour both contracted it and were partially paralysed as a result. Fortunately we all escaped TB, another prevalent illness in those days (not helped by the disgusting habit of spitting. Spittoons were ever provided in Pubs for this purpose!), but the influenza epidemic which swept Europe and other countries in 1918 and 1919 caused more deaths than the actual war. Many of our relatives developed it and two died as a result.

Sex was a word we never heard, but I do remember being surprised when Jack was being bathed to see that he had something sticking up between his legs! It was many years before I realised the sexes were different!

8. SHOPS, FOOD AND CLOTHES

Luxurious shops had sprung up, especially in Bond Street and Piccadilly, London, where the wealthy Edwardians spent thousands of pounds on dresses, coats, shirts and shoes. More good shops were also appearing in the suburbs. In 1909 Gordon Selfridge, who had experienced the efficiency of large American shops, built his ornate store in Oxford Street. He employed 1,800 staff and displayed £100,000 worth of goods in light, airy surroundings. Chain stores grew, including those belonging to Thomas Lipton and Sainsbury's. Nothing was prepacked, so customers could see the produce before purchasing it and choose the particular bacon, butter, cheese and other foods they preferred.

Most shop assistants were treated almost like slaves. In the bigger shops they had to live in and were boarded in cramped, dirty dormitories. Miserable meals were provided in basement dining rooms, and hours were long, holidays few. H. G. Wells has well described these conditions in *Kipps (1905)* and *The History of Mr. Polly (1910)*. Like many other bad practices, the war brought a change, as there was alternative work for employees to choose, and wages and conditions improved considerably.

Pocket money obviously varied according to parents' incomes, but most middle class children counted themselves lucky if they had a penny a week as young children, rising perhaps to sixpence for teenagers.

There was a great difference between the diet of the wealthy and that of the poor people during Edwardian days. The former ate very well: Kind Edward VII had a massive breakfast, an eight course lunch and a ten course supper in the evening, a form of diet common to the aristocracy. Not surprisingly, many were grossly overweight, which added to health problems.

Middle class families had plainer food, but plenty of it, with such things as porridge, fried egg and bacon, toast and marmalade, coffee or tea with milk or cream for breakfast. For mid-day dinner there would probably be a roast joint with a variety of vegetables, followed by a substantial pudding. Before the evening meal, consisting of more meat, a sweet with biscuits and cheese, and a drink, there was tea, with bread and butter and marmalade.

Servants had a much plainer diet, but they were also able to finish off the food left over from the meals upstairs, so in this way were better off than other poor families existing on a pittance.

Cooking was done in heavy iron pots, heated on top of or inside coal or coke ovens. There were no machines to grind, grate or blend the flood, so it was all done by hand. Very labour intensive, especially as there were few tinned foods, and of course no frozen ones, but they produced some delicious meals, much more tasty than those of the Nineties!

As soon as war was declared, there was a rush to the shops as people stocked up against possible shortages. Britain depended much on her imports, and soon there were long queues at many shops. The wealthy were able to afford expensive meals at hotels like the Ritz, and to buy all that they wanted: it was a very different matter for the impoverished. The poor potato harvest in 1916 added to their problems. Wheat, too, was desperately short and substitute breads made of potato or bean flour appeared. Fuel was in equally short supply and people again queued with prams, wheelbarrows, sacks and boxes outside railway coal-sidings. This was rationed in October 1917, based on the number of rooms in the house. Land was dug up for allotments and to grow food in parks and school-fields, and even the waste land beside railways. By 1918 an extra three million acres of farmland had been added

Long food queues as the submarine campaign deprived Britain of food.
(Tramlines in foreground).

Ivy Ross's mother (Jane Anderson) with two friends (twins).

to the eleven million acres farmed in 1914. Girls who had joined the Land Army were ploughing and handling threshing machines as competently as the men. Fortunately the 1917 harvest was a record one because food stocks were dwindling fast. It was not until rationing was introduced that year that there was a fair distribution of the available food. At first there was a meat card, and a food card for butter, cheese and margarine, but in July the first ration cards were withdrawn and replaced by books of coupons for all rationed foods. Prices remained high, but immediately the queues vanished.

It was not until some time after the war ended that stocks returned to normal: Europe, too, had been impoverished by the war, and costs had spiralled.

There was no synthetic material available for clothing, so in the winter ladies wore woollen garments, with silk or cotton in the summer. Skirts touched the ground, and when shortage of materials led to a shortening of them, some were shocked if an ankle was exposed. Women would not consider venturing out into the street without a hat, and men also wore either caps, bowlers or top hats. The wealthy wore very elegant gowns of velvet and embroidered silk, changing their wardrobes frequently and thinking nothing of spending hundreds of pounds on one gown.

During the war those who worked in factories had to wear heavy, bulky overalls and caps on their heads, which were both hot and uncomfortable. Only those who worked on the land dared to wear trousers!

Hair was usually worn long by children, often plaited or curled; when they grew up they wore it in a bun. Later the bob became fashionable, and it was found particularly appropriate for those working on machinery in factories.

Shopping expeditions were enjoyed by Betty Bindloss.

We always looked forward to shopping - chemists' shops had enormous glass jars full of coloured liquid, red, green and yellow in the window. Our chemist had a wonderful cough mixture called Maribine, which cleared up colds and sore throats rapidly. Grocers' shops had sackfuls of goods like currants, raisins, sultanas, and sugar. The amounts one needed were measured out into blue paper bags. Biscuits were not sold in plastic packets but loose - plastic was unknown then. Very little was pre-packed, one could buy two or three screws or nails, buttons, wooden clothes pegs and so on.

We had very little pocket money, only a penny to start with, though by the time I was eight I had sixpence, and perhaps a shilling a week at ten years old. We bought our presents for people at Woolworth's, where nearly everything cost six pence. We purchased our own comics. I was given an extra twopence a week, one penny for my subscription to the Brownie Pack or Guide Company, and the other penny for a packet of fish and chips to eat on the way home. Our church collection was also given to us.

Very little food could be bought that had already been manufactured, except sausages and pasties and pies. Far more cooking took place at home, on the range, even bread was largely home-made, and smelled and tasted wonderful. We shopped in the Market once a week - every farmer's wife made butter with the farmer's 'signature' pattern on the top of the pat. A sweet stall had home-made fudge, peppermint bullseyes and round flat glycerine suckers.

The stall holders were our friends, as were the drovers of the sheep and cattle. We knew them by name and they knew us. A market town was a friendly community, with family shops in a fairly traffic free shopping street, full mostly of pony traps and errand boys on bicycles.

The Caledonian Road Market was a very popular shopping area for Margery Clow and her family.

Around 1919 I used to go to the Caledonian Road Market with my mother by tram. It was a great treat for us, because we always had an 'okey-pokey', which was like an iced custard, the forerunner of ice cream. We had a big block for a penny and wandered round after my mother, licking at it. They lasted a long while. Then Mother bought secondhand clothes, all from wealthy people, beautiful serge suits, lined with pure silk. She bought them for about one and sixpence. This was after the First World War, when the long skirts and the styles had completely changed. The dresses were fitted to the waist and then flared out down to the ankle: they had gone out of fashion. She bought them cheaply, removed the linings and made our dresses. Then she would make whatever we needed from the serge suits. They had long skirts, beautifully made. Once she made me a tammy hat to go with a dress. I had no idea of fashion!

Mother was very clever with her needle and once she made me a blue cotton dress. She worked french knots all round it and made up her own pattern. I wore this dress to school for ages. Every now and again it would be let down. Mother was always dying clothes - she could not pass the shop that sold dyes without buying something. The blue dress had faded so she dyed it red. I went to school the next day, never having new clothes, and felt I was a queen. I was wearing this new dress and as I went to my seat one of the others said, "Go on, it's only your old blue dress dyed", and I was deflated.

After the war women wore stockings, either brown or black, with their shorter skirts. They were artificial silk up to the calf, and then cotton up to the thigh. Through the years the artificial silk went higher and higher.

Kathleen Hogg lived in London and had branches of the bigger chain stores near her home.

There were four corner shops within reach, handy if we ran out of anything, but most of our shopping was done on the main road not far away. There were three of the chain grocers - Liptons, Pearks, and the Home and Colonial Stores. Each had its mountain of eggs at one end of the counter, sold to us in paper bags. There was a large marble slab, with a giant cube of butter, and the assistant skilfully slapped this into quarters, halves and pounds with a pair of wooden pats. He did the same with the cheese, cutting it through with a wire slicer, with a little wooden handle at right angles to the end of the wire. Biscuits stood around in large square tins, their lids removed so that we could see the contents. We bought them loose, in quarters, halves or pounds.

In a Cornchandler's shop on the way home from school, arranged on the floor were sacks of lentils, macaroni, butterbeans and other commodities, all with their tops rolled back to display their contents. Sometimes I bought a large bag of broken wafer biscuits here for a penny, and my mother might ask me to get her an ounce of pepper, which the assistant wrapped in a twist of blue paper. There was a fresh fish shop, where my mother would send me when my father was home, for 'a nice haddock about seven pence' for his supper. Nowadays people might lift their hands in horror at the lack of hygiene, but I don't think any of us were the worse for it.

Kathleen M. Robinson = HOGG
aged 1 year 6 months.

Our milk was delivered to us in lidded cans, which jangled as the milkman pushed his cart along, with a large churn from which he filled the cans. Later in the day he collected the empty cans for sterilising; and if we wanted more milk we took a jug to be filled at the dairy just round the corner.

There were several regular street callers: a man pushing a cart loaded with a barrel and calling out, 'Your vinegar, mam, mother'; the crumpet man came mostly at the week-end, ringing a bell and carrying his goods on his head; men collecting jam jars in exchange for toffee apples (forbidden us by my mother) and windmills; and, of course, the cat's meat man, selling little steaks of not very fresh horse flesh, pierced through with skewers.

One thing that strikes me forcibly when comparing the last decade of the twentieth century with the first two decades is the quality of the most ordinary things. Our toys were beautifully made, often by hand. We had kid-bodied dolls with charming heads, often in china, which somehow survived; dolls' cots with drop sides and our hoops all made of wood. Some years ago my husband and I were selling our house, built at the turn of the century. The surveyor, used to dealing with modern properties, called his assistant to the loft. "Come and see this roof", he cried excitedly, "It's built like a cathedral".

Mrs. Grace H. Knight (née Ashford) is now living in Storrington, Pulborough, but she enjoyed the sights and sounds of the different kind of shopping she found in the London streets of her childhood.

Living in the East End of London as a child in the early part of the twentieth century, one of the customs I remember quite clearly was street vending and the cries that heralded the approach of sellers of many differing commodities.

It is extraordinary that in those days food was trundled around streets, sometimes on wooden barrows, sometimes on trays slung round the necks of the vendors, often in horse-drawn carts and sold from a flat at the back, uncovered and exposed to the air. One old chap brought fresh fish round in a home-made box of wood mounted on old pram wheels. He weighed the fish on a spring-scale. His cry of 'Hake...Hake' brought housewives to their doors, for they were sure the fish would be fresh and full of flavour.

On Sunday afternoons between lunch and tea, regularly summer and winter, the shrimps and winkles barrowman appeared with shouts of 'Shrimps, Winkles - all fresh', and people went out to the barrow with their basins and dishes to buy their tasty Sunday tea-time treat. I often had the job of getting the winkles out of their shells with a long pin (usually one of Mum's hatpins), putting them in a dish and covering them in pepper and vinegar for my father's tea (with some for us too). Shrimps were fiddly, but very tasty. Sometimes there were prawns, which were easier to peel. Each serving cost but a few pence.

The cats' meat man came round regularly; he carried his skewers of horsemeat on a tray slung before him, and his stuttering cry of 'M-M-Meat, M-M-Meat' brought cats from far and wide following him with plaintive meows.

Streets singers were common and their tuneless dirges performed in the middle of the road were not at all entertaining. Rude children would make fun of them; but kind-hearted householders often came out and gave them a coin or two.

The lavender-sellers, carrying baskets of the sweet-smelling herb, were more tuneful and the song they sang was lovely:

> 'Won't you buy my sweet-scented lavender?
> Sixteen branches for one penny.
> You'll buy it once, you'll buy it twice;
> 'Twill make your clothes smell sweet and nice.

The ringing of a hand-bell and the shout of 'Muffins...Muffins' easily identified the frequent sight of the muffin man, with his white apron and tray of muffins carried on his head. His wares were always in demand.

The knife and scissors' grinder made periodic appearances, calling 'Knives to sharpen-- Scissors to grind'. His contraption, with its stone wheel turned by a foot pedal, was always the centre of attention for little boys, and business was usually brisk.

With cries of 'Rags and bones' or 'Rags, bottles or bones', the ragman would slowly drive his horse and cart along the road. He often rang a hand-bell, too, and would pause from time to time to ring it and give people a chance to gather any articles they wanted to get rid of. These he would scrutinise and then make an offer of what he considered to be a fair price. This was usually accepted.

Flower girls brought baskets of brightly coloured blooms around the streets during the growing season. They had no song, as the lavender-sellers had, but called our 'Flahers, luvly flahers', all the while tying the blooms into bunches for sale.

The lamp-lighter, with his pole carried over his shoulder, conjures up memories of cold, dark streets being gradually transformed into lighted walkways with glowing pools of soft radiance, so comforting to anyone who happened to be abroad after dusk.

I also have affectionate memories of the Sunday Scout Church Parade with its bugles and drums, marching round the streets. This was usually followed by several urchins marching in step. The hit or miss performance of the buglers rudely assaulted musically attuned ears.

Organ-grinders were a common sight and the sound of their jangling, often badly out-of-tune renditions (you could not call it music!) either entertained or irritated you. My mother told me that in her childhood they used to dance round the street-organ, but this practice evidently died out.

These street vendors added colour to what was usually a quiet, uneventful life in the back streets of East London.

A highlight in the week for Mary Blott used to be shopping by tram with her mother on a Saturday.

It cost a penny on the tram for adults to go to Kingston from Hampton Court and a halfpenny for me. Frank Bentall was the draper in Kingston, a large shop to me in those days. They used to put money for purchases in a round tin, then it went on a wire to the office for the change. It was very noisy and I was frightened by it. Very often when the tin came whizzing back there was a packet of pins instead of a farthing change.

Mother also went to Sainsbury's for butter etc. They used butter pats to take a piece of butter from a large lump, weigh it up and then stamp it with an imprint of a thistle or a rose! I remember Mother telling Father at teatime one day that Sainsbury's now had an imitation butter, which was cheaper - margarine.

Shopping was very different before 1920, as Eileen Amsdon describes.

Shopping was done nearly every day. Mothers did not go out to work then, unless the family were very poor. We carried our own baskets and did not collect piles of plastic shopping bags - they had not been invented. Most eatables, like bacon, butter etc., were sold by the pound. The amount you wanted was cut off and wrapped. Quite often you had a friendly relationship with the shop assistant. Biscuits came from large tins. The broken ones could be bought very cheaply for puddings.

Although the summers were quire often very warm, we managed well without fridges or freezers. The milkman came in a pony and trap, with the milk in a large churn. The housewife went out to him and he gave her milk from his own measure, which hung by the side of the churn. On Sundays the muffin-man walked round the roads, holding with one hand a tray of muffins, covered with a white cloth, on his head. With the other hand he swung a bell, so that you heard him coming.

Ice-cream was a treat bought by cornet or wafer from the sweet-shop, when we were given our weekly pocket-money. However, whenever I stayed with Auntie Lou I liked to go with my cousins on Sunday mornings to the baker's and bring back hot rolls for breakfast. What a wonderful aroma they gave out!

Dor Curgenven remembers all the shops and services in Zelah when she was young.

At the corner of Bowling Green Lane, Miss Hoskin kept a small shop selling a few groceries and sweets. There were also two other shops in the village, a grocer's and a general store, run by Miss I. Lanyon and Mrs. M. A. Lanyon. Mr. C. Rawlings ran the Post Office from his cottage kitchen in The Square. There was a pork butcher's business housed in a shed in The Square by sisters Mrs. Broad and Mrs. Tyack every Tuesday morning. They toured the surrounding villages with the remainder of their stock.

Two thriving blacksmiths carried on their trade almost opposite one another in The Square and at the corner of Back Lane. The Reading Room situated behind the Mission Hall was used by ladies of the village from 12.00 to 4.00 pm every Tuesday for sewing bees and generally for social events. The doctor's surgery was held in Mrs. Powell's home opposite the Hawkens Arms. The doctors came on horseback from Perranporth twice a week and Mr. Willy Joy, who was totally blind, brought the prescriptions which had been dispensed in the surgery, walking all the way from Rose every Thursday. A nurse who lived at Tolcarne with Mrs. Read cared for all the St. Allen parish and St. Erme, covering this considerable area on her bicycle. We raised the money for her salary by various social events, but the main occasion was Easter Monday when a carnival was held at the school, with a band parade through the village. This was in the afternoon, followed by a sit down tea. Stalls of home-made produce and secondhand goods were very popular. Then in the evening there was the carnival dance. This was an opportunity for the young people to socialise, and if you met someone you particularly liked you might go off together on your bicycles later.

Mr. W. Mitchell from Henver made coal deliveries once a week by horse and wagon. Three threshing sets were owned by the Lanyon brothers and Mr. Bassett. Mr. H. N. Jewell combined his talent as a butcher with acting as MC for the many varied social events in the village.

Blewetts' Baker called twice a week and The Red House also called on two other days, so there was always fresh bread and cakes in addition to all the home baking that was done!

We had two carpenters' shops, one at each end of the village, run by Mr. Hoskin and Mr. Paynter. A man called Waters repaired footwear. The general store carried wool, materials and footwear, and the women knitted and sewed practically all our clothes, so the village was almost self-sufficient. The people themselves produced the bulk of their food.

Shopping was very different from today in Dor Thorneloe's time.

There were no cars, but plenty of horses and carts. Anything could be delivered. The milkman's float came round two or three times a day, and the milk was measured into jugs on the doorstep. The greengrocer's cart had a sloping tailboard at the back and was like a shop inside. Women went to the back of the cart and chose their goods. The lamplighter came round at dusk and again in the morning; he used his long pole to put the high gas lamps on and off at several points in the road. Many people came to the door trying to sell things, also women wanting to buy rags, and gypsies selling pegs (or plants taken from other people's gardens!) or to tell fortunes.

Mother seemed to go to the grocer's each day, and to the butcher's very often. The meat, bacon and butter were kept in the meat safe, which was in a cool outhouse joined to the back of the house. I used to think my mother was a terrible talker, because when we went to the shops she stood talking to another woman. Then perhaps she would meet more friends: it seemed ages to me. It probably was not such a long time, and now I realise that without wireless, TV or telephone, women's lives were pretty insufferable unless they could chat with other people. Another break Mother had was the *Woman's Weekly*, at twopence a week.

I remember the contents of our food cupboard and how restricted was the range in those days. The weekly grocer's order barely changed - flour, sugar, butter, margarine, syrup, cereal and porridge. Pineapple was the only tinned fruit and when Mother opened a tin on Sundays it was a special treat. She managed to make a family cake each week, no doubt using a wartime recipe. When that was gone occasionally my brother, six year's my senior, was allowed to take me to the village shop to choose six penny worth of pastries. We put our hands into the shop window and pointed out to the serving lady which ones we wanted. They were seven for sixpence, and lovely.

Cyril Davies recalls the prices of food and other items before the First World War.

A quartern white loaf was 4d.
Eggs a shilling a dozen;
Coal a shilling a hundredweight.
Boots and shoes could be soled and heeled for about
eighteen pence.

At the beginning of the twentieth century, chickens had not been programmed to produce eggs all the year round, so at certain times of the year they were scarce, as Mary Horseman's Mother knew.

Every summer, when egg prices fell low enough, my mother bought a lot and preserved them in a bucket of waterglass. This sealed the shells and they kept until eggs were scarce (and expensive) in the winter. They were used for all cooking purposes, but fresh ones for boiling, as they did not taste as good. They worked well in cakes and puddings.

We never bought jam or marmalade. Cook used to make it. Again, fruit was bought when it was cheap or was grown in the garden. I got on very well with our cook in particular, and she used to let me 'make pastry' with her, which was a great treat as normally we did no often go into the kitchen.

We were regularly dosed with castor oil, and later Gregory powder, at weekends, as it was considered very important to have a good turn-out once a week! I have hated liquorice ever since, but at least it was an improvement on castor oil, although I found both revolting.

Joyce Booth had a first-hand experience of fashion between 1912 and 1920.

Aunt Kate was invited to spend a fortnight's holiday in Glasgow - she stayed three years! Something about a divorce and Scottish Law being the reason. Her forbears had been theatrical costumières, which might have accounted for her love of personal adornment!

She wore a costume with a sable fur and muff, dainty shoes with louis heels, and a large hat with an osprey plume. In the summer she wore a costume of tussore silk, trimmed with Maltese lace. Her second husband-to-be was at sea and plied her with silks, lace, exotic fruits and tea. Her long skirts were edged with brush braid underneath, which afforded some protection against the Glasgow mud. Cleaning it was a messy ritual! Under her stays was a finely tucked chemise, over them a crêpe-de-chine camisole, pink directoire knickers and a taffeta petticoat with a pleated frill. Her looks were important and she had jars of Ponds cream and Icilma, and a bowl of face-powder. She carried a little book of 'Papier Poudre' leaflets in her large handbag, and she touched up her hair with henna.

News came that an uncle had been killed, so garments were hurriedly sent to be dyed black. There was a lot of black about: fashion houses had special departments and there were shops which sold nothing else but mourning and half-mourning. Whitby jet jewellery, last worn when Queen Victoria died, was repaired and jet bracelets were added to the gold curb bracelets. When my father died in 1919, my mother wore a veil and widow's weeds for six months before going into purple. I wore a black sash at the waist of my Swiss cotton summer dress. Aunt Kate never lifted a duster but covered all the chairs with her 'pen-painting' on black satin cushions, and attended soirées in aid of wounded soldiers, with other fashionable ladies.

Babies wore enormous bonnets, but I loved a toffee coloured satin coat and a bonnet with oyster organdie ruching. A beautiful satin and lace dress never came out of its box. A friend, a professional singer, used to send gifts for which she rarely paid, so discreet enquiries would be made by my father and the garment returned to the shop! Toddlers wore chemises and cotton drawers (the button flat variety) edged with lace. The buttons would get squashed in the wringer, and the neck tapes of the cotton and flannel petticoats became knotted strings.

Joyce Booth

Aunt Kate's divorce came through, she married her sailor and went to London, caught 'flu in the great epidemic, and died. Mother and I went to visit the friend with whom she had been staying. When she went out of the room I whispered, "Why is that lady wearing her nightdress?" "Hush", said my mother, "it's a teagown." I hated London, all the yellow-brick houses with outside WC's and noisy flag-waving crowds pushing me to the front to see the King and Queen, separating me from my mummy. I was terrified!

When we were young it was the sweet shops that we found most attractive! Jars of unwrapped sticky sweets, bars of chocolate (also unwrapped!), brilliantly coloured 'duck and sweet peas', 'baby's comforter' and other such delights, liquorice sticks and liquorice braids. Pocket money in those early days was a penny, but you could buy four liquorice braids or a bag of other sweets for that. Not far from the sweet shop was the baker's, and the delicious smell of home baked bread filled the air early in the morning. Mother made much of our bread, and if Father was around she got him to do the kneading: he made a very good job of it!

Another shop nearby was the chemist, and we would stare fascinated at the large glass containers filled with coloured liquids, sometimes seeing our reflection in them. Inside there was a strong smell of disinfectant: the chemist was always prepared to effect first aid, if required. Doctors dispensed their medicines in those days, but many poorer people could not afford their fees so relied on the chemist.

Once war began there was soon a shortage of many things, especially sweets, as sugar was one of the main imports. Being confronted with the rigours of war for the first time, the government had no conception of the need for rationing until it was forced upon them in 1917. So we were fortunate to be living away from London, first in Winchester and then in Bath, and escape the long queues outside shops in the city. It was easy to get eggs and chicken, and plenty of home-grown vegetables. There was more meat around, too.

It was not until we returned to London in December 1918 that I saw any large shops. We sometimes went to Clapham Junction, where there were branches of some of the multiple stores like David Greig, Woolworth and Sainsbury's, and also Francis' delicatessen. The delightful aroma of coffee being roasted engulfed us long before we reached the shop, where Mother often bought cream and cheese as well as coffee. Across the road was the largest store, Arding and Hobbs, but I was not interested in the arrays of fashion, underwear, furniture, kitchen appliances etc. However, at Christmas time it was quite different, because they had Father Christmas' grotto. Having purchased a ticket we wandered through what seemed like endless tunnels filled with sparkling lights, with gnomes and fairies in decorated groves. Then at the end we met Father Christmas himself, and he gave each of us a present. It was always exciting to unwrap the parcel and discover the contents. Once I had a toy set of pots and pans, and another

a small tea service. I little realised that my parents had had to pay for them!

Clothes did not seem very important to me in those early days, but I do remember Mother wearing long, sweeping black skirts, with a high-necked white blouse or a beautifully embroidered collar. Ankles were invisible, but I expect she was wearing black woollen stockings. She certainly wore boned stays, that were pulled in tight with strings to produce the fashionable narrow waist. Occasionally one of the steel rods

Jessie Solkhon (née Wilson)

| Jack | Kit | Arthur | Jessie | Mr. Wilson | Sallie |
| Wilson | Wilson | Solkhon | | | |

in the garment came out! They must have been extremely uncomfortable and restricting. She loved hats and always wore one, and gloves, when she went out. She looked most elegant. I never liked hats, but when we were at Winchester in 1916 Mother bought new hats for us. They were rather like poke bonnets, decorated with blue and pink flowers, and quite attractive. I remember the first Sunday we wore them. Kathleen and I had gone for a walk across the Arbor, and were confronted by a gang of about six ragamuffins (as we called them then). They danced around us calling out 'Jampot hats; jampot hats' and would not allow us to return home. They were much older than us and we were afraid, but I told Kathleen to take no notice. They shepherded us for some distance until we were in an unknown part of Winchester, a very poor area. When the ringleader reached her house they suddenly dispersed, and we were allowed to return home.

9. BOOKS, MUSIC, ARCHITECTURE

The early days of the war inspired many young poets to write of their experiences in France. Among them was Rupert Brooke who wrote a sonnet in 1915 which became very popular, especially as he himself was killed not long after on his way to Gallipoli:

> *'If I should die, think only this of me:*
> *That there's some corner of a foreign field*
> *That is for ever England. There shall be*
> *In that rich earth a richer dust concealed;*
> *A dust whom England bore, shaped, made aware,*
> *Gave, once, her flowers to love, her ways to roam,*
> *A body of England's, breathing English air,*
> *Washed by the rivers, blest by suns of home ....*

Another popular poem was 'Into Battle' by his friend, Julian Grenfell. Ian Hay's *The First Hundred Thousand,* describing life in Kitchener's Army, became a best seller. Baronness Orczy's *Scarlet Pimpernel* and other books provided a respite from war themes. E. M. Forster describes in *Where Angels Fear To Treat* (1905) the pleasant life of the Herriton family in suburbia. In 1910 he wrote Howards End, another book of the times. There were best-sellers like Florence Barclay's *The Rosary*, A. E. W. Mason's *The Four Feathers* (1902), and Edgar Wallace's *The Four Just Men* (1904). H. G. Wells was another popular contemporary writer, with *The War In The Air* (1908), *Kipps* and *Tono Bungay* both in 1909, and *The History Of Mr. Polly* (1910). John Galsworthy's *The Forsyte Saga* is well-known to many nowadays as are some H. Williamson's books. Also appearing were new cheap reprints of the classics by World's Classics, Collins' Classics and Everyman's Library. The *Strand Magazine* contained among others popular stories about the adventures of Sherlock Holmes. Public libraries also grew considerably, with stocks doubling between 1901 and 1914.

The early years of the twentieth century saw great changes in the perception of painting. Pierre Auguste Renoir (1821-1919) was influenced by Claude Monet, the French Impressionist painter. He painted out-of-doors, which was a new development, and experimented with different shades of light.

In 1905 the group known as 'Les Fauves' in France used colour to express their feelings rather than to portray what they saw. Matisse, Derain and Vlaminck were among the leaders. Then came Pablo Picasso (1881-1976), a Spanish artist who founded the Cubist movement. He said, "I paint objects as I think them, not as I see them". In 1909 Marinetto, Boccioni and Severini developed Futurism in Italy.

The Armory Show, an exhibition of art in New York in 1913, attracted much criticism, although a few approved. The painting of *A Nude Descending A Staircase* by Duchamps was castigated as 'revolting art' by the press. He belonged to the Dada group and produced his first 'ready-made' art - a bicycle wheel, as a new form of visual art. That same year he began a large abstract work *The Large Glass* of *The Bird Stripped Bare By Her Bachelors, Even.* A further development in 1914 led to the formation of the Voticist movement, led by Wyndham Lewis. He was interested in the Italian Futurist painters. In his magazine *Blast* he wrote: 'We stand for the reality of the present - not for the sentimental future, or the sacrosanct past'.

Music, too, was undergoing change. Schunberg and Stravinsky abandoned conventional sounds and rhythms. When Diaghilev's Ballets Russe arrived in Paris from Russia in 1900 it was to inspire Stravinsky and others to compose music especially for the ballet. Nijinsky was appointed choreographer and worked with Debussy on the Prelude '*L'apres Midiè D'un Faune'* and Stravinsky on *The Rites Of Spring.*

Nijinsky choreographed Stravinsky's music and it was performed in a Paris theatre. The first scene was of a Russian forest, where pagan rites were imitated by mass movements of dancers. This was very different from the classical ballet the audience had come to expect and the music with its unusual harmonies offended their unaccustomed ears. There was an uproar, and so much noise that the orchestra became inaudible and Nijinsky had to shout counting so that the dancers could continue. It was to become popular in later years.

In 1916 Gustav Holst, born in Cheltenham in 1874, completed *The Planets.* He taught for nearly thirty years at St. Paul's school for girls and composed the St. Paul's Suite for their string orchestra. He and Vaughan Williams were great friends. The latter was much influenced by English folk music but also by the Bible, Shakespeare, Bunyan and some English poets. *Fantasia On A Theme Of Tallis* is probably his most popular work, and in 1914 he composed the *London Symphony*. Edward Elgar, who was born in the Worcester area in 1857 and died there in 1934, is another popular English composer of that period; he composed the *Enigma Variations* in 1899 and this was followed by *The Dream Of Gerontius*. Then came the *Coronation Ode*, which included the tune to become the celebrated *Land Of Hope And Glory*. Symphonies, a Violin Concerto and other works were produced before the First World War, but very little afterwards.

Frederick Delius was born in England in 1862 but emigrated to America when he was twenty-one to avoid going into his father's wool business. Two years later he went to France, where he lived until, blind and paralysed, he died in 1934. However, the pastoral influence of the English countryside pervades much of his work. It was Sir Thomas Beecham who made him so well known in England. There were many eminent composers overseas during this period, too.

Such songs as *Annie Laurie, As I Was Going To Strawberry Fair,* and *Oh! No John, No John, No John, No!* were popular at that time, but the wartime songs soon became firm favourites.

> *Pack up your troubles in your old kitbag*
> *And smile, smile, smile.*
> *While you are troubling to light your fag,*
> *Smile boys that's the style.*
> *What's the use of worrying.*
> *It never was worth while, so*
> *Pack up your troubles in your old kitbag*
> *And smile, smile, smile.*

Another was *It's A Long Way To Tipperary,* and *Goodbyee, Don't Sighee.* When the ill-fated Dardanelles expedition was on its way came the popular Charlie Chaplin song:

> *Oh! the sun shines bright on Charlie Chaplin,*
> *His boots are cracking,*
> *They want a blacking;*
> *And his little baggy trousers*
> *They want patching*
> *Before we send him*
> *To the Dardanelles.*

For architecture there was a major event in Saxony in 1919, when the Bauhaus school was opened. Using new building methods, with reinforced concrete and steel, skyscrapers were to be built, airy buildings with large windows. It became the most famous art and design school of the twentieth century.

Among my earliest memories are those of being cosily tucked up in bed whilst Father told us a story or Mother read to us. Books were part of the furniture of the house! So it was natural that we learned to read whilst quite young, but even so it was still a thrill to listen to a book being read. It was Rudyard Kipling's Jungle Books that made the greatest impression in those early days, and Mother's rendering of Rikki-Tikki-Tavvi was so dramatic that for many years I was scared of snakes. One day we were walking by the river at Winchester and there was a one-plank wooden bridge across a small stream that was flowing into it. Through a hole in the wood I saw a snake (eel?) crawling, and I was terrified, although I was yards away.

One of my father's brothers, Harry and his wife Hannah visited us every Christmas after the war and brought us Annuals as presents. These were all devoured avidly. But it was when I was seven that my godparents gave me the first real book: Knock Three Times by Eleanor Farjeon. This was a fascinating, and at times frightening, story of a boy and girl whose amazing adventures began with a disappointing birthday present - a pincushion. This was left on the dressing table and when a shaft of moonlight shone upon it it suddenly began to roll off the table, along the floor and out of the door. The two children followed it and saw it knock three times on a tree, which opened to let it in, so they did likewise. An evil gnome had been locked up in the pincushion which had been activated by the moonlight. It was many years ago that I read the book and details are vague, but it included looking for a black leaf and various frightening experiences. In later years I gave a copy of the book to one of my godsons and he said he was too scared to finish reading it! Many other books followed - Rudyard Kipling's Just So Stories and Kim, G. A. Henty's books and many others. Then came the schoolgirl craze and Angela Brazil, but it was not long before we were deep into the classics.

My father had a deep appreciation of poetry and introduced us to Shakespeare and other poets at an early age. Poetry also was a popular part of English lessons. I particularly enjoyed the rhythm and alliteration and vivid pictures of John Masefield's *Cargoes.*

> *Quinquireme of Nineveh from distant Ophir*
> *Rowing home to haven in sunny Palestine,*
> *With a cargo of ivory,*
> *And apes and peacocks,*
> *Sandalwood, cedarwood, and sweet white wine.*

Stately Spanish galleon coming from the Isthmus,
Dipping through the Tropics by the palm-green shores,
With a cargo of diamonds,
Emeralds, amethysts,
Topazes, and cinnamon, and gold moidores.

Dirty British coaster with a salt-caked smoke stack
Battling through the Channel in the mad March days,
With a cargo of Tyne coal,
Road-rail, pig-lead,
Firewood, iron-ware, and cheap tin trays.

Then there were the haunting poems of men caught up in the First World War, like Julian Grenfell's INTO BATTLE. He died in 1915 making doubly poignant the verse:

The blackbird sings to him, 'Brother, brother,
If this be the last song you shall sing,
Sing well, for you may not sing another,
Brother, sing.

Rupert Brooke also died in 1915 and his poem CLOUDS has a premonition of death about it:

They say that the dead die not, but remain
Near to the rich heirs of their grief and mirth.
I think they ride the calm mid-heaven, as these,
In wise majestic melancholy train,
And watch the moon, and the still-raging seas,
And men, coming and going on the earth.

His photograph had a melancholy beauty about it.
Music also was much part of our early life. My father played the violin quite well, and mother strove to accompany him on the piano, but with a young family had little time to practise. However, she loved to sing and we learned many of her favourites -
***Annie Laurie, As I Was Going To Strawberry Fair, Oh Merry Goes The Time, Oh No John, No John, No John, No,* and many others. She taught us all the nursery rhymes and soon we were singing with her, but it was not until Father returned from the war that we had our first gramophone and records. Nothing like the modern music centres, but heavy records that played for only a short time, with steel needles that needed replacing frequently, and a handle with which to wind it. Often the record would run down during the play with the accompanying slowing of the music till it ended in a low groan. However, before the days when we were old**

enough to go to concerts it was a wonderful joy to be able to listen and dance to an orchestra.

Art was flourishing during that period, but my painting, although very enjoyable was extremely amateurish.

Books and music played a large part in Lady Helen Asquith's family life.

My mother's parents had a very wide circle of friends - artists and literary people who visited them in their house in London and also stayed at Mells.

When we first went to St. Paul's school in London and began our formal education we were growing up and my mother had friends like Hilaire Belloc and Maurice Baring, and a very nice friend called Desmond McCarthy who was a literary critic. They came to supper with us, which we liked very much, and talked to us as though we were grown up.

In the holiday at Mells, we had a very happy life; we played tennis, went for picnics, climbed trees and went swimming, but we also did a lot of reading. We had books around us all the time and then at St. Paul's we became excited about music. My sister learned the violin (she was more musical than I was), but I had many musical friends so I learned the clarinet in order to get into the school orchestra with them. There was a large music staff and a wonder musician, Gustav Holst, was Director of Music. His daughter, Imogen, joined the school at the same time as I did and became a great friend. So music loomed very large in our lives, and living in London, we were able to go to very good concerts.

We all learnt to read quite easily at a very early age and thereafter books were perhaps our most cherished and favourite source of recreation. We had plenty, though in those days there were no public libraries accessible to us, so we read and continually re-read the books we were given or borrowed from friends. My mother loved fairy stories so we became familiar early with Andrew Lang's Red and Blue Fairy Books, Jacob's Old English Fairy Tales, a book of Celtic Fairy Tales and Andersen's Fairy Tales. My great aunts, three elderly ladies who had lived in Mells all their lives, had a huge library of very pious Victorian children's books; they were largely about children doing good works in villages, but also on desert islands and even in Siberia. We used to borrow them and devour them. No modern child would understand or tolerate them. A rather more highbrow author of the late nineteenth century was Charlotte M. Yonge, who wrote excellent historical stories, The Little Duke, The Lances of Lynwood, Unknown to History, The Chaplet of Pearls, which my mother liked and encouraged and also long family chronicles which she didn't care for so much but we loved: The Daisy Chain and the Pillars of the House and a more famous one called The Heir of Redclyffe, whose characters became almost a real world to us.

Contemporary friends introduced us to Baroness Orczy's Scarlet Pimpernel and E. Nesbit's Treasure Seekers; and in the library at Menabilly, we found the complete works of Captain Marryat which we devoured and Trollope's Barsetshire Chronicles.

My mother loved Scott and used to read the Waverly Novels aloud to us; I fear we did find them rather heavy going. But by the age of 12, I had enjoyed Charlotte Bronte and Dickens and even Jane Austen though without consciously appreciating the latter's irony. At the same time, we were kindled by 'school stories' which were just coming into fashion, mainly those of a very meretricious writer called Angela Brazil. They were enjoyable but completely unreal and my mother was distressed when they inspired me to plead to go to a boarding school. She had high standards about literary quality and was always trying to lure us into reading 'worthwhile' books. We were rather proud when we did manage to read and enjoy some non-fiction - Macaulay's Essays or Stevenson's Travels with a Donkey, but I fear 'stories were what we chiefly devoured.

Poetry played quite an important part. In the nursery a very comprehensive anthology by Louis Chisholm called the Golden Staircase was a great standby; a collection of verse made by E. V. Lucas was perhaps better quality and we loved Stevenson's Child's Garden of Verses and learn quite a lot by heart. When I was about 12, I began to enjoy a remarkable anthology of prose and verse by Robert Bridges, called the Spirit of Man, which was a favourite with my mother at the time, and I developed great enthusiasm for the poems of Keats and Shelley.

We also enjoyed Shakespeare, whose plays and sonnets my mother knew by heart. In the years between the war and 1922, the Anglican rector of Mells had a remarkably artistic and gifted wife who used to produce a Shakespeare play every August on the Rectory lawns with a mainly village cast. We were too young to take much part but we always went to see them and the Merry Wives of Windsor, the Tempest and Cymbeline were very much a background of our lives.

William Butler Yeats, the Irish poet with Nanette Hales (née Porter).

Books were an important part of life for Nanette Hale's family.

My mother read aloud well and we listened as a family. I remember *John Halifax Gentleman, Cloister And The Heart, Last Days Of Pompeii, Ben Hur, Treasure Island*, Mark Twain's *Tom Sawyer*, Fennimore Cooker's *Last Of The Mohicans* and others. I read for myself *Secret Garden, Sara Greeve, Little Women, Pilgrim's Progress* by Bunyan, Kipling's *Jungle Book* and especially loved tales of Robin Hood. My 'best' friend had a home with grounds where there was a wooded section. We played Robin Hood there, with grape juice (a Ribena-like drink) for wine and a ditch with a board over it for the fight between Robin Hood and Little John.

My grandfather used to give me large, beautifully illustrated books; among them were *My Book Of Beautiful Legends*, Mary Magregor's *Story Of Greece* and *Story Of Rome*, and Mallory's *King Arthur*, which had illustrations by Arthur Rackham. I liked Stevenson's *Child's Garden Of Verses* and the *Cambridge Book Of Poetry For Children*, and I learned by heart the whole of *Horatius At The Bridge*. I wrote very trite little poems myself.

When I was nearly eleven my mother went to California to recuperate from an operation, and I was taken out of school to go with her. We were staying at a hotel in Pasadena, when an odd looking man came into the dining room. "That man is either a fool or a genius", my mother said. We enquired and found that he was William Butler Yeats, the great Irish poet. The next morning I saw him sitting alone in the hotel lobby. I went to him and said, "You write poetry, and so do I." Happily he was not annoyed and let me sit by him. Belatedly modest, I declined to recite any of my poems so he entertained me with stories of rabbits and of his tower in Ireland. Some photographers approached and he said, "I will only be photographed if you take me with this little girl."

After Pasadena we went for several weeks to a small garden hotel above Santa Barbara. The American poetess, Susan Teasdale, was there recovering from a broken heart. I suppose I was a lonely little girl, with no other children and my mother resting, so Sara Teasdale befriended me. We used to go out in the evening and she would tell me the names of the stars. She liked Orion to have the emphasis on the first syllable, as being more musical. I was given Yeat's poems, but alas, found them too difficult! I have still never written any good poems! When I was eighteen I started studying painting.

Mary Horseman remembers the early days of the telephone and radio.

We had a telephone at home. The mouthpiece was fixed to the wall and the ear piece hung beside it. Our number was 58 and our grandparents' 8, so we must have been among the first to have telephones locally. In those days there was no direct dialling, and on Saturdays sports fans rang up the operator to get the latest local football and cricket results.

My uncle made us a wireless set. It had enormous coils and valves, and took up as much room as a whole music centre nowadays. It used batteries, which had to be taken to be recharged quite often. It also had a cat's whisker, which had to be manipulated delicately to make it work.

Kathleen Hogg enjoyed the sound of music when she was young.

In the early years of the twentieth century women often sang about their work. My mother had a great store of songs, including many Irish ballads, which I still find myself singing to this day. The back gardens rang with cheerful melodies as the housewives hung out their washing. In the streets men whistled on their way to and from work. Whoever hears anyone whistling in the streets nowadays? Yet every delivery boy whistled as he sailed by on his bicycle. The tuneful airs of those early days were ideally suited to whistling.

When we were young, families and friends gathered round the piano at weekends and sang the latest popular songs, as well as old favourites like *The Mistletoe Bough, Little Dolly Daydream, The Old Rustic Bridge By The Mill,* and *Daisy, Daisy, Give Me Your Answer Do.*

Music has been a lifelong pleasure to Arthur Room.

In 1913, when I was nine years old, I was able to join my father in the choir of All Saints Church at Benhilton, Sutton, Surrey. He was a dedicated bass in the choir there. Mr. Baker, the organist and choirmaster, taught me to play the piano. As a result, I was able to accompany my father when he sang at social evenings during the First World War. That was the beginning of my love of music.

I had my first experience of taking part in Handel's Messiah with an augmented choir. A normal Sunday meant choral Matins, Eucharist and Evensong, with children's services in the afternoon.

10. RELIGION

At the beginning of the twentieth century, although there was an awareness of other religions such as Islam, Confucian and Taoist, Buddha, Brahma and the Hindu worshippers, few people had met followers of these faiths, and not many had even had contact with Jews. As more immigrants arrived from foreign lands, there followed mosques and temples as well as synagogues in the British Isles, so that in later years we have become a multi-faith society. Various attempts have been made throughout the twentieth century to unite the various denominations of the church. The International Missionary Conference at Edinburgh in 1910 led to the formation of the International Missionary Council in 1920, but it was not until 1948 that there was the first meeting of the World Council of Churches.

Around 1880 there was a mighty outpouring of the Holy Spirit in Russia, to be followed some twenty-five years later by a similar experience in Armenia.

There had been a prophecy by an uneducated Russian boy that all Christians would be massacred by the Turks unless they fled to America. Eight Armenian families took the prophecy seriously, and in 1905 emigrated to Los Angeles, California, thus escaping the fulfilment of the prophecy. They established a Pentecostal church in the home of Demos Shakarian. A group of them moved eventually to 312 Azusa Street, where a former Methodist church had recently been used as a horse stable and needed much clearing to make it habitable. What has become known as the Azusa Street Outpouring followed.

Many were baptised in the Holy Spirit and more and more people joined them, so that meetings continued day and night. There were many miracles of healing. Other Pentecostal churches and missions began to spring up, and missionaries went to many parts of the world. Among those affected was Aimee Semple McPherson, who became a world famous Pentecostal, preaching to thousands. Other revivals followed in England, Wales and Scotland.

Another who was to have a great influence on the Pentecostal movement was David du Plessis, who became known as Mr. Pentecost. He was born in Basutoland, South Africa, and when he was eleven years old was asked by Reinhardt Gschwent, a young Swiss missionary, to borrow his horse to ride the eleven miles to the village post office to collect his mail for him. As David was returning home he was caught in a violent thunderstorm. Lightning struck the ground in front of him, the horse stopped suddenly and threw him off. In fear David knelt in the mud and called on Jesus to save him - and he knew he had. As the storm abated he made his way safely home. The following year, he was baptised in water but he had to wait a further year before he was baptised in the Holy Spirit.

One day he asked the school's principal if he could have the following day off. He was asked why and said he wanted to fast and pray so that he might receive the Holy Spirit. His unusual request was granted, but for three days nothing happened: then a young girl, who had recently been baptised in the Holy Spirit, joined him in the coffin shed where he was sitting, spiritually and physically exhausted. She said to him, "David, I think the Lord has given me something to say to you. He has told me that if you will confess the thing that's on your conscience, He will baptise you in the Holy Spirit." David remembered an occasion seven years earlier when he was taking care of his baby sister whilst his parents were away. He was swinging a string with a small metal trinket in the end. Accidentally he let it slip and the metal hit the baby on the head, leaving a slight scratch. His parents asked him what had happened and he said he did not know.

As soon as he remembered this long forgotten lie, he went to both his parents and confessed. He was filled with joy and began to laugh and shout 'Hallelujah', but instead found he was speaking in a strange tongue. A sailor, Bob Masser, who was standing nearby recognised it as Chinese.

From that time on until his death some years ago he travelled all over the world, sharing his experiences and enabling others to be baptised in the Holy Spirit.

George Müller had died in 1898 but his wonderful life of faith was to influence many future generations. Because of his compassion for the many children who had been orphaned he opened the first orphanage in Bristol, with little financial support. He never asked for money, believing that God was the supplier and would answer believing prayer. So one day when there was nothing to eat for breakfast, and no money to buy food, he sat the children down at the empty table and said grace, thanking God for what he was about to provide. Almost immediately there was a knock at the door and the milkman asked if he would like some milk, as he had too much and in those days before refrigeration he knew it would soon go sour.

Not long after there was another knock. This time it was the baker who said the Lord had told him to cook an extra batch of bread that morning. Often he would find food and fruit left on the doorstep, and so much money poured in from supporters that eventually he was able to open 117 orphanages worldwide.

The Church of England was well-served at the beginning of the twentieth century first by Frederick Temple (1821-1902), who was Archbishop of Canterbury from 1897 and had done much to foster education after the Forster Act of 1870; then his second son, William (1881-1944) was to become a much-loved Archbishop of Canterbury in 1942. However before that he had followed in his father's footsteps and done much to foster educational reform. He became the first president of the Workers' Educational Association, which was to give to the working classes previously inaccessible opportunities.

From 1910-1914 he was headmaster of Repton but then entered the church as the rector of St. James, Piccadilly, and was one of the founders of the Life and Liberty movement. He was made a canon of Westminster in 1919 before he became Bishop of Manchester in 1921. He was always very accessible to the man in the street and the author of many Christian books.

During the carnage of the First World War Tubby Clayton instituted TocH to care for the spiritual as well as the physical and moral needs of the soldiers, and it gained universal appeal. Woodbine Willie was another who ministered to the soldiers' needs. Many lost their faith during the war, but many found it for the first time.

I am very grateful that both my parents were Christians. From the earliest age I can remember my mother praying with us by the side of the bed at night. 'God bless Mummy, God bless Daddy, God bless Jessie, God bless Kathleen.' Later Jack and Biddy were added. There was that more difficult one:

> 'Gentle Jesus, meek and milk
> Look upon a little child;
> Pitty MICE IN PLICITY
> Suffer me to come to Thee.
> Feign I would to Thee be brought
> Gracious God, forbid it not.
> In the kingdom of thy grace
> Give a little child her place.'

For a long time I wondered what was happening to the mice and why they needed prayer, but never thought to ask! I don't know when I realised it should have been 'my simplicity'. I was too simple! Also, as my name was Grace it was good to know I had a place in God's kingdom. In those days small children were not usually taken to church, and the first service I remember was during the war in Winchester Cathedral. There was an army parade there and my father was among the soldiers, so that was an important part of the proceedings, but I also remember being overawed by the size and magnificence of the naive and the beauty of the singing.

Religious instruction was definitely part of the school syllabus, and there was always a morning assembly. I do not remember them at Winchester and Bath, but at Swaffield School in London Miss Jones, the Headmistress, always began with "Hands together, eyes closed." There was an orchestra with out-of-tune violins to escort us in and out of the hall. We all joined in the Lord's prayer, but other details I have forgotten. In those days there was no difficulty with multi-faith immigrants, and I do not recall meeting any Jews, although there were many in the country.

Jessie Young and her family always observed Sundays.

Sunday was a very special day, and we were told several times, 'Remember what day this is', if we made a noise. We all went to church in the morning, with both parents when Father was at home. An older sister or the 'Big Quine' stayed at home to look after the dinner and there was usually a baby who was too young to attend church.

After a very special dinner we younger children went to Sunday School, which we enjoyed; then after a walk and tea off we went to church again. Before retiring, my father had family worship, when we were all present, a custom with most families in those days. I can never remember resenting this procedure at all. We just followed in our parents' footsteps and accepted it as normal living.

There were two churches in our village of Hopeman, Morayshire, the Church of Scotland, which we attended, and a Baptist Church. There were also several other sects, Brethren of different types who all stuck to their own beliefs. Our church, built in 1850 had no organ at first, and the singing was conducted by a Precentor, my grandfather. When money was collected for an organ some people objected to the worldly gadget and left the church. One old man walked two miles to the next village where the church had no organ!

Our instrument was hardly necessary as there were so many wonderful voices, basses, tenors and sopranos. I will never forget hearing *Lead Kindly Light* from our pew. We were surrounded by talent (not in our family) and the sound still rings in my ears at times. Beautiful!

I used to feel sorry for the children who did not come to our Sunday School, therefore missing our annual picnic in the summer and soirée in the winter, to which we all contributed poems or songs. No need for the expense of entertainers - we were easily pleased.

Our ministers did not come and go. The first in our church stayed for his whole forty years, the one in my time a mere twenty-five years!

Elsie Paget felt the spirit of Christianity whilst living on the Isle of Islay.

It was St. Columba who in 563 AD first brought the news of God's redeeming love from Ireland to the island of Iona in Scotland. He spoke of its cost and the gift of forgiveness and everlasting life through his Son, Jesus Christ.

The 1611 translation of the Bible, a gigantic and thrilling task, was greatly helped by the quiet, careful reign of James I, the combined monarch of England and Scotland.

Years later, the Scottish metric version of all the Psalms was completed. Having been educated there, I had the joy of learning psalms in easy rhyme and metre. All children had to learn many psalms as well as the very fine Scottish catechism. We loved it, for such was the attitude of our teachers.

Many of the beautiful poetic psalms have now been included among the hymns of various denominations:-

Psalm 23.The Lord's my Shepherd.

Psalm 46.God is our refuge and our strength;
In stress our present aid.
There, although the earth remove,
We need not be afraid.
O God, our help in ages past,
Our hope for years to come.

Psalm55Ho, ye that thirst, approach the spring
Whence living waters flow
Flee to that Sacred Fountain,
All, without a price, may go.
This is usually sung to a tune called 'Felix', for it was composed by Mendelssohn, who loved the Hebrides and wrote some de-

lightful music there. Perhaps the qualities developed in the midst of wild winds and dangerous seas, and the many other influences, have been used by our Heavenly Father to build a robust faith, available to everyone, everywhere.

Church played an important part in the life of Mrs. Dorothy E. Curgenven, who has spent all her life in the pleasant village of Zelah in Cornwall. There were hard times and happy times in those 'good old days'.

I was born on 11th February 1912 in Zelah Lane, and I'm lucky to still be around. From my earliest days I was a member of St. Allen Parish Church, walking there twice every Sunday across the fields from Trerice along the public path. There were also two thriving chapels, the Bible Christian at Zelah Lane and the Wesleyan opposite the school, both of which I also supported. Both chapels had annual tea treats to celebrate their anniversaries, and these included processions through the village with the Newlyn East Band.

Rogation Sunday falls in May and was the time of the St. Allen feast. There were horses, donkeys, clay pigeon shooting etc., followed by a tea for all. Another big event was the dance held in the evening on either the Saturday or Monday of that special week. The Rector's wife from St. Allen church, Mrs. Buck, travelled the parish in her horse and cab, driven by a coachman, for several days each Christmas, delivering saffron cakes and mince pies to every home. That to me was wonderful!

Anderton and Rowlands' fair came to Church Lane, and something took place every night in the school, the church and the chapel.

For most people Sunday was a day of rest from work, but obviously farmers had certain restrictions. They got up early in the morning to care for their animals, to feed and water them and, if necessary, milk them. That had to be done again in the evening, but they had the rest of the day free. Mothers, too, had to look after the family and do the cooking as on a weekday, but older children gave a hand.

Religion was an essential part of life for Isobel Wookey's family.

At the turn of the century and until after the Second World War, religion was very important.

It was the custom for children to go to Sunday school. My brother and I had many prizes for regular attendance at St. Mary's church (Anglican, high) on the corner of Knox Road and Elsden Road. It is a huge church, whose towers can be seen for miles.

My mother was a high church Anglican and my father a Primitive Methodist. My brother once said, "A lot of the trouble between Mum and Pop was their difference of religion."

When they became Primitive Methodists, my grandma and aunt Florrie used to invite all the lay preachers to dinner on Sundays. She gave them parsnip wine: "It isn't alcoholic", she said. Whether it was or not, they used to sleep right through from after the meal until the evening service at 6.00 pm!

On Sundays no cooking was allowed and no reading, not even the Bible! We used to sit in her parlour bolt upright - no talking, laughing, or even smiling. The only walks were to chapel or to the cemetery to put flowers on the Brooks plot, where my two aunts were buried. They had died when quite young of some kind of fever, which caused their hair to come out. Aunt Florrie caught the same disease but survived, the only difficulty being that her hair did not grow again for many years. In the meantime she had to wear what was called a 'transformation' - a pad of false hair about half-an-inch thick, placed squarely on the head. Though strict, she was a very kind person, but 'not easily provoked to laughter!'

On the wall of the room behind the shop was an oblong religious tract, with a dark green background and silver lettering:

> *Christ is the head of this house,*
> *The unseen guest at every meal,*
> *The silent listener to every conversation."*

To the Primitive Methodists, Catholics were wicked people who danced on Sunday! In the chapel no flowers or candles were allowed, and hymns were mournful ones - no joyful celebration of our Lord's life.

I was baptised at Charfield Parish Church, Gloucester, as was my brother. I can remember, too, my young sister, Mary, being christened at the same church. In the churchyard is a communal grave for the victims of the Charfield train disaster; buried in a separate grave are the bodies of a boy and girl killed at the same time but never identified. For many years, on the anniversary of the crash, a heavily veiled lady would visit their grave, leaving flowers.

As for most households early in the twentieth century, Sunday was kept as a very special day for T. C. in Cumberland.

On Sunday we went to church in our best clothes and flat heeled shoes. I remember with great affection a white straw hat with roses and forget-me-nots round the crown, sewn on to rose pink velvet ribbon which hung down the back. We walked through the village and were not allowed to look into any shop window that had not drawn blinds. We had also to think about our posture: 'chests out and bottoms in', my father used to say, and Mother impressed on us that if we didn't look at the Vicar during the service we would not hear what he was saying. No hanging about after the service gossiping, but straight home thinking about the sermon.

After lunch we sat down for at least half-an-hour reading a book from the study shelves. I chose *The Baronet's Wife*, but this was quickly removed and replaced by *Muses From An Old Manse*. We were also given six chosen chocolates from a huge box which was locked away in the study during the week.

Mrs. Hilary Hellicar (née Fenby), born 1907, spent her early years in Clapham, London, but she is now in a nursing home in London.

I used to attend the Ascension Church in Lavender Hill, Wandsworth, London. I remember one Sunday service in 1912 or 1913 when a frail, short and elderly figure of a priest sat in honour in the sanctuary during the ceremonies. He was an Anglo-Catholic priest who had been imprisoned for refusing to give up certain ceremonies of worship, and in his nineties was revered as a hero of the High Church tradition.

I also have vivid memories of a sermon preached at the same church in 1916. The priest inveighed against the scourge of the Germans, giving details of their troops in Belgium killing babies with bayonets. He called for a response to this. My animosity towards the Germans dated from such experiences in the First World War rather than the Second.

The vicar of the church from 1916 was Father Arthur Montford, a notable Anglo Catholic priest. He was a good orator, who impressed even those who did not like him on such occasions as Speech Day at the school. His sermons at the Ascension attracted bus loads of poor people from Battersea and other parts of London.

My devotion to the Catholic wing of the church as opposed to the Protestant tradition was reinforced by these experiences, which made me less content with the establishment of the church.

Margery Clow had different experiences of religion.

When I came home from the Shaftesbury school, I was very religious. I slept with my mother and when she got into bed she hadn't said her prayers. I said to her, "Mother, you haven't said your prayers." She replied, "I say everything but my prayers, and those I whistle." I still said my prayers for quite a while, but my grandfather was an atheist. He did not lecture us at all, but he was a true socialist. He would go without himself to give to others. He said to me, when I was praying about my food, "You're praying to God for your food, but see how much he gives you when you've got no money or food."

He used to speak in Finsbury Park on Sunday morning and we went with him. We saw the crowds of people and really thought that Finsbury Park belonged to my grandfather! Wet or fine he used to be there on his rostrum. He was known as Jack Webb and as soon as he began to speak the people cried, "Jack's up, Jack's up." All the other groups would be depleted of people as they came to listen to him. He was a marvellous speaker: he could hold the crowd. He was never taught - just natural.

Grandfather had an old harmonium, and he gave it to Mother. We had great fun with it, trying to play. As my grandfather was an atheist we did not go to ordinary Sunday school. Instead we went to the Socialist Sunday school. On Sunday mornings he used to take me to a Welsh milk shop in nearby Tollington Park and give me a glass of milk. I hated it but drank it out of respect for my grandfather. He used to say, "There you are, my girl, now when you grow up choose your friends from those that drink milk!" He was a lifelong teetotaller.

One time he wanted me to learn *The People's Flag,* the socialist song, so that I could recite it in the park on Sunday morning from his rostrum. It took me ages and ages to learn, but at last I knew it by heart. My mother made me a very nice sailor suit in black satin, with pink french knots round the hem and round the little pockets and collar. I felt very smart in it! He stood me on top of the speaker's stand and I had to recite:

> *"The people's flag is deepest red*
> *We shroud it o'er our master's head..."*

My grandfather stood me down when I had finished and everybody came up and filled my pockets with pennies, each one put in a penny until I was bulging with them. I thought it was lovely! I went round to Grandfather's the next evening to ask him what I could learn next!

FRANK BUCHMAN
Founder of the Oxford Group Movement

Frank Buchman was an American of German origin. In 1899, when he was twenty-one, a cousin quoted from one of Bacon's essays to him: "He that hath wife and children hath given hostage to fortune, for they are impediments to great enterprises, either of virtue or mischief." Buchman took this to heart and remained single all his life.

He graduated from Michlenberg College and then went to Philadelphia to attend the Lutheran Theological Seminary at Mount Airy in Germantown. At that time his ambition was to be a farmer, author and hymn-writer, but he also enjoyed the fashionable social life.

In 1901 he and a group of colleagues opened a Sunday school in Kensington, one of the poorest districts in Philadelphia and it proved very popular. His desire was to minister to the needs of the deprived children and others in the area.

After he had graduated from Mount Airy in 1902 he was invited to start a church at Overbrook, with no building and no funds, but a month later due to his endeavours the Church of the Good Shepherd was opened. A year of intense hard work found him exhausted, and his doctor recommended a long holiday. His father generously provided the funds for him to go to Europe with friends. While he was there he was impressed with the work done by Hospiz in Switzerland and Germany by providing accommodation in a Christian setting for students and others. So when he returned to Overbrook he determined to provide similar accommodation himself. A hospiz was founded in May 1904. This proved so popular that the Church's Home Missions Board decided to open one to hold fifty young men, calling it a hospice. Buchman was appointed to run it and again it was very popular, but his vision was for a place with good food and the comforts of a Christian home. He was soon in conflict with the Board, who wanted the enterprise to be self-supporting and not loss-making as it was under Buchman. In the end he was dismissed and felt much bitterness.

Again he suffered from severe exhaustion, and his father provided the funds for him to go to Europe in January 1908. In July he went to the Keswick Convention in England, hoping to meet F. B. Meyer, the well-known Methodist, but was disappointed to discover he was not to be there. However, the Lord had other plans and one Sunday he dropped into a small chapel, where he found only seventeen other worshippers, with a lady leading the service. It was Jessie Penn-Lewis. Her description of the Cross and what it cost Jesus to suffer there so that we might have forgiveness of sins so affected him that it changed his life. The words of the hymn challenged him:

> 'When I survey the wondrous cross
> on which the Prince of Glory died,
> My richest gains I count but loss
> And pour contempt on all my pride.'

He had recognised his own pride and that although he was in the right it was wrong to harbour ill-will against those who had rejected him.

When he returned to America he was a different man, much happier and calmer, although he was without a job. However, it was not long before he was offered the post of Y.M.C.A. secretary at Pennsylvania State College. He was to be in charge of religious work at what Mott had called 'the most godless university in the country.' He had a very difficult beginning but soon won over many of the students. Some of his meetings attracted over a thousand men. However, Buchman was not satisfied and felt the changes in their lives were too superficial to be permanent. At that crucial time a visitor to the college (probably F. B. Meyer) answered his questioning by saying, "You need to make personal, man-to-man interviews central, rather than the organising of meetings." He also asked him whether he set apart a time when he could listen to God and know from him what he should do.

This was another big step forward for Buchman. He decided to set apart an hour, 5.00 - 6.00 am, for a 'quiet time', when he would listen to the Holy Spirit. He found that names of people came to him and when he followed them up there were changes in the lives of the most unlikely people. He also ran annual 'Y' week campaigns, which drew people from many other colleges who came to discover the basis of his extraordinary influence on men.

In 1912 Buchman decided to set up a home on the campus where he could encourage the friendless, the lonely and the sick, giving them good food and fellowship. He gave so much away that often he had barely money enough for his own needs.

Garth Lean in 'Frank Buchman, a Life,' (p.43) sums up Buchman as a man of contradictions.

'An ardent advertiser of his own activities, he was also surprisingly self-effacing; the product of a conservative and cautious religious tradition, he was strikingly radical in his methods; extrovert in manner, he was at heart profoundly reserved.'

He was to leave Pennsylvania State College for good in April 1915, although he did not realise this when he set sail for India, a place he had long wanted to visit. There he became friends with Rabindranath Tagore and Amy Carmichael. He found the Dohnavur Fellowship she had created near Tinnevelly 'the place nearer heaven than any other spot on earth.'

He was able to help a very difficult, rebellious schoolboy, Victor, whom he met at a boys' camp. He saw Victor twirling bamboo canes like a bandmaster's baton. Buchman congratulated him and wished he could do it, so instead of running away as he had done previously, Victor told him to try. He failed, and that pleased Victor, but it also opened the way for conversation. Buchman told him that he went to camp once, and hated it, so Victor went on to tell Buchman that he did, too, and so was making a nuisance of himself. He added "There's something inside me. I'm sorry."

"How much sorry?" asked Buchman. "Do you know what remorse is?"

"That's being sorry and then doing it again," said Victor.

"Then what do you think you need?" asked Buchman.

"Repentance."

"What's that?"

"Oh, that's when a fellow's sorry enough to quit." (page 48).

From this opening Buchman was able to talk to Victor about Jesus Christ, who was the only one who could take away sin. Victor knelt with Buchman and prayed, "Lord, manage me, for I can't manage myself." He knew that a great weight had been lifted from him and was able to share this with his friends. Buchman used his definition of remorse and repentance for the rest of his life.

He sailed for Canton in February 1916 and was able to touch many key men there, but returned to America that August, partly because of his father's ill health. He was offered a part-time job at the Hartford Theological Seminary in New England and became Extension Lecturer in Personal Evangelism. This gave him the liberty he needed as he could arrange his lectures when it suited him, and he also had an expense account for travelling. His conviction that work with individuals was the key to evangelism did not please everyone, but there was a small group that supported him in a companionship of 'fellowship and silence'.

He consider their first work should be among influential Chinese leaders, training them so that they could train others. In June 1917 he sailed to China again with three friends from Hartford and two from Yale. China had a very weak and unstable government at that time, with massive debts. Mao Tse-tung was a student but not yet a Communist. He believed in absolute moral principals and the power of the mind.

Many of the prominent Chinese felt that only Christianity could save their land. Then enthusiastic reports of Buchman's work caused opposition from the established missionaries, who did not like his methods or approve of his treatment of the Chinese as equals. During this tour Buchman met Samuel Moor Shoemaker, a Princeton graduate who was helping at a business school for Chinese boys. The numbers in his Bible class had declined, and Shoemaker asked Buchman if he could touch one of the leaders, as this might affect the whole student body.

He was shocked when Buchman suggested he should do this himself, and even more so when Buchman told him that sin might be the barrier he was finding in his life. It took much heart-searching before Shoemaker could accept that Buchman was right and he needed forgiveness from God for trying to do His work his own way. He also asked Buchman to forgive him for his resentment.

Buchman asked him what was the next step, so Shoemaker told him he had a long-standing agreement to have tea with one of his bible class boys. Then he asked, "What shall I tell him?"

"Tell him just what you've told me. Be honest about yourself," replied Buchman. Shoemaker did this and the boy wanted the same thing for himself. He was shown the way and responded.. Thus began a twenty year association between Buchman and Shoemaker.

In 1918 there was the summer conference at Kuling and Peitaiho. Buchman was asked to lead both but opposition grew from many quarters. Hsu Ch'ien, acting prime minister whilst Sun Yat-sen was in Japan, spoke of the moral evils in China, 'despotism, militarism, autocracy, opium-smoking, liquor traffic, concubinage, foot-binding and slavery.' However, he considered that Christians were powerless in China because of their private sins. Buchman and others publicly confessed sins in their own lives: this Buchman had found most efficacious in evangelising. Some of the missionaries present were furious at his plain speaking; others found him extremely helpful. When he talked of unhealthy 'crushes' or 'absorbing friendships' there was even more indignation. Some had complained to Bishop Roots and after fifteen months of passionate campaigning Buchman was asked to leave China.

His letters to Bishop Roots, while acknowledging that he might have seemed harsh, explained that it was only because he was so concerned at the failure of the churches and some of the missionaries. They did not like the fact that he spoke out about sin.

Meanwhile his father's health had been deteriorating and in March 1919 Buchman sailed for the United States. He arranged for his father, who had had a stroke the previous autumn, to be cared for in a nursing home near Hartford whilst he took his mother on a holiday. He accepted a renewed offer from Hartford, which gave him freedom to travel for nine months of the year as well as giving a series of lectures on the 'how' of personal evangelism. However, as Buchman felt he should go as and where the Spirit let him, even if he was expected at Hartford, this inevitably led to friction amongst some of the staff.

He was concerned that Russia should have submitted to an atheist regime but even more at the deterioration in his own country, with the aftermath of the war. He wanted to remake the world!

At the Northfield Conference in the summer of 1919 Buchman had a profound effect on members of the Princeton delegation. They appointed his friend, Sam Shoemaker as secretary of the Philadelphia Society, the university's student Christian association. Buchman visited them most months and between them they influenced the lives of many students.

By this time he had formed the basic tenets of the life of faith; the standards of absolute honesty, absolute purity, absolute unselfishness and absolute love. These formed the basis of the Oxford Group Movement, to be founded in the Thirties.

ALBERT SCHWEITZER (1875-1965)

Albert Schweitzer, a German, might well have become an eminent theologian, philosopher or musician, for he excelled in all three. He studied philosophy and theology at the universities of Strasburg, Paris and Berlin. Then because of his Christian beliefs he felt compelled to preserve life and decided to qualify as a medical missionary, which he did in 1913. He opened a hospital at Lambarene in the Cameroons and lived in comparative obscurity whilst he looked after the desperately poor, sick Africans. Many of them would travel miles on foot, often carrying a sick child, to seek the caring help of the hospital there.

He had already written some scholarly theological books, among them *The Mystery Of The Kingdom Of God* (**1901**) and *In Quest Of The Historical Jesus* (**1906**). Other books were to follow, among them his Pauline studies. He was also well known as an organist, and from time to time left Lambarene to give world-wide concerts to raise money for his missionary work. The music of Bach was his speciality, and later in the Twenties I was privileged to hear him both speak and play at the Guildhouse, Eccleston Square, Victoria, London.

11. POLITICS

Queen Victoria's long and gloomy reign came to an end when she died on 22 January 1901. She was followed by King Edward VII, a very different personality who enjoyed an extravagant mode of life. Although he died in 1910, the characteristics of the Edwardian period really continued until the outbreak of war on 4 August 1914. He was succeeded by King George V.

The Boer War had proved extremely expensive to Britain, and she was no longer the wealthiest nation in the world. It had also changed her relationship with Germany and France. Until then the French had been considered the potential enemy, but Germany had encouraged Kruger during the Boer War and Britain was now drawn to Ententes with France and Russia. In 1905 there were secret military talks between the British and French which increased their commitment.

The Liberals were still in the ascendant and won the election of 1906 with 377 seats, as against 157 for the Tories, 29 for the young Labour party and 83 Irish Nationals. In 1909 the House of Lords refused to pass the Liberals' budget, which imposed a supertax on the wealthy and for the first time taxed landowners. The money was needed to provide for the new social services that were being introduced. Free school meals (1907); old age pensions (first considered by Asquith before he became Prime Minister in 1908, but brought to the Commons by David Lloyd George, who succeeded him as Chancellor of the Exchequer). Labour Exchanges were introduced by Winston Churchill in 1909 and the first National Insurance Bill by Lloyd George in 1911. These were the beginnings of the Welfare State, not appreciated by the Lords. Money was also needed to finance the building of a fleet of Dreadnoughts needed to match the rapid expansion of the German navy.

The Liberals could not function without finance, which the Lords would not approve, so there were two more general elections in 1910, when the Liberals were again in power, though with a reduced majority. In 1911 the Parliament Act limited the Lords' veto to two years.

Scott of the Antarctic died in 1912, and that same year the TITANIC, the largest and most modern ship in the world, considered unsinkable, sank. Warnings of a large iceberg were ignored. The ship was divided into watertight compartments and it was considered that even if three of them were flooded the ship would remain afloat, but five were affected when the TITANIC hit the iceberg, enough to cause the bow to sink. To make matters worse, there were lifeboats for less than half the permitted number of passengers. Precedence was given to the wealthy first class passengers, and many women and children travelling third class were drowned. True to their tradition, the crew kept to their posts until the last minute, and 686 out of 875 men were drowned, as well as two of the 23 women.

To satisfy their Irish supporters, the Liberals introduced the third Home Rule Bill, which became law under the provisions of the Parliament Act in 1914, though it lay dormant during the war. Andrew Bonar Law who had replaced Balfour as leader of the Unionists in 1911 would not tolerate this, and Ireland was on the verge of civil war in 1914 when the outbreak of the war with Germany delayed action.

Trade Unionists, who had greatly increased in numbers since 1903, sought to improve the lot of the working class by a series of strikes after 1910, culminating in the first general railway strike of 1911. There was also increased action by the Suffragettes, first by Mrs Fawcett's National Union of Women's Suffrage Societies and then by the Pankhurst's Women's Social and Political Union (1903). To gain votes for women the latter were prepared to use violence against politicians and property, and also to go to prison and suffer the indignity and hardship of hunger strikes and forced feeding. This led to the 'Cat and Mouse Act', when suffragettes weakened through hunger-strikes were released from prison only to be re-arrested when they had regained sufficient strength. They curtailed their activities and supported the war effort wholeheartedly, and gained through co-operation what they had not obtained through violence.

The German invasion of Belgium in 1914, contrary to the guarantee of their independence signed by both Germany and Britain in 1870, led Asquith and his Cabinet to declare war on Germany in support of the French. Although the navy had been strengthened, Britain's ground forces were feeble compared to those of Germany and France. Lloyd George, who had been strongly opposed to the Boer War, made a rousing speech in the Queen's Hall, London, on 19 September 1914, stating that this was a moral war on behalf of the small nations like Belgium.

Most people considered that the war was just and necessary, and many volunteered for service believing they were fighting for their families and the nation.

The Cunard ship *Lusitania*, the fastest ship on the Atlantic, was torpedoed by a German submarine in 1915. Among the passengers were 159 Americans and this turned the USA against Germany, so to avoid bringing her into the war the Germans desisted for a while from further such attacks.

Drunkenness in Britain was widespread. Before 1915 public houses were allowed to stay open all day until midnight. War production was affected so pubs. were restricted to opening only at lunch time and during the evening. The strength of the beer was also reduced and these measures resulted in a dramatic decrease in alcoholism.

In 1917 the Russian revolution and their withdrawal from the war meant that Germany was no longer fighting on two fronts. She decided to risk antagonising America and returned to U-boat warfare. So many ships were sunk that Britain was on the verge of starvation until Lloyd George forced the Admiralty to accept convoys, with warships protecting them by using depth charges against the submarines.

Germany had assumed that she could beat the Allied armies before America had a chance to mobilise, and she almost succeeded.

Many women had served at the front, especially in medical field hospitals. Among them was Nurse Edith Cavell, who was martyred by the Germans for assisting British and French prisoners of war in Belgium to escape. Other women had done valuable work in munitions factories, on the farms and elsewhere. Sex barriers had been eroded and it was no longer possible to deny women the right to vote, so in 1918 women over thirty were given the vote.

Labour and the trade unions had also been strengthened by the war. Membership of the latter had almost doubled to reach over eight million by the beginning of 1919. There were dissensions in the Liberal party, although Lloyd George had taken over from Asquith in December 1916 and proved a very popular Prime Minister during the latter part of the war. The rump of the Liberal party under his leadership was in coalition with the Conservatives. They were to become the majority party.

At the election in December 1918 Lloyd George was given the credit for winning the war, and coalition MPs numbered 526, with only 57 Labour and 26 Independent Liberals. He had campaigned for 'a land fit for heroes' and there were programmes to extend health and educational services. More important still was the subsidised housing programme, when over 100,000 houses were publicly built between 1919 and 1922.

There was a short boom, but depression soon followed, with many ex-service men unable to find work.

In 1919 the Treaty of Versailles brought peace to Europe, but Britain's wealth had been consumed by the enormous expense of the war, leaving many problems for future generations.

THE FIRST WORLD WAR

The First World War was sparked off by the assassination of the Archduke Franz-Ferdinand, at Serajevo in Bosnia on 28 June, 1914. He was heir to the throne of Austria-Hungary, so in retaliation Austria declared war on Serbia, Russia's ally. The Russians backed Serbia, the Germans the Austrians. As France was Russia's ally, Germany knew she also had to make war on France. Belgian neutrality had been guaranteed by Britain, as well as by France and other powers, so when the Germans began an assault on Belgium, the British gave an ultimatum to Germany to withdraw. Otherwise they would consider themselves to be at war as from 11pm on 4 August.

It was the bank holiday weekend and the fleet was already preparing to go to sea; the regular army was mobilised on 3 August. Panic buying hit the shops as people began to hoard food. Mr. Asquith was Prime Minister (1852-1928) and stated in the House of Commons that Britain had a duty to Belgium and was bound by honour to support France. The brutal way the Germans treated Belgium was enough to silence any critics: they pillaged towns, and shot several thousand hostages as reprisals when civilians tried to fight back. Many refugees escaped to Britain across the North Sea and were offered hospitality. Later they helped the war effort by making munitions.

The first taste the mainland had of the war was on 16 December that year when German cruisers shelled Hartlepool, Whitby and Scarborough on the east coast. Then on 24 December an aeroplane dropped a bomb on Dover. Later the Zeppelin airships, with their ability to carry many more bombs, were to cause much more damage. Black-out of London was introduced in September. Lord Kitchener was Secretary of State for War and recognised the need for volunteers to support the small regular army. Over two million had volunteered by the time conscription was introduced early in 1916. Because of the shortage of equipment they had to drill with broomsticks and learn to shoot with dummy artillery, and it was 1915 before they were provided with uniforms. The vain hope that war would be over by Christmas was soon dispelled, and after the first Battle of Ypres began the horrors of trench warfare. Many wounded were already returning to Britain.

1915 saw more Zeppelin attacks, at first on East Anglian towns but later on London. Searchlights were able to pin-point them, and occasionally one was set on fire by artillery attacks. When the Cunard Liner *Lusitania* was sunk by a German submarine on 7 May, over a thousand people, including children, were drowned. Public uproar led to the internment of Germans between the ages of seventeen and forty-five.

Casualities at the front were already so great that the Government realised it would have to consider conscription. Everyone between the ages of fifteen and sixty-five was entered on a National Register in July: all had to carry registration cards. Workers in coalmines and on munitions were exempt from military service. Men too old to be soldiers could serve as special constables, replacing policemen who had volunteered for the army. After a day's civilian work, the constables went out for three or four hours guarding gasometers, railway lines and suchlike. Women, too, undertook voluntary work in hospitals and in knitting garments for the troops.

On the industrial front Britain was ill-prepared for war. Essential products like ball bearings and optical devices had been imported from Germany until the outbreak of war, and the chemical industry was small. It was not until the dynamic David Lloyd-George became Minister of Munitions that production of shells and other essential munitions began to equal demand. Former suffragette groups organised a huge procession of women on 27 July 1915 to dedicate themselves to war work. Thousands of them took jobs in commerce, banks and government offices. Others went to work in the munitions factories. By the end of the year there were three times as many women as men in munitions. Other women swept roads, took over milk and coal deliveries, and even helped with funerals.

Lloyd George also took steps to counter excessive drinking, which was hampering the war effort. He restricted drinking hours, reduced the strength of beer and made it more expensive. Spirits became luxuries that were almost unobtainable.

In January 1916 the first Military Service Act deemed that all single men between eighteen and forty-one had enlisted. The second Act of May 1916 extended conscription to married men. There was a clause allowing exemptions based on a 'conscientious objection to the undertaking of combatant service.' These men were called before Local Tribunals who considered their cases. Most agreed to non-combatant service such as forestry and road making. The Quaker ambulance units contained some of the bravest men at the front. About 6,000 'absolutists' were imprisoned, and of these seventy died.

Meanwhile, women were employed more and more, driving motor cars and vans, collecting tickets at underground stations, acting as conductorettes on buses and trams, and working on the land. This led to a change in female attire, as more practical uniform trousers replaced skirts, and short hair the long tresses that could easily be caught in machines. Shortage of material led to shorter skirts, and because for the first time in their lives some women had money of their own, they could indulge in the luxury of wearing 'silk' stockings.

There had been few facilities for women in factories, but now canteens selling cheap but good food were introduced, also medical rooms and nurses, proper bedrooms and wash-rooms, and even nurseries for women workers children.

Saturday, 1 July 1916, saw the first day of the terrible battle of the Somme, as the French and British tried to break the Western Front. More than one and a half million shells had bombarded the German positions during the previous week, but when the order was given to go over the top it was found that many shells had not exploded and the Germans had been untouched in their deep dugouts. Nearly 20,000 British soldiers died that first day, and twice as many were wounded. Asquith's eldest son was among those killed. Many of them were the early volunteers of 1914, seeing their first action. By November only a small muddy piece of occupied France was wrested from the enemy. For the first time long lists of the dead appeared in newspapers, revealing to the public the full extent of the slaughter.

At home, Zeppelins were also causing death and destruction, especially on moonless nights, but an explosive bullet had been invented that would ignite their gas-bags. These were fired by Britain's BE2C aeroplanes flying to defend London. The first was destroyed on 2 September, when the blazing wreck crashed in Cuffley, north of London. On 23 September another was hit by artillery fire and a third Zeppelin also went down in flames. On 28 November the destruction of yet two more Zeppelins brought an end to their usefulness, but then a single aeroplane dropped six bombs on London, heralding a new phase of warfare.

Women joined the armed forces to take up non-combatant duties to free men for battle. Of the 100,000 girls involved, most joined the Women's Auxiliary Army Corps (W.A.A.C.). Others went to the Women's Royal Air Force (W.R.A.F.) and Women's Royal Naval Service (W.R.N.S.). Many became V.A.D. (Voluntary Aid Detachment) nurses in hospitals at home and in all the major theatres of war. Yet others joined the Women Police.

Mud at Ypres

On 31 July 1917 the British attempted to strike from Ypres towards the Belgian coast, but exceptionally wet weather combined with the effect of millions of shells fired at German positions had turned the area into a sea of mud. The drainage system was destroyed and many men drowned in the swamps. There were 324,000 casualties in the four mile advance to Passchendaele ridge over four months, but in November there was a break through of massed tanks at Cambrai which brought some relief.

The Germans now produced first twin-engined Gothas and then huge four-engined Giant machines. They attacked the Kent coast during the spring; then on 13 June 1917 there was a mass attack on London. They attacked again on 7 July, causing more deaths. General Smuts was put in charge of London's defences, and brought in mobile guns on lorries to follow the raiders. Some fighter squadrons were recalled from France and barrage balloons, trailing curtains of steel streamers, were introduced.

In September the Germans launched a sequence of day and night raids on London, using incendiaries as well as explosives. People sought shelter in Underground stations and elsewhere. The blackout was rigorously enforced. Boy Scouts sounding their bugles to announce the All Clear were most welcome. The air-raids continued until May, 1918, with twenty attacks on the capital. Compared with the blitz during the Second World War, casualties were very few, but the psychological effect was great.

Taking shelter during an air raid.

Even children were enlisted to help the war effort. They collected silver paper, wool, rags and even horse chestnuts. Some helped on farms or allotments, and they were encouraged to invest in War Savings. Schooling was disrupted in many areas, as the army took the buildings over or they were used as hospitals; the children sometimes had only a half-day at school.

Germany's all-out war on shipping caused a massive loss of boats; in April alone 526,000 tons went to the bottom, and this

214

was having a devastating effect on food supplies. To combat it, Lloyd George introduced the convoy system, whereby merchant ships sailed in groups protected by destroyer escorts.

The entry of America into the war in April 1917 brought new hope and when the first American soldiers marched through London in August there was a portent of eventual victory for the Allies.

1918 belatedly brought food rationing, first sugar, which was in extremely short supply as it had mostly come from German beet, then meat and bacon, butter, cheese and margarine. The meat ration was fifteen, bacon five, and butter or margarine four ounces each week. At once queues disappeared and there was a fair share for everyone. Only tea, cheese and bread remained unrestricted.

The great contribution of women to the war effort was rewarded by the Representation of the People Bill, granting the vote to women over thirty, as well as to nearly all men. This became law in June 1918.

However, there were more problems in France. Germany had concluded a peace treaty with revolutionary Russia, so she was free to divert the troops from that area to bulster those against the allies. She launched a formidable attack on the Western Front and the allies had to fall back. Many more casualties arrived at Charing Cross station. To counter this desperate situation, the age of conscription was raised to fifty-one. Added to war carnage, Spanish influenza arrived in Britain in June 1918. Three-quarters of the population were affected, and of these 150,000 died. This was to be added to the 745,000 British soldiers killed during the war.

The German advance spent themselves by July, and a massive British attack on 8 August using four hundred tanks caused the whole front to begin to collapse. In September and October Germany's allies, Bulgaria, Turkey and Austria surrendered. There was mutiny in the German navy and signs of revolution at home, so the generals began negotiations for an Armistice. Finally on 11 November 1918 at 11 am the Armistice was signed. In many future years the date and time were remembered: all work, including movement of buses, trams and trains, ceased for two minutes of remembrance. Crowds filled the streets and assembled outside Buckingham Palace and in Trafalgar Square and elsewhere. Again church bells rang and lights shone in the streets. Peace at last, but at what a price!

For most of the contributors to this book, who were barely in their teens by 1920, memories of politics are dominated by the events of the First World War.

War was to cause a great upheaval in our lives. Everything was very happy and peaceful until that eventful day, 4 August, 1914. In those days before radio, if there were any special news small boys ran down the streets yelling "Special news. Late extra." My father obviously heard the boy that day, and took me to the corner shop to buy a newspaper. He was a big man, over 6'2", and my little hand could just grasp one of his fingers. As we neared the shop I saw a placard with 'W A R' written in very large black letters. I had just begun to read and so said, "What does WAR mean, Daddy?", making it rhyme with car. I don't remember the answer, but was to discover all too soon!

Lance Corporal Jack Wilson, Christmas 1914.

It must have been only a few weeks later that my favourite uncle, mother's only brother Jack, came to visit us, and I could sense the tense atmosphere. When he picked me up to give me a kiss, as he always did, I found his clothing was quite different, all rough and scratchy, and it had a peculiar smell. I didn't realise he was wearing khaki and had come to say goodbye. That was the last time we saw him. The following year my father volunteered. As he had fought in the Boer War with Pagets Horse Brigade, he was offered a commission, but at that time he was on the staff of the London County Council and although they made up the salaries of other ranks, they did not do so for officers. With a wife and three children to support he felt he could not afford it so he became a sergeant in the Royal Army Service Corps and was stationed at Winchester. Later the LCC relaxed the rules and he was able to take a commission.

He was sent to Winchester, and the first thing he did was find a place there where we could all live, and soon we were off to Arbor View to join him. It was the first time I had been in a train

Kit Beard neé Wilson   Jack Wilson   Jessie Solkhon neé Wilson

and I was travel sick, but soon forgot that in all the excitement of our new home. Apart from the many army personnel around it seemed far from the air raids in London, and we enjoyed the peace of the countryside. Sadly this came to an end in 1916, when our father was given embarkation leave and he decided we should return to our own flat in London. There had been a lull in the air raids and he considered it would be safe, but we arrived just in time for a devastating period of day and night bombing. I think much of the noise was from the anti-aircraft guns on Wandsworth Common, and we found shrapnel in the garden, but I was terrified, and continued to have frequent nightmares of raids right up to the Second World War. It was not until many years later that I mentioned this to Mother and she told me that Kathleen, with whom I shared a double bed, often complained that I kept her awake at night because I was shaking so much! Although I was in London for the blitz, that was not nearly as bad as my memories of the First World War!

Fortunately for us, it was decided not to send Father's contingent to France at that time after all, and he was returned to Winchester. We went there with him, but in the meantime Mrs Beard had let two of her rooms to Mr Scrivener, a retired school master, so we did not have the use of the front parlour, with its assortment of stuffed birds in glass bowls and other exotic ornaments.

One day there was great excitement as a friend of my father's had made a model tank, and it was decided that Jessie should 'drive' it, whilst photographs were taken by the press. It was a new weapon of war!

217

Jessie Solkhon in model tank, 1917.

Then Father was moved to Bath, where he again found us accommodation. Shortly after our only brother was born, on 6 December,1917, my father's unit was eventually sent abroad, but to Italy, and by the time they disembarked the war there was almost over. Then came Armistice Day on 11 November, 1918, and soon after that we returned home.

There were also casualties on my father's side of the family.

First his brother William George, who was Chief Petty Officer and engine room artificer on HMS PEMBROKE, died on 3 January 1919 following an accident. According to the Imperial War Graves Commission cemetery register he was buried at All Saints, Nunhead, Kent. There was a German submarine in the vicinity at the time, so the ship was in darkness. When the order came to go below decks William was the last man down, so it was left to him to lower the hatch. In those days the ladder went straight down and in the darkness he slipped and fell. He developed a large lump on his stomach, but it was nearly a year before he could be put ashore and taken to Gillingham Hospital. Cancer of the stomach had developed and he was given only a few weeks to live. He decided he wanted to die at home so discharged himself and walked home. He was so weak he had to sit on a doorstep on his way. He died three weeks later. He left a widow, our aunt Isobel, and a daughter Connie.

Chief Petty Officer
William George Solkhon

Harry Solkhon

Registration Card

Only a few weeks later Father's younger sister Alice Josephine lost her husband, Regimental Sergeant Major Jim Hall, in the devastating influenza epidemic that followed the war. He had successfully nursed other members of the family through the illness but when he developed it himself was so exhausted that he succumbed.

The third casualty was John, the oldest of the eight children. He was so badly gassed in the war that he was advised to emigrate to Australia, where the climate would be more amenable. I never saw him and his

219

family. Father's other brothers Fred, Frank and Harry survived, as did his sisters Nellie and Jo.

[handwritten note]

9-1-19.

Writing pad etc. received
yesterday.
Parcel not yet to hand.
Am on Guard Tonight
but will write then if
I can manage it.
     Fondest love.
          Will
Hope all colds are better.

Photographs posted from France after the Armestice.

Left: Writing on back of photo:-

9-1-19
*Writing pad etc. received yester-
day. Parcel not yet to hand.
Am on Guard tonight. Will write
then if I can manage it
     - Fondest love W.H.
Hope all colds are better.*

Miss Connie Grant was born in 1907 and all her life she has been interested in children, first when she took them for Sunday School and then when she went to Furzedown College, a London County Council Teacher Training College. She became a much-loved Headmistress of Brookwood Primary School in Woking and is now enjoying a retirement in the attractive village of Chilworth, near Guildford, where 'children' still go to visit her. However, this was all to be in the future.

When I was seven my parents moved from Wimbledon Park to Knoll Road, Wandsworth, London, and I was enrolled at Swaffield School. Mrs Soper, mother of the great preacher and owner of our Knoll Road house decided I should not go to the Infants' department as they had a measles epidemic - quite a serious disease in those days. So I began in the 'Big' Girls and was there throughout the First World War. The Headmistress then was Miss Odam - an unfortunate name.

My teacher in 1918 decided all her class should learn the Te Deum, ready to give thanks to God when peace was declared on Armistice Day. So when 11 November arrived and we heard the exciting news that the war had ended, we had to return to school after lunch. My mother said that my father would take me up to town, to join in the celebrations that evening, but she insisted that I went back to school for the afternoon. I was really annoyed at having to go back just to sing the Te Deum, and obviously my face showed it, for on the way a strange gentleman stopped and said, "Why are you not happy, little girl? Don't you know the war is over?" I replied "I know, but I've got to go back to school to sing the Te Deum!"

Kathleen Hogg (née Robinson) remembers her childhood in London during the First World War.

I had just passed my sixth birthday when war was declared on the 4th August 1914. This had an immediate impact on my family as my father was an Army Reservist, and he was impatient for action. Every day when he came home from work he demanded to know whether his call-up papers had arrived; and although it must have been a distressing time for my mother it was a great relief to us all when he was finally called up on the 14th August.

The next time we met him was at Paddington Station, where we went to see him off to "somewhere in England". (Security meant we were forbidden to know where the men were sent.) He was among a number of men in uniform who broke ranks at the station, and we went into a restaurant for tea and cakes and a last farewell.

We saw little of him after that during the whole war. He had a few leaves from France, which were very exciting, culminating in his departure from Victoria Station where hundreds of soldiers and their families stood around till their train was due to go.

Once my mother took us children to a picture palace to cheer us up, but alas the movie (silent in those days) turned out to be a lurid drama about the Incas in South America, with a great pyramid of steps at the top of which was enacted a human sacrifice. We all hated it, and it was the last thing we wanted on such an unhappy occasion.

I suppose the first memory I have of the war, apart from my father's call-up, was the arrival of large numbers of Belgian refugees, who had crossed the Channel to escape from the Germans when they overran their country. They assembled in Earls Court, and during the next few weeks we would meet little groups of these strange people with their exotic language. This did not last long as they gradually disappeared, never to be seen again, and I imagine they had been dispersed over the country.

We soon became accustomed to the sight and sound of columns of recruits tramping through the main roads, to embark at one or other of the main London stations for training. They would burst into song every now and again - *"Tipperary"* was their favourite; housewives would run out to give the men sweets and cigarettes; and if my sister and I were out shopping with my mother we were allowed to delve into her bag for bars of chocolate which we ran to give to the recruits, and which they accepted gratefully with a smile and often a kiss.

Conscription was a long way off, hence the conversion of any empty shops into recruiting offices. These were manned by two or three men in uniform, and we often saw a sergeant filling the open doorway, and casting a beady eye on any civilians who happened to pass.

I don't know when the posters of Lord Kitchener began to appear. There was a huge one on a wall which I passed on my way to school, a picture of the Field Marshal with a finger pointing, and the words "Your country needs you" printed below. From whatever angle I saw it he always seemed to be pointing directly at me, a thoroughly unnerving experience for a small girl.

Air raids were much less frequent than in the Second World War and not so intense. The alarm was sounded by scouts blowing their whistles, and the "all clear" by blowing their bugles.

A neighbouring widow appeared at our door regularly as soon as she heard the air raid warning. She would sit with my mother, her fingers smothered with rings and clutching a deed box in which we understood she kept her precious documents, while we children played and giggled under the kitchen table until the "all clear" sounded.

In 1916, when my brother was about to be born, I was packed off to Bury St Edmunds to spend two months with my mother's younger sister and her family. Air raids were a nightly occurrence on the East Anglian coast, and we all slept in hammocks in the cellar, save for my uncle who spent most of his nights on duty as an air raid warden.

Quite early in the war I remember a tremendous succession of bangs which we thought must be a daylight raid. However it proved to be a huge explosion at an ammunition factory at Silvertown in East London, miles from where we lived, and the sound reverberated for many minutes.

On one memorable occasion a zeppelin was shot down over Cuffley by an airman named Leafe Robinson, who became quite celebrated for his feat. My sister, two years older and more daring than I, ran barefoot and wearing only her nightdress to the corner of the road, where she had a splendid view of the airship floating down in flames.

We had no radio in those days, and depended for information about the war from newspapers. Several editions were rushed out during the day, and boys would bring them round the streets. When there had been a big battle housewives would rush out to buy the papers, and carry them into their houses, shutting the doors behind them so ;that they could read alone the long casualty lists.

The first Christmas of the war was a very exciting one for us children. People were anxious to make the season as happy as possible for those of us whose fathers were on active service. They arranged parties with Christmas trees in the Town Hall, Church Halls and other meeting places. I remember particularly one very tall tree completely covered with beautifully dressed dolls, and the agony I suffered making a choice of one of these delectable creatures. The greatest treat of all was a visit to a pantomime at the Kings Theatre Hammersmith arranged by a kind anonymous benefactor. We gathered outside the theatre and were ushered into the two front rows of the dress circle. We were given bags of sweets, and lemonade and buns during the interval. I only remember one scene from the pantomime after all these years, but it is clear and vivid to this day. It was a farmyard, with a rustic bridge, at one end of which stood a milkmaid and at the other a young soldier in khaki uniform with puttees wound round his legs. He sang with great gusto "K-K-Katy, beautiful Katy, You're the only little girl that I adore, And when the m-m-moon shines over the cowshed, I'll be waiting at the k-k-kitchen door".

The parties continued as the war progressed; they were less lavish but still as enjoyable.

As the war years passed, and before rationing was introduced, many things were hard to come by. My mother would hear on the grape vine of a certain store which had received a supply of sugar, for instance, and we children were despatched to join a queue to collect a small ration which we carried home in triumph.

Life went on normally, and we accepted the war without question. We continued to have our breakfast of porridge made overnight in a steamer from oatmeal delivered to us regularly in 7lb jars from the Army & Navy Stores. Then we would bowl our wooden hoops round the square, where we exchanged greetings with the milkman as he trundled his cart. The metal cans rattled around the churn of milk, from which he filled them using a ladle and delivered them to the doorsteps.

Kathleen Hogg (neé Robinson) as May Queen at school in 1916.

After this we set off for school, which continued in its usual pattern of lessons, thirty to forty in a class and all exceedingly well-behaved. We still enjoyed our usual festivals - Empire Day, when we assembled in the school hall and sang patriotic songs like "Rule Britannia" and "Land of Hope and Glory". We also sang songs from the Dominions. My favourite was one from Canada - "The maple leaf our emblem dear ...."

May Day was a great occasion. Each class chose its own Queen, who in her turn chose two maids of honour. Then, wearing long white dresses and wreaths on their heads, and two maids bearing their trains, the Queens processed through the playground to a dais with the senior girl taking her place in the centre as May Queen. A maypole was erected and the classes took it in turn to dance round it, and with various country dances we entertained our parents and friends.

The school was opposite a park, part of which was given over to allotments for the duration of the war. The school had a large area where we worked in shifts, each class doing its share. I was not a natural gardener, but I remember dibbing holes for small lettuce plants. My greatest joy was at the end of the session buying some of the produce to take home. I particularly remember a spectacular cauliflower costing $2^1/2$p which I carried home with great pride, nibbling florets on the way.

Cookery lessons produced some unusual menus. Maize and lentils figured prominently; and I remember an ersatz spread, to take the place of butter and made from haricot beans.

Towards the end of the war when shortages were acute, Lady Rhondda (who I think must have been the wife of the minister of food) came to give us a talk about economies. She particularly stressed the need to chew every mouthful at least thirty times, an idea that appealed to us youngsters. She left us with a slogan "Chew! chew! chew!" and offered a prize for the best account of her lecture. My essay was chosen as the best, but alas Lady Rhondda died suddenly soon after her visit so I never received the promised prize.

The columns of men had by now changed in character. The young men were no longer strong and healthy-looking and raring to go, and the older men were even older. However the war was coming to an end, and it would be nice to think these conscripts never reached the front lines. By this time, too, bus and tram conductors had been replaced by conductresses. These women wore navy serge coats and skirts, and black stockings with black boots laced up to their calves. They proved very efficient and continued after the war.

Two things stand out in my memory as if they happened only yesterday. One was the chilling sight of women of all ages going home from their morning shift at the munitions factory by the Thames. Their faces and necks, their foreheads, hands and forearms, every inch of exposed skin, were all bright yellow. In my extreme youth I found this more horrifying than any other wartime experience. I tried to avoid meeting them, knowing approximately when they would be around, but there were times when I forgot and I would turn a corner and find them coming towards me in weary groups, always unnaturally quiet and all uniformly yellow.

The other outstanding memory is of being in a group of friends outside the school gates returning from our midday meal - there were no school dinners in those days. Our chattering was suddenly halted by the dreaded hum of enemy aircraft, and we stood silent and still gazing up at a large flight in square formation moving above us across the sky. We watched spellbound - until suddenly we realised the risk we were taking. We fled into the school and flung ourselves face downwards on the classroom floor where we remained till the "all clear" sounded.

We never heard that any bombs were dropped that morning and as far as I know it was the only day-time raid in our area. It was, indeed, unlike a raid, more a farewell flypast, as the war was coming to its end and I do not remember any more night raids.

The end came on the 11th November 1918, and the women and children were in a fever to see their husbands and sons and fathers again.

Miraculously my father came through the whole of the war without the smallest injury. To our delight he was awarded the Military Medal, and was mentioned in despatches - which pleased him much more.

The stress of those long years, however, had taken their toll. He had joined the ranks in 1914 with a thatch of chestnut hair, but when he finally reached home in the spring of 1919 he was almost completely bald!

Mrs. Dorothy Taylor was brought up in Widnes, but now lives in Morden, Surrey. Her grandfather was a well-known West Bank man who owned the Gandy Boatyard. Boat repairs were carried out there on the dredgers which sailed up the river Mersey. Dorothy shares memories her mother, Ethel, has of her brother Edward's return to Widnes after the disastrous battle of the Somme.

My uncle Edward was a corporal in the King's Royal Rifle Corps. He was one of the lucky ones as the rest of his batallion was practically wiped out in the battle of the Somme.

He came straight from the trenches across the Channel to board the train to London at Dover. Then he travelled on to Runcorn station and over the old Transporter Bridge to Widnes. When he walked up Mersey Road all the neighbours came out to greet him. He said, "I'm not fit to shake hands with these people". He was caked in mud, so Mother's sister Lucy had a boiler of hot water in the shed and the old zinc bath ready for him to take off his clothes and have a bath. Then Lucy washed his uniform and clothes to make him feel more comfortable.

Edward had to return to the front and managed to survive until Armistice Day. After the war he became a ship's carpenter there at his father's boatyard.

Mother has an amusing memory of Trinity Methodist Chapel, West Bank, Widnes, which she attended. One week the organist, a very smartly dressed man, started to play the organ at the beginning of the service, but there was no sound at all. In those days there was a second man in the basement, where there was a pipe connected to the organ. This man operated the bellows that circulated air round the organ. When someone went to investigate the problem it was found that the man was fast asleep!

Memories of the war years were not so pleasant for May Goodman.

I was nine years old when the First World War began. There were no air-raid shelters and, as far as I know, no ration books. We seemed to queue for bread, meat, potatoes, nearly everything.

Early in the war the munitions factory at Silvertown, near Woolwich, London, blew up. The explosion was heard many miles away and the blaze lit up a very wide area. A considerable number of civilian lives were lost. Of course there was no radio or television, so first-hand news was lacking.

The warning we received of a potential air raid was a policeman on a bicycle ringing his bell and wearing a placard saying, *'Take Cover'*. In our area there was one anti-aircraft gun placed on One Tree Hill, so called because Queen Elizabeth the first planted the tree, so the story is told. There were plenty of searchlights (long beams of light) in the sky. One bomb was dropped at the gates of Dulwich park, the crater no more than 8 to 10 feet wide and about 3 feet deep. One of the raiding Zeppelins (a huge airship) was brought down at Cuffley in Essex. This I saw happen, a direct hit and it burst into flames and broke in half. I can clearly see that picture to this day.

As the war continued we school children wrote letters to the 'Tommies' at the front line in France, and knitted socks and balaclava helmets. My pen friend was a Mr Thomas. He did reply to my letters but eventually I heard from Mrs Thomas that he had been killed.

When the war ended in 1918 I was thirteen years old. It was a great time of celebration when the armistice was signed at Versailles, but millions of young men had been killed and maimed during those four years.

Cyril Davies' schooldays were affected by the outbreak of the First World War.

My early school days occurred at an eventful time, as war was declared with calamitous effects. It was a small school run by the School Board for London and was adjacent to the *Pavilion* cinema in Clapham High Street. There were no sirens or police cars touring around in those days. What I do remember is gripping my mother's hand as I accompanied her to help carry the shopping. A policeman with a flat cap, no helmet, came cycling along the curbside shouting out, 'Take cover. Take cover', and on his back was a piece of white cardboard about one foot square, with an improvised piece of string round his throat to represent a handle for this card. On it was hastily scrawled the words, 'Take cover. Air raid'. At the same time he rang his bicycle bell continuously. Young mothers gathered up their children as there was no time to lose, and directed them into adjacent shops, doorways, basements or anywhere that would provide some cover.

My arm was nearly pulled out of its socket by Mother, who was seeking cover for us, whilst I was gaping into the air to see what was coming over. Uncannily it did, because we had hardly reached the foot of some basement steps when to my mystification I saw droning about a hundred feet up, following the tramline course, a grey fabric-covered dirigible, which was a Zeppelin. It seemed only a few seconds before there was a terrific bang. They had dropped a bomb on to Clapham Road Station some hundred yards ahead of us. As it proceeded towards Stockwell, I remember Mother cuffing my ear to get a move on towards our home.

When I left school I was coached privately and then eventually obtained a job at a solicitor's office at Bloomsbury off High Holborn. From there I moved to a clerical position in Cornwall, where I now live.

The First World War affected Catherine Field's family in various ways.

My father was a carpenter but things were very difficult for him during the war, as bombs were devastating many houses and it was useless to rebuild whilst the air raids continued. So he had no choice but to get work in a munitions factory. As we lived quite close to it we were the object of many air raids, but escaped a direct hit. When the war was over he returned to cabinet making at Southall.

During the war I joined the WVS and had the job of organising offices where people could come to make enquiries about casualties. It was a very grim time between 1914 and 1918. Much food, including potatoes and sugar, was in short supply, and before rationing was introduced I had to leave home at 6 am to join the queue outside the butchers. You did not say, "I would like half a leg of lamb", or whatever, but just took what they offered you. With the shortage of food it is not surprising that members of the family went down with TB. Rationing later saved people who were not rich enough to pay for what they wanted: the lesson was learnt by the Government and before the Second World War ration books were prepared in good time.

Bill Hogg can well remember the First World War.

We had ack ack guns nearby, and when the zeppelins flew over it was very noisy. There were casualties when a tram was hit. The Germans also tried to bomb the railway near us. One day my father, who was a special constable, noticed that one of the street lamps had been left on, so he climbed up and put it out.

Meat was very scarce and we had to queue for most food. Rationing was not introduced until later in the war.

As with many families during the war years, Mary Blott experienced the pain of a brother being notified as missing during the battles in France.

My eldest brother worked in a bank in the city, so he joined up fairly soon after war was declared. He was trained as an officer and was sent to France in 1915. Eighteen months later my parents had a telegram to say 'Lieut. Cook was missing, presumed killed.' This was happening all around to friends and acquaintances, and we learned to live with it. Life had to go on, but it cast a heavy gloom at the time. Then my younger brother joined the navy.

Music was mostly popular war songs like Tipperary, and with the blackout there were no gatherings until after the war, when we started going to dances.

In spite of the war, my parents gave me a very happy childhood. Then eighteen months later we had a letter from my eldest brother, who was a POW in Germany. The relief and happiness were unbelievable! He returned home in January 1919, when all who survived came back to England. It was a bitterly cold winter and we had nights skating on the Long Water at Hampton Court. We made bonfires on the bank and roasted potatoes - no other food was available, but we thought it was utopia.

Kenneth Jones experienced a number of German raids during the First World War.

At the outbreak of war in August 1914 Alleyn's school lined up to see the Camberwell Gun Brigade, with guns, on its way to France.

Zeppelin raids began and an anti-air crafty gun on a lorry ran up and down the road. We saw the first Zeppelin brought down over London, and the following day hundreds of people converged on Potters Bar to see the remains. My brother, who was working at Lloyds, was among them and was run over by a bus in London. He was taken to St Bartholomew's Hospital, where he made a full recovery from many injuries. He fought in both World Wars.

During school holidays we went to relatives at Lowestoft. There were Zeppelins overhead during the night and we went down to the cellars. Later some of our relatives were in Lowestoft when it was bombarded by German cruisers. One holiday when my mother was in the Royal Free Hospital I went to relatives in Birmingham. During my first night there was a raid by German planes.

We spent a night in the Tube (an underground passage) at Christ's Hospital when seven Zeppelins switched off their engines and drifted over the school, finally crashing in France. At home during the holidays the German raids changed to Gotha planes and a man was killed in Dulwich College Lodge. Mr Gregory, music master at the girls' school at Hertford, was killed during a raid on that town.

Nancy Ramsey has some isolated memories of life during the war.

A number of girls when they left school went to work in Cox's Bank. This was somewhere in the west and was much favoured, I believe, by young army subalterns. Cause and effect?

Bolingbroke hospital was, at least in part, turned into a military hospital, the 3rd London General. I remember one Christmas a party of us went out carol singing to provide comforts for the wounded there.

The assistant school caretaker, Taylor by name, left to go into the army. On at least one occasion the school sent him a parcel of comforts.

Mr Arthur G. Room now lives in Rustington, Sussex, but was brought up in Sutton, Surrey. He remembers the First World War.

I was born in 1903. I shall always recall the fourth of August, 1914, when I was eleven. It was a Bank holiday weekend, and the day war was declared. I went for my first country walk with my parents from Dorking to the Silent Pool at Albury, and loved it. After this I was taken on many country walks by my parents, who taught me to appreciate the countryside.

In the Spring of 1917 I went to the Sutton Secondary School for a two year period. At that time education was at a premium, with very little sport. Playing fields were turned into allotments in the 'Dig for victory' campaign. On a quiet summer's evening we could stand in the garden and hear the gunfire in France. Soldiers were billeted throughout the area. During the war I saw Croydon Aerodrome developed. It was within cycling distance of my home and I was lucky enough to see one of the first Handley Page 0400 bomber aircraft.

Miss Connie Grant was born in 1906 and all her life she has been interested in children, first when she took them for Sunday School and then when she went to Furzedown College, a London County Council Teacher Training College. She became a much-loved Headmistress of Brookwood Primary School in Woking and is now enjoying retirement in the attractive village of Chilworth, near Guildford, where children still go to visit her. However, this was all in the future.

When I was seven my parents moved from Worcester Park to Knoll Road, Wandsworth, London, and I was enrolled at Swaffield School. Miss Florence Skinner decided I should not go to the Infants department as they had a measles epidemic - quite a serious disease in those days. So I began in the 'Big' Girls, and was there throughout the war. The Headmistress was Miss Odam - an unfortunate name!

Miss Skinner decided all her class should learn the Te Deum, ready to give thanks to God for Armistice Day. So when 11 November 1918 arrived and we heard the exciting news that the war had ended, we had to return to school after going home for lunch. I was really annoyed at having to go back just to sing the Te Deum, and obviously my face showed it, for on the way a strange gentleman stopped and said, "Why are you not happy, little girl? Don't you know the war is over?" I replied, "I know, but I've got to go back to school to sing the Te Deum!"

Doris Russell has some poignant memories of the war.

Many boys at the age of twelve during the war had a simple test at school to assess their skill at writing and arithmetic. If they passed they went to work on local farms to replace the men sent to join the army in France. Very few returned.

The Canadian soldiers had a soup kitchen underneath the Museum in Egerton Park, Bexhill, and gave free soup to children and the poor during the First World War. My outstanding memory of this period is of the Army veterinary surgeons and buyers walking up and down the streets of Bexhill, looking for strong, young, fit horses suitable for war work. The only horses not bought for the army were too old or mares in foal. It was a very sad sight to see horses taken out of their van, trap or cart, unharnessed and taken away to the railway station. Their harness was thrown into the vehicle, and the carter or owner was left to get the vehicle to the nearest stables or yard for collection. Very few of these horses were brought back from France after the war.

War had no direct impact on Jessie Young, living as she was in a remote part of north-east Scotland.

I was eight years old when the First World War began. Young men from our village disappeared, returning like strangers dressed in khaki. My oldest brother was among them, and a sister went to work in a munitions factory. As time went on another brother joined the Navy. War to us younger children meant new spellings, such silly words that did not look right: sergeant, lieutenant, camouflage, and many more. Black-out was not as important then as it was in the Second World War, but as our church was on a hill the evening service was held in the afternoon during the winter.

War seemed very remote to us children, but sweets disappeared from the shops and we had to spend our pocket money on locust beans, which were sweet for a minute then tasted just like wood. Horrible! Naturally we sensed that war was serious on hearing of lads being killed, which happened in most families. One of my uncles and a cousin were among them, and my brother was wounded. This shortened his service as a soldier but probably saved his life.

My father did his war work at Scapa Flow for several years, so we were all involved.

The outbreak of war in 1914 caused changes in Elspeth Burns family life.

My father was a keen Territorial and responsible for enrolling the men who volunteered in droves. Most of them joined the Argyll and Sutherland Highlanders. I remember one morning my father came downstairs in his kilt and my sister, in great delight, said, "Oh, Daddy, ooz got bare knees like me!"

In 1915 my father, like many older officers and men, was seconded to the 23rd battalion The Rifle Brigade and sent to India, while the regulars serving there came home to go to Flanders. We did not see my father for four-and-a-half years but we always wrote to him and at last he did return, to find his 'wee girls' had grown into school girls. I think adjusting to home life was quite difficult for him and many others.

During the war years Granny Macpherson had died and uncle John came to live with us. Hillside was a Red Cross Hospital. One of the patients was an Englishman called 'Flowers', and on Sunday evenings they loved to sing the hymn:

> 'Birds and beasts and flowers
> Soon will be asleep'!

Mother often gave tea to wives and children who came to visit the patients - not easy with rationing.

Noreen Beaumont reveals details of life during the First World War which are contained in letters kept by her mother, Norah Hook. Some were written by his relatives to Leslie 'Lewie' Stuart, who was Norah's first love. After he joined the army she did not hear from him again. The following year her future husband, John O'Donoghue, began to write to her of his experiences.

A letter to LEWIE Stuart in York, 29 May 1915 from his sister in Edinburgh.

Dear Lewie

Just a note to let you know that I received your letter this morning and wondered what was wrong when it was addressed to me. However I was not long in discovering the reason. We all got quite a shock but were not really surprised. Mother has evidently thought of it before but never said anything. We were all amused at the Regiment you have chosen. They are recruiting for it here. We have also a few battns. of them stationed in different parts of the town. They are really a fine set of men. Have you written to Alec? We have had two letters from him today. He expects to leave Monday night or Tuesday. He seems quite pleased at the prospect. Jim has been threatening to go, but as yet has made no move. Bob has been in France for three weeks now. Dave and Bill are still at Queensferry.

When are you going away and where will you be stationed? Is it Plymouth? Mother was wondering if you are sending your belongings home, or just keeping them in York. I suppose you will let us know everything in good time, so I will not ask any more questions in case you get tired answering them. Mother will have to see about your insurance when you are once settled. She is quite pleased at your going and I am sure we all are and only wish you success. Charlie says you will not have so much time now to brush your hair and wash your face as previous.

I will now close hoping to hear from you soon again, if there is anything I can do for you.

With love from us all,

Your loving sister, Liz.

There followed a letter from their mother, postmarked 1 June 1915, from 15 Atholl Terrace, York.

Dear Lewie,

I was just waiting to get your letter, before I would write to you. I cannot say but I am sorry that you have to go, but still think you have done right. I know of a good few here, who won't allow their sons to go, and yet other mothers' sons have to fight for them. I think that is the proper way to see it, you will do for others what others have done for us at home, and I trust you and Alec will both be spared to come back. I had such a nice letter from Alec yesterday. He wrote me whenever he got your letter, telling me not to worry that you were sure to get on all right, still, my boy you will find this work a little different from your usual but you will just peg along as you used to do, and always do your best. Poor Alec has had a hard enough time of it, but he is always to the front in the best of health and spirits and he is with a lot of nice lads. I am glad you are sending home your things, for we will look after them all right. You will give me all particulars after as I will have to tell your society. Are you getting any allowance off your office? Most of the large places here are giving their employees something, some of them all their pay. I wish you had been coming nearer us, instead of going farther away, but we will just be looking forward to seeing you shortly, and I am proud you will wear the kilt and represent your own country. I have no news to give you but hope you will write again soon. I must just again wish you the best of luck from

Your loving mother.

P.S. Charlie is proud of his two soldier brothers and only wishes he were big enough to go, though I hardly think he realises what that means.

Although born in the west of Ireland, John O'Donoghue was liable for military service as a subject of the British Crown. He enlisted in the Army Pay Corps in London in November 1914 when he was twenty-one years old.

A bomb-net over York is the ostensible theme of John's first letter to his new-found friend, Norah, for he is now billetted at York. It is May 1916.

Dear Miss Hook,

Regret atmospheric conditions did not permit my seeing you on Friday, and hope; that same did not cause you any inconvenience.

You will, however, be glad to hear that certain authorities are 'thinking out' a scheme whereby they can cover the whole of York with one large umbrella, which on the very few occasions when the sun shines may be changed to a sun shade, and at other times may be used as a bomb-net.

As the censor will not allow a deluge of correspondence on the subject of bombs I refrain from further comment thereon...

After this Heath-Robinson-type humour, John asks her to meet him at a certain cinderpath, and concludes,

I am

Yours very sincerely

John O'Donoghue Sgt.

In January 1917 a post card depicting a summer scene of white cliffs, topped by green turf on which sits a lone maiden drooping under a large white hat, arrives from Folkestone. A pencilled message informs Norah,

"Have arrived here. Awaiting embarkation. Will write as soon as an address is possible."

There is something strangely shaky about the writing, besides envelope as well as letter being inscribed in pencil, and in the arrival postmarked 10 June 1917. It is, however, completely legible, including three kisses following his signature.

The letters concerning John's wounding in France and subsequent discharge are contained in the chapter on Health.

His discharge certificate adds that he was first posted to the Army Pay Corps, also previously served in 87th Training Reserve Battn. (probably in Autumn 1916 when he went to Pocklington for Active Service Training) and Northumberland Fusiliers. He was, however, discharged from the Royal Dublin Fusiliers. I have heard elsewhere that the regiment was so severely depleted that it amalgamated with the Northumberland Fusiliers and ceased a separate existence.

I recall an anecdote which John recounted to me many times with great glee.

He and another wounded soldier had left the main thoroughfare O'Connell Street and were proceeding down an alley (presumably returning to the Mater Hospital). At this time the slums of Dublin were notorious as being the worst in Europe. *"Poor women wearing shawls were standing around"*, John would say. In later versions he described them more frankly as prostitutes. One woman identified the approaching couple and vilified them.

Noreen Beaumont's father John O'Donaghue in short jacket with right arm bandaged.

"Look at yez!" she shouted. "Look at the state of yez! Isn't that what comes of fighting for the Brits?" Suddenly a second woman burst forth from a doorway with a cry of "Up the Dubs!" (The Dublin Fusiliers), clawed at the shawl of the vilifier and set to pulling out handfuls of her hair. The first woman retaliated and in the ensuing melee John and comrade made their escape.

The war was now over and John discharged from the army. He was issued with a ration book at York food office in April 1919. Photographs show him sitting in a boat on the River Ouse near Poppleton, York, or standing in white flannels manoeuvring an oar. Others reveal him holding a bicycle in company with cousins of Norah in rural Lincolnshire. He looks well fed and well dressed, and well pleased with himself. The friendship of Norah and the hospitality of her family are helping him in that awkward gap between leaving the rough protection of the army and finding work in a country not yet back to peace-time employment.

Norah coached him for an examination which he passed with success. He became a civil servant in an executive capacity and took up his post in London in about 1920.

Maidie Stokes and her mother suffered some of the traumas of the First World War.

My mother became pregnant and had her second daughter, Joan, in September, 1915. My father had to leave without seeing her or knowing how mother was. My cousin Mary and her mother came to stay with us, because her husband was in Gallipoli. Father was away a long time. The ship had been turned into an armed cruiser and had been to Suez collecting troops, etc.

One day Mary's Mother heard the *Echo* boy calling out as he walked down the road. This was the only way we heard news in those days when we had no radio. He was calling out "IVERNIA torpedoed in Gallipoli". We tried to prevent Mother hearing him. We waited anxiously for months for news, then one day there was a telegram. Mother took me on her lap. She was crying and showed me the telegram which said, "Safe. Phipps." Dated January 1917, Crete. A few months later Father arrived home in a mixture of clothing. Apparently he had dived into the water and was picked up by a British ship and taken to Crete.

He never mentioned his journey home. I know he would not trust life boats and said he would dive into the sea and swim. I think it was a small ship which picked him up. He had help from a monastery with clothing, as he was wearing some women's clothes when he returned home.

Mr Inglis Gundry, is still living at Mill Hill in north west London, near the school where he was a pupil and later librarian for some years. He has vivid memories of the ending of the First World War.

My first term at boarding school happened to be in 1918, so I was a new boy of not more than two months' standing when the Armistice occurred on 11 November.

As far as I remember, we were not told about the Armistice until lunch-time, but then we got more and more excited. It was an ordinary afternoon and at that season of the year games preceded work, so we were free till 4 pm. Somebody suggested a march round the very attractive countryside, so we soon formed ourselves into a procession which took the course of the 'Six' or some other well-known route. We made as much noise as we could, shouting and singing to let everybody know we were celebrating the occasion.

When we returned we expected to be rewarded with a half-holiday. Had not the war lasted four years and the Old Boys decimated?

I shall never forget the actual scene that confronted us! The elderly Headmaster, his shock of white hair flowing in the breeze, strode across the loggia separating the School House from the block of classrooms, ringing the bell as much as to say: "Cross me if you dare." A great shout of disappointment welled up from the school ranks. There was near mutiny. But the Headmaster got his way in the end. It was understandable. Perhaps he had suffered too much hearing of his sixth-formers, as they had been only a year ago, mown down at the front. But the older boys among us had suffered, too, and they had been suddenly saved from almost certain death.

12. SCOUTS, GUIDES
AND OTHER CLUBS

By 1900 the Boys Brigade, founded by William Smith in 1883, was well established. It catered for boys over twelve and had a Christian as well as a military background. Boys were taught drill and there was also a weekly Bible class, but other activities included educational classes, physical training and games. Camping became very popular.

When Baden-Powell returned from the Boer War in 1902, he found that his booklet *Aids to Scouting* was being used by the Boys Brigade and others, so he rewrote it in a more suitable form for boys. His original intention was that Scouts and the Boys Brigade should be integrated as one unit, but there were fundamental differences and so many boys not connected with the Boys Brigade wanted to become Scouts, that Baden-Powell left the army in 1910 to take charge of them. Girls were not to be left out and soon there was provision for them as Guides. First it was Baden-Powell's sister Agnes who took charge, but later it was his wife Olive who became Chief Guide

Cubs and Brownies naturally followed on, and all are still flourishing. Many older people still speak glowingly of times they had as Cubs and Scouts, Brownies and Guides, and what a difference it made to their lives.

THE BIRTH OF THE BOY SCOUT MOVEMENT

Robert Stephenson Smyth Baden-Powell was born in 1857 and had already had a distinguished career before the turn of the century, but it was his defence of Mafeking during the siege in the Boer War that brought him national acclaim.

It was his experience in training Scouts at this time, as well as the many tracking games he had played whilst at school, that laid the foundation for Boy Scouts. He rewrote *Aids To Scouting*, which originated at Mafeking, to make it suitable for the boys, and in 1907 held the first camp at Brownsea Island for twenty boys, ten from the Boys Brigade and ten from the sons of friends at

Preparatory or Public Schools. This breaking down of class distinction was unknown in those days. They were divided into patrols of five, with the senior boy in each being the patrol leader. It was B-P's personality that gave life to the movement. As P.W. Everett recalled:

> 'I can see him still as he stands in the flickering light of the fire - an alert figure, full of the joy of life, now grave, now gay, answering all manner of questions, imitating the call of birds, showing how to stalk a wild animal, flashing out a little story, dancing and singing round the fire, pointing a moral, not in actual words, but in such an elusive and yet convincing way that everyone present, boy or man, was ready to follow him wherever he might lead.'

Lord Baden-Powell (Robert)

After the camp, Baden-Powell issued a twopenny pamphlet called *The Boy Scout Scheme*, giving details of his methods, and soon many patrols and troops came into being.

Scouting For Boys by B-P (Lieut.Gen. Baden-Powell, CB) was published in six parts at fourpence each, the first in January 1908. The first complete edition published in May that year cost two shillings. At first there was no definite uniform and it was not until 1910 that the age of admission was fixed at eleven to eighteen. That year B-P resigned from the Territorials, so that he could devote more time to Scouting.

Already there was keen interest overseas, and in January 1912 B-P set off on a world tour so that he could study the problems of Scouting in the Dominions and Colonies. His tour also included China, Japan and the United States. It was whilst sailing on the *Arcadian* to the West Indies that he met Miss Olave St.Clair Soames, who was to become his wife and the mother of their three children, Peter (1913), Heather (1915) and Betty (1917).

The movement was growing apace and on 4 September 1912 10,000 Boy Scouts gathered at the Crystal Palace, where B-P took the salute as Chief Scout. It was there that he discovered a small band of girls, wearing Scout hats and scarves with their dresses. When B-P asked who they were, the leader replied that they were the Wolf Patrol of the Girl Scouts and they wanted to do Scouting like the boys. Following this, Girl Guides soon came into being, with Olave Baden-Powell a Chief Guide.

In January 1913 the Baden-Powell family sailed from Southampton for Algeria; beginning at Biskra they set out on a tramping camp amongst the desert mountains. When he returned he was soon involved in work again. As Master of the ancient Mercers' Company he attended meetings connected with its educational and benevolent trusts and funds; the position also meant he became chairman of the Governors of St. Paul's School, formerly attended by three of his brothers so especially close to his heart.

The Exhibition of Scoutcraft at Birmingham in 1913 for the first time enabled members of the public to asses the valuable work done by the movement. The following April there was an important conference at Manchester and in June Queen Alexandra inspected 11,000 London Boy Scouts. For the first time the juniors, the Wolf Cubs, joined in the rally. Then, sadly, the outbreak of the First World War meant that many of these ordinary activities had to be left in abeyance.

On 1 August 1914, B-P offered the services of the Boy Scouts to the War Office and soon they were doing much of the work later done by auxiliary forces. They acted as messengers in Government offices and elsewhere, patrolled railway lines, guarded bridges and helped in hospitals. Later they were used in the collection of waste paper and other salvage, harvesting, and as buglers to sound the 'All Clear' after air raids. Sea Scouts provided a valuable coastguard service. Many Scoutmasters volunteered to join the army, but patrol leaders continued the work, sometimes assisted by women, and most of the them did very good work.

Although B-P paid a number of visits to France he was not engaged on active service: his work with Scouts was considered to be of greater importance. It was in 1915 that Olave B-P became Guide Commissioner for Sussex and the following year she was appointed Chief Guide Commissioner. This established the importance of Girl Guides, and in 1918 she was elected Chief Guide.

Once war had ended, B-P was able to devote his attention to the building up of the movement. This included putting the training of Scoutmasters on a permanent footing; deciding what to do for older Scouts; and the expansion of the movement through the Empire and the world. The first was dealt with by the acquisition of Gilwell Park, near Chingford, which was away from any main road and bounded on one side by Epping Forest. A pioneer camp was held there at Easter 1919 by some Rover Scouts from East London, and shortly afterwards parties of local Scouts began work clearing the overgrown gardens and grounds. It was formally opened on 25 July and that September the first training camp for Scoutmasters was held under Francis Gidney.

To solve the problem of older Scouts, the Rover Scout scheme was evolved. Service and the general principles in the ideas underlying the orders of chivalry were the foundations of the order. It included service to self, by getting himself established in a career, to develop his health in outdoor activities like hiking and camping; and to work energetically at his employment as his contribution to the national welfare

Then there was service to the Scout movement, which for many meant becoming Scouters. Finally there was to be service to the community. It was not until 1922 that B.-P. published the book *Rovering to Success*, covering the many problems of young manhood, and it was found very helpful by men outside as well as inside the Scout movement.

It was in 1920 that the first international Jamboree was held at Olympia, London. There was a camp in the Old Deer Park, Richmond, to sleep some 6,000 Scoutmasters and Scouts, with many countries taking part. It was towards the end of the Jamboree that B.-P. was acclaimed as Chief Scout of the World. At the service on the opening Sunday the Archbishop of York (Dr. Lang) preached to a congregation of 8,000 Scouts. His final words were:

The World is so Full of a Number of Things.

AND this is one of them.
It is the end of the day at Little Mynthurst Farm, and we are just taking the goats for a walk, an occupation which allows not a little time for leisurely reflection ; so while " Mrs. Brown " and " Roughton " are devoting their attention to the green things of the roadside, swallowing with expressions of astounding enjoyment the most thorny delicacies that the hedge can produce, there is ample opportunity for reviewing the events of the day in their order.

*   *   *   *   *

" There are some Scouts coming to-day," shouted Peter this morning, as he descended the oak staircase in the full insignia of a Scout, complete with haversack and billy can.

" And some Girl Guides," amended Heather (who always has the last word) struggling with the Chief Guide's cockaded hat, which would topple over her eyes and obliterate the view.

Betty murmured something incoherent, but she was in *mufti* and, therefore, spoke with less authority on these matters. But from the depths of her perambulator she smiled in the superior manner of one who knows all.

Then the avalanche descended (which is merely another way of saying that the Headquarters Staff arrived), and the quiet old courtyard rang with cheery greetings as the Chiefs received their sixty guests, and we sorted ourselves for lunch in the dining-room and in the barn.

There were other good things besides food in the barn, for everything on the walls and in the cases round the room has a thrilling story attached—if the Chief can be caught to tell it.

You always have to work for your living at Little Mynthurst, and after lunch the real hard work of the day began. Everybody had to take his share in one or other of the fearful and wonderful competitions which began to take shape in various parts of the garden.

For the long-limbed, " nail-planting " offered itself, wherein the competitor must go forward on his hands from a given spot, plant a nail in the grass, and return to the starting point without moving his feet.

For the fleet of foot a race along the straight road outside the gate ; for the steady of nerve a balancing game on rocking stepping stones ; for the straight of eye a nut-throwing stunt ; for the energetic and thirsty a " sipping race " ; for the still more energetic a tug-of-war—or rather several tugs-of-war. Indeed, tugging and warring was so popular that it might have gone on for ever if the rope had not had enough and given way.

Thus did everyone perform with cheerful countenance the most gruesome tasks that were set before him, while the instigators criticised from a safe distance. Only Heather and Peter, being under age, received special exemption.

But there were other rewards than virtue when the job was done, and they were worth some effort, being paintings and sketches by the Chief Scout. There was also a concert for which we sat on cushions in the cool drawing-room to listen to recitations and songs, and—best of all—to the Chief Guide's fiddle.

Tea in the barn and in the garden completed the cooling and soothing process, to be followed by a paper chase and a personally conducted tour by the Chief round the museum before train-time.

Then we sat with our hosts on the friendly lawn in front of the house and basked in sunshine and brotherliness ; and the babies brought themselves and their chairs and their faithful steeds Sharker and Jonathan, from whom they are loath to part. Peter, carrying out his Scout Law about kindness to animals, had thoughtfully tied a bunch of feathers round Jonathan's nose " to keep the sun from hurting his eyes."

Then the party melted away, the flag was unfurled, and the sun went down, leaving in its train more golden glory than ever the hand of Midas created to curse.

And Lady Baden-Powell remembered that the dogs and the goats had not been for their evening stroll.

*   *   *   *   *

The goats at last have finished their supper, and the Chief has returned from a final expedition to the station. The babies have gone to bed, and the doves to roost, and silence reigns once more in the old garden.

To-morrow to work again—but the memory of this sunny day will outlive many duller jobs and " plain days."

We have a heated discussion as to who has enjoyed the party the most—and the Chief swears that he has.

There are some occasions when even the Chief Scout's statements have to be disputed   ANON.

'You are now a great power, which can make for peace. I exhort you to take this as your aim - the bringing into existence of the peace of the world. This is my message to you, Boy Scouts. Keep the trust.'

B.-P.'s talk to the assembly ended with the words:

'If it be your will, let us go forth from here fully determined that we will develop among ourselves and our boys that comradeship, through the world-wide spirit of the Scout brotherhood, so that we may help to develop peace and happiness in the world and goodwill among men. Brother Scouts, answer me. Will you join in this endeavour?'

The answer was a resounding 'Yes': then B.-P. was picked up and carried across the arena, to wave after wave of cheering. So the Jamboree came to a close, but it was to be the first of many, as the Scout and Guide movements grew and developed.

243

Peter   Betty   Heather   Baden-Powell.
September 1920.

Mr. Frank V. Smith OBE was born in 1906 at Sparkhill, near Birmingham. He had a distinguished career, including that of technical consultant to the Board of Trade, where he was concerned with the setting up of several new factories in South Wales. When he was young he spent many happy hours with Cubs and Scouts. He now lives at a Retirement Home in Bovey Tracey.

I very much enjoyed Cubs and Scouts, where we played games and I learned to tie knots and other useful things. I was a Sixer in the Cubs. Friends from the church had property at Droitwich, where I was able to camp on my own as well as with the Cubs and Scouts. We used to hire a van for transport, which took our kitbags and tents as well as boys.

I was a good cook and enjoyed making stew and porridge. Of course we used a wood fire and all the wood had to be collected, as was milk and water. It was the Vicar of St. Margaret's Church, where I was a chorister for nine years, who taught us to swim. Later I was in the choir at St. Martin's-in-the-Fields, one of the first to broadcast. That was in the time of Dick Sheppard.

As Lord Baden-Powell was to Boy Scouts, so was his wife, Olave Soames, to be for the Girl Guide movement. Yet her early life would hardly seem to have been one that would equip her for this demanding role. Like many other children of wealthy parents in the Edwardian era, she was brought up to a life of ease and luxury. The household included many servants to take care of every domestic chore, and in her early years there was a governess for the children. Formal education was not considered necessary for Olave and her sister, Auriol, but her brother Arthur was to go to prep. school and thence to Eton.. She considered he was spoilt! Yet the girls learned many skills. They handled boats on the lake at Renishaw, played tennis, went riding and swimming as well as going for long walks; all pursuits that helped to make her strong and healthy, ready for the vigorous life ahead. There was also an active social life, with visits to theatres and concerts in London.

It was in 1912 that there was to be a dramatic change in her life. On 3rd January Olave and her father set sail from Southampton on the *RMS Arcadian* en route for a holiday in Jamaica. Some Scouts were waiting to greet their beloved founder when he arrived on the boat train from London to embark on the same ship. For the first time Olave saw B.-P., the hero of Mafeking, and two days later she was introduced to Lieut. General Sir Robert Baden-Powell They met again at the Captain's table for dinner. Immediately the two were aware of a bond between them. In spite of the wide difference in ages, it was love at first sight.

The romance was kept secret on board and it was not until 20 September that the engagement was officially announced. They were married quietly on 30 October, before the announced date, to avoid the crowds. They had only a week's honeymoon at Mullion Cove, before B.-P. had to attend the many Scout functions booked ahead..

He was exhausted by continuous overwork and his doctor said he must have a complete change and rest. First they went to see J.M. Barrie's play, Peter Pan, to fulfil a promise they had made together earlier. So it was on 14 January, 1913, that they set sail for Algiers from Southampton. After a week exploring the countryside around Algiers, Robin (Olave's nickname for B.-P.) announced that they were going for a week's camping expedition in the mountains edging the Sahara. Although they had two mules with Arab guides to carry the tents, equipment, food and water, they went on foot and did their own cooking. This was an entirely new experience for Olave and one she thoroughly enjoyed.

There was to be another co-incidence, as their son, Peter, was born on 30 October 1913, their first wedding anniversary. So Olave's activities were curtailed for a while, but in 1914 she joined B.-P. in many of his Scout visits. When war was declared on 4 August, B.-P. wanted to return to his regiment, but Lord Kitchener felt he had a more important role to fulfil with Scouts. Many of their leaders had volunteered for active service, and in 1915 Olave helped with the Scout troop in Ewhurst village, where they lived at that time. The following year she went in Scout uniform to help with the Recreation Hut for soldiers in Calais. It was in 1915 that she had her first daughter, Heather.

On her return from France later that year, she decided to get involved with the young Girl Guide movement and was granted a warrant from Headquarters to organise guiding in her own county of Sussex. She was so successful that in October she was appointed Chief Commissioner of the Guides. This was to be followed eighteen months later by her appointment as Chief Guide for the whole of the British Empire. During her short time in office the number of Guide Commissioners had risen from a hundred and sixty to three thousand. Every county had its complete organisation.

At the end of 1917 she was to write in her diary:

'I do seem to have got myself fully embroiled in the Guides now and hold rather too many positions. Sussex County Commissioner, Chief Guide and Vice-Chairman too. So 1917 is over and it has been a busy year and we have done quite a lot:

(1) Had Betty. (2) Moved to Little Mynthurst. (3) Matlock Conference. (4) Became Chief Guide. Toured Scotland and visited Herts., Lancs., Cumberland, Staffs, Kent, etc. , etc.'

(Olave Baden-Powell. The Authorised biography of the World Chief Guide, by Eileen K. Wade. Hodder and Stoughton, 1971.)

In 1916 the first booklet of *Policy Organisation and Rules*, compiled by Miss Thorndike, was issued, to be followed in 1918 by B.-P.'s new handbook *Girl Guiding* and Olave's companion volume *Training Girls as Guides*. The latter cost just one shilling, but contained everything that a Guide Commissioner should know, based on Olave's own experience.

Early in 1918, Olave went to France again, this time as Chief Guide, one of a small party of 'women of standing' sent to investigate the Women's Auxiliary Army Corps. One or two girls had become pregnant and sent home, and there were fears about the general morality in the forces. The group toured various WAAC camps in Boulogne, Etaples, Abbeville, Dieppe, Le Havre, Rouen and Calais. On their return they were able to give an account of

Little Mynhurst Farm 1918. Baden-Powell's home.

the splendid work the girls were doing and the suitability of their hostel accommodation.

Many other countries had taken up guiding, so Olave devised an informal International Committee, composed of her personal friends who had travelled or had links with some particular country, to act as friendly correspondents and interchange news and report progress or needs. Olave herself was Chairman. Also she appointed an Overseas Council to keep in touch with British guiding overseas. These became the nucleus of the great World Association.

When the war ended, many women who had served in the forces became leaders in Guides under their young leader. Princess Mary, who succeeded B.-P's sister Agnes as President in 1920, was anxious to be properly enrolled as a Guide, so Olave went to Buckingham Palace to carry out the ceremony. Princess Mary became a very active and much loved President.

It was Olave's intent, and B.-P's, that guiding should be fun, but it also has its religious basis, with Promises and Laws to live up to. Olave was given her own personal standard, and most counties and many divisions had their own. Guide flags and standards were carried in procession or used at camps and other ceremonials, to lend dignity, colour and significance to the event. At world centres Olave and B.-P. believed that those who worked together, camped, cooked, and washed up, as well as climbing, dancing, singing and praying together, would not want to wage war on those they had known as friends.

On November 12, 1918, the day after the Armistice was declared, Robin and Olave put their bicycles on the train for Farnham, and went in search of a new home. By chance they passed a FOR SALE notice outside Blackacre Farm, and decided to explore it, although they had no introduction. They pushed their bicycles up the hill to the house, and found the place of their dreams, high on a hill, facing south, and with a wide view over the Surrey and Hamphire hills. However, when they enquired about the price, they found it was beyond their means, so were very grateful when Olave's father generously paid the balance. They named it Pax Hil , because they had discovered it just after the Armistice and it was a hill of peace.

They were able to enjoy Christmas together with the children, but this was shattered on Boxing Day when Olave had an urgent phone call saying her father had been drowned. Just four months

Pax Hill 1918. The Baden-Powell's new home.

later her sister Auriol was to die in the deadly 'flu epidemic.

Robin and she had already accepted an invitation to tour the United States and Canada in the early spring of 1919, so, much as she disliked leaving her mother at that time, they decided they must not disappoint all the thousands of youngsters who were looking forward to their visit.

A Mrs. Juliette Low had met them on the *Arcadian* in 1912, and was so impressed with what she heard that she had started guiding in America. However, as in that country the name 'Guide' was not appropriate, she called them Girl Scouts, and the name remained.

The Baden-Powells' home town.

They should have sailed on 23 April, but were delayed by a dock strike, so eventually embarked on *SS Baltic* on 29th April. They visited many cities in Canada and the USA, where gatherings of up to 3,000 Scouts and Guides gave them an enthusiastic welcome. They were also entertained to luncheons and dinners with up to 1,200 guests, all done on a lavish scale and promoting Scouting and guiding. This tour was an eye-opener to Olave, and was the fore-runner of many similar tours, which she and Robin carried out for the rest of their lives.

After two weeks, they returned to Canada and stayed with the Duke and Duchess of Devonshire at Government House, Ottawa. There was a lack of organisation among the Guide leaders, so Olave and B.-P. went their separate ways, leaving Olave to devote her time to Guide matters.

They were both exhausted after their tour and glad to be able to stay in their cabin and sleep, so that they had recovered by the time they reached home in June. Following Auriol's death, Olave's mother had taken her three small daughters to Pax Hill. She was now a wealthy widow, so she helped pay for extensions to the house. A large music room was added at the same time. Many Guides and Scouts were to appreciate the hospitality at Pax Hill, some camping in the grounds and some in the house.

Olive's enthusiasm and leadership enabled the Guide movement to spread world wide and give inspiration to many, many girls and women. She and B.-P. will always have a very special place in people's affections.

Olave Baden-Powell 1920.

Robert Baden-Powell 1920.

Peter   Betty   Heather Baden-Powell

The great enjoyment Betty Bindloss found in Brownie pack and Guide company when she was young led her to devote much of her life to guiding. Before her retirement she was Chief Commissioner for the whole of south west England.

Of all the many activities and interests in which I was involved, being a Brownie and then later a Guide were what I enjoyed most. Being a Brownie appealed to my imagination and was a challenge. I was first of all an Elf: our special song was :

> *Here we come, the laughing Elves,*
> *Think of others, not ourselves.*

Later I was a Gnome. Their song was :

> *Here we are, the che-e-r-ful Gnomes,*
> *Helping Mother in our homes.*

We danced round the Brownie circle, which had a big red toad-stool with white spots in the centre, and when we had all sung our 'Six' songs we sat down and put our pennies under the toad-stool. Then we had a 'pow-wow', where we could only speak if we put two fingers into the circle and waited our turn.

When we were ten-and-a-half we could 'fly up' into the Guide company. Immediately we felt older and even more challenged. So much to learn: first the 'Tenderfoot' tests, then the 'Second Class' tests, finally the 'First Class': this latter not to be achieved for some years. Tests were a challenge, but always fun and always with a 'Be Prepared' object.

Mrs. Maude Clode (née Maudie Bell) was the youngest of a family of eight children.

They lived in Geraldine Road, Wandsworth, not far from East Hill Congregational Church where her older sisters Barbara and Peggy had joined the recently formed Fifth Wandsworth Girl Guide Company.

I joined the Brownie Pack until I was old enough to go with my sisters to the Guides. They were a very friendly group and I thoroughly enjoyed all the games and activities. We were each in a group of six Brownies, led by a Sixer. I was in the Pixie patrol and was quickly promoted to be Sixer (leader) of the Pixies. At one point in the evening we all sat on the floor around a large Toad-stool and put down the pennies we had brought towards the funds. We wore brown tunics and a cap to match. Then we each recited our own patrol poem about the Pixies, etc. We learned the Brownie promise: 'A Brownie's motto is 'lend a hand' '. We took our Second class test to win our badge, then other badges fol-

Mrs. Maudie Clode - Brownies

lowed. Some managed to pass their First Class and then were allowed to 'fly' up to the Guides when old enough.

When I was eleven I became a Guide. Miss Kathleen Chilcott, who had only recently left a Teacher Training College, was the Captain. She was a very gifted person - a wonderful story teller but she also had a love of dance and singing, and taught us many beautiful and also some humourous songs.

My first camp was at Thakeham in the grounds of Mr Harris' farm. We slept in converted stables and Captain made it all great fun. We enjoyed collecting wood for the fire as well as milk and water for cooking. Then the patrol on duty for the day cooked porridge for breakfast (no non-stick pans so it often burned!) and probably cooked bangers and mash for lunch or possibly a stew, with dumplings. If the weather was hot it could be quite exhausting stirring things over the fire!

In the morning we all went on parade where we were inspected, then there was a short service whilst the Union Jack was raised to the top of the pole. There was a similar gathering in the evening when the flag was lowered. After that we had cocoa and biscuits and gathered round the camp fire whilst Captain told us one of her yarns and we sang some of the Guide songs and rounds. The climax of the day, was at night, was when each patrol stood at their tent doors and across the skyline we could see the officers leading us in 'Taps':

The day is done.
Gone the sun
From the sea, from the sky, from the hills,
All is well,
Safely rest.
God is nigh.

They were wonderful days!

Whilst we were living at Bath in 1917 and 1918, Jessie joined the Brownies. Maddy Horton, the daughter of our landlady, became a Guide and so introduced her. I was only five, and really too young, but as usual I seemed to have tagged along with my older sister. I remember she was most embarrassed that I could not say the Brownie promise correctly. I think I said something like 'The Brownie's hand is lend a motto'! Maddy was very proud of her uniform, including the pole!

When we returned to London I joined the Brownies there, and enjoyed the fun and games, but it was in Guides I was to find my real fulfilment. I was so used to being with older children that I think I was out of my element with Brownies.

Maddie Horton in Girl Guide uniform at Bath.

Growing up in the Twenties and Thirties has been covered in earlier books. To many 1920 saw the dawning of the great disillusionment. They had been feted when they returned from the front, many of them wounded physically and mentally by the merciless bombardment of the guns and the filthy conditions of the trenches. They were told they would find a country fit for heroes. Instead, many were to face degradation of unemployment and homelessness. The peace following the war to end wars was to last barely twenty-one years.

There were some gains. Wartime inventions were to be converted to peacetime use, and for those in work wages gradually rose. It was a relief to be without blackout and the fear of air raids, but the many widows and wounded were to prove a permanent reminder of the cost which had been paid.

Bibliography

I am very grateful to have received permission from publishers to quote from the books marked *.

* Olave Lady Baden-Powell. *Window on my Heart.* Hodder & Stoughton 1973.

Nancy Emery. *When I was Young.* Franklin Watts Ltd. 1989.

* Trevor Fisher. *Portrait of a Decade 1910-1919.* Batsford 1991.

* Peter Gammond. *Illustrated Guide to Composers of Classical Music.* Salamander Books Ltd. 1980.

Cherry Gilchrist. *Finding Out About Life In Britain In World War 1:* Batsford 1985

Renke Huggett. *Growing Up in the First World War.* 1985.

Denis Judd. *The Life and Times of George V.* Werdenfield & Nicholson Ltd. 1973.

Freda Kelsall. *How We Used To Live 1902-1926:* A & G Black with Yorkshire T.V. 1985.

* Christopher Martin. *The Edwardians.* Wayland Publishers Ltd. 1974.

* Christopher Martin. *English Life in the First World War:* Wayland Publishing 1974.

Stewart Ross. *How They Lived: An Edwardian Household.* Wayland Publishing 1974.

* E.E Reynolds. *B.-P. The Story of his Life.* Oxford University Press.

A.J.P.Taylor. *English History 1914-1945.* Oxford Pelican 1965.

* Eileen K. Wade. *Olave B.P.:* Hodder 1989.

List of Contributors

I much regret that the following ** have died since contributing to the book.

ADDRESS	CHAPTER	ADDRESS	CHAPTER
Mrs Eileen Amsdon Redland, Bristol, BS6 6NG.	2, 5, 8	Mrs Margery Clow Sutton, Surrey, SM26 6RE.	2, 3, 5, 7, 8, 10
Lady Helen Asquith, OBE Mells, Frome, Somerset, BA11 3PX.	1, 2, 5, 9	T.C. Herefordshire.	1, 10
Mrs Lily Barry Liverpool, L8 OSL.	2, 4	Mrs Dor Curgenvon Zelah, Truro, TR4 9.	2, 5, 8, 10
Mrs Noreen Beaumont Southampton, SO15 5DH.	2, 3, 7, 11	** Mr Cyril Davies (RIP) Zelah, Truro, TR4 9	1, 2, 5, 8, 10
Miss Betty Bindloss Bovey Tracey, TQ13 9LE.	1, 2, 4, 6, 8, 12	Mrs Marjorie Davies Main Road, Brailsford, Derbyshire.	1, 5
Mrs Mary Blott Kings Lynn, PE30 1HT.	1, 2, 4, 5, 7, 8, 11	Miss Katherine Field	1, 6, 7, 11
Miss Joyce Booth Ruislip, Middlesex.	2, 5, 8	** Mrs Elsie Gomm (RIP) Tracey House, Devon.	1, 2, 3
Mr Havre Brown Chichester, West Sussex, PO19 4EG.	4	Mrs May Goodman Bovey Tracey, TQ13 9	1, 2, 11
Mrs Elspeth Burns Edinburgh, EH9 3EH.	1, 2, 5, 11	Miss Connie Grant Chilworth, Guildford	11
Mrs Winifred Chandler Haytor, Bovey Tracey, Devon.	1, 2, 3, 5	Mr Inglis Gundry Mill Hill, London, NW7 2RA.	11
Mr Gervas Clay Wiveliscombe, Taunton, Somerset.	2, 4	Mrs Nanette Hales Henfield, West Sussex, BN5 9TS.	1, 2, 5, 9
Mrs Maudie Clode Sutton, Surry SH3 8JG	12	Mrs Gwendoline Harris Bovey Tracey, Devon, TQ13 9BZ.	1

ADDRESS	CHAPTER	ADDRESS	CHAPTER
Mr Arthur G. Room Rustington, W. Sussex, BN16 3PL.	2, 3, 9, 11	Mrs Doris Thorneloe Littlehampton, W. Sussex, BN17 5NG.	1, 2, 7, 8
Mrs Ivy Ross Westcliff-on-Sea.	4, 7	Mr Terence Watkins Newton Abbot, Devon, TQ12	4
Mrs Doris Russell Zelah, Truro, TR4 9HN.	1, 11	** Mrs Isobel Wookey (RIP) c/o Mrs Mary Shirley, Dawlish, EX7 9AB.	1, 2, 10
Mrs Florence Slade Harrow Weald, HA3 5EL.	1, 3	** Mrs Marian Yates (RIP) Tracey House.	1, 2
Mr Frank Smith Tracey House, Bovey Tracey, Devon, TQ13 9LE.	12	Mrs Jessie Young Chepstow, Gwent, NP6 7DQ.	1, 2, 6, 10, 11
Mrs Maidie Stokes Ledbury, Herefordshire, HR8 2EU.	1, 2		